The Ordinary Adventurer

Many Happy Trails!

The Ordinary Adventurer

Hiking Vermont's Long Trail:

A Primer for Baby Adventurers,
and Other Musings on the Nature of the Journey

Jan Leitschuh

Jerelyn
Press

Titusville, Florida

The Ordinary Adventurer

Copyright © 2007 by Jan Leitschuh

First Edition

Printed in the United States of America.

Cover Design by Jonathan Scott
Map by David Miller
Photographs by Jan Leitschuh and Clyde Dodge
Cover photo editing by Ken Westcott
Interior photo editing by David Miller
Editing by Nina Baxley Rogers

"The Road Not Taken" from THE POETRY OF ROBERT FROST
edited by Edward Connery Lathem.
Copyright 1969 by Henry Holt and Company,
publishers, New York.

Library of Congress Control Number: 2007929909
ISBN 978-0-9797081-0-7

Jerelyn Press
Titusville, FL
www.Jerelyn.com

CANADA

JAY PEAK ▲ ● JAY

● JOHNSON

MT. MANSFIELD ▲

JONESVILLE ●

▲ CAMEL'S HUMP

▲ MT. ABRAHAM

VERMONT

APPALACHIAN TRAIL

RUTLAND ●
▲ KILLINGTON
PEAK

THE
LONG
TRAIL

MANCHESTER ●
▲ STRATTON
MTN.

BENNINGTON ●

MASSACHUSETTS

Contents

*"An adventure is only an inconvenience rightly considered.
An inconvenience is only an adventure wrongly considered."*

—G.K. Chesterton

Preface

It starts as an uneasy sleep, a deep restlessness. That's how it began for me. Perhaps for you, too.

Underneath the slick, secure, same surfaces of daily life, "things" begin to stir. Soft whispers are heard, faintly, in the heart; a restlessness moves in the solar plexus. These stirrings, easy to ignore at first, remain as tenderly persistent as a plant pushing through asphalt. The restlessness seems like the enemy within, threatening to blow up the status quo.

And, of course, it will. That's the news I want to convey.

But it is no enemy. It is, in fact, the very best friend you have.

Initially, resistance is steadfast. You remain a rock. Uncertainty and risk, after all, are unwelcome. In the domain of the map-wielders, there is always certainty; "X" always marks the spot. Best to stay safe, stay put, you think. No logical reason to break routine.

Yet resistance, as they say, is futile. Part of you knows this. Opposition crumbles steadily, helpless as granite decomposing before the elements. The restlessness will have its way.

At some point, you surrender logic. You see that the same ancient pulse that sends birds and butterflies to new continents, that moves bison, wildebeest and lemmings over the miles, still throbs inside us today.

When this force makes itself known, it may come unbidden, but you ignore it at your peril.

Congratulations. You have been warned.

Introduction

This story actually begins with another story.

Words can invoke powerful energies. So I pick them carefully—often imperfectly, but not without regard. Words can redraw our inner maps, can cause the world to wobble on its axis.

The words of an Indiana woman did that for me. Jean Deeds was in her fifties when she solo-hiked the entire Appalachian Trail. She later chronicled her experience in a book, *There are Mountains to Climb*. I read that book.

I was in my late forties. As I took in Deeds's words, something shifted. I tried the massive idea of thru-hiking on for size: "I'm not yet 50 ..."

I was in denial at first, dismissing the impulse to adventure. It was inconvenient, radical; the timing was all wrong. But while I rationalized during my waking hours, the tectonic plates began shifting in my sleep. I would wake up at 3 A.M. in a cold sweat. Some part of me, I knew, was actually considering a thru-hike of the Appalachian Trail.

The very concept fried my circuits; such an undertaking was too large, too long, too tough, and too lonely. I'd never even backpacked before. I had too many responsibilities at home. The logistics would be immense. The whole idea frightened as much as it captivated. Jean Deeds could do something like this. I couldn't.

Eventually, though, I yielded to this overtaking notion—this wild and inconvenient "thing," as my brother called it, that sprang up from nowhere I could identify. I wanted to have a go, at least. I wanted to try to hike the whole "A.T.," all the way from Georgia to Maine.

So why am I writing about the Long Trail?

I decided to walk the entire Long Trail of Vermont because, while I couldn't yet escape for the six months the A.T. required, I *could* take a month off. I could field-test this inconvenient notion on a smaller scale.

This is my story. And because you're reading this, I know something about you. In some respect, this is your story, too.

Most of us are ordinary, unremarkable people. We're stalwart citizens. We get up, go to work, and come back through the same door at night. Wrest two or three weeks, perhaps even a month, of vacation time annually. Most of the time that's perfectly okay.

Once in a while, it's not.

Tell the truth. Can you feel it? Sitting on the porch on quiet summer evenings, lightning cracking the black air, rain dripping from nearby bushes, a clean-scrubbed breeze stirring the nostrils … there "it" is. Lurking.

This is not the first time this vague internal itch has crept up on us. A seemingly innocent thing, this restless gust that rucks the surface of our psychic seas. "It" is a yearning, a craving for … what? Not the television, useful narcotic though it is. No, the longing is for something more substantial, if we could just put our collective finger on it. Pine tang? The odor of damp earth? The snap of a campfire? The ring of boot against solid rock? A sky dark enough to splay out the galaxies? Space and movement? Simplicity of purpose? Adventure?

Awe?

Such stirrings are quickly tamped down. What hope is there for such tugs of the spirit? "Real" life holds us firmly in its claws. We're ordinary. We have commitments. What can an ordinary, restless, semi–broken-in, responsibility-enmeshed person do to reconnect with adventure, the natural world, one's own interior spaces?

Let's make an assessment, shall we? Reasonable health. Could be in better physical shape, sure. A little adventurous, sometimes downright foolhardy, but when you get right down to it, not all that brave. Smart enough to know when we've just done something really stupid. Can chew gum and … walk.

Walk! (Smack to the forehead!) Yes, walk! Why not? The very word "walking" has a healthy twang to it. Walking is a slow, simple, *doable* mode of locomotion. Ah yes, *feet:* the perfect vehicle for an ordinary adventurer.

But not just any "walk," we think, growing excited now. Not a walk to the corner store, were there still corner stores. Not a walk in the park, either. No, sir! To stir the soul, this walk needs to have scope. Dimension. A hint of the epic.

This walk also needs a destination. It must lead from "here" to "there," with no backtracking. This walk needs a purpose; otherwise, it's a stroll, not a walk. Strolls have their place, but they're dreamy, aimless. Walks, on the other hand, are substantive. They have meaning. They are journeys, complete with destinations.

Thus the very idea of a journey takes root. Before long, it seizes control of most waking hours. We start justifying. Isn't walking the ultimate exercise? Isn't the clock ticking on this ordinary adventurer, and wouldn't exercise be a good thing? Don't all markers of health improve with walking?

Wouldn't it be amazing to be buff, in the best shape of one's adult life, *and* middle-aged?

The daydreams start, full force. What pleasure it would be, we think, to escape for five to seven months and wander free, hiking the Appalachian Trail, one of the world's great long-distance paths. To don a little pack stuffed with one's basic needs—shelter, sleeping bag, food, water, bandanna—and just begin … walking. Ah, to roam unfettered down a pleasant pine-needled footpath, far from calendars, stoplights, paperwork, responsibilities. To follow the rhythms of the sun and earth. To live a life of freedom.

"Ha!" we counter once the shimmering edges of the daydream evaporate to a ringing phone or buzzing alarm. Even if we *could* wrangle time from work and family, would our soft, traffic-dulled selves even have the grit to set out on such an epic adventure, much less *finish* it? Lewis and Clark we're not!

Take note, adventurers. This shrill little voice is the mechanism by which ideas of journey and freedom are stuffed into the furthermost recesses of our minds. But a thing ignored does not leave; it simply goes underground and toys with us in silly and ignoble ways.

It makes us cranky to live with, for one.

Of course, there wouldn't be bad news without good. The yin of that yang is that, for those with ties and responsibilities, escape and adventure *are* possible—as are communion with the natural world, jaw-sagging awe, and butt-sculpting exercise. In other words, one doesn't have to quit the day job. One needn't sell the house or get a divorce. No need to give away the dog.

A short long-distance hike—a trek of a month or less—may be all we need to revitalize city-sluggish spirits. After all, adventure is part of our heritage, is it not? The red blood of nomadic ancestors still runs in our domesticated veins.

Was it so long ago that we first decided to stay put, scratched a few grains into the dirt, tossed up a hut, and put a brush fence around it all? Then, since we didn't have to tote everything on our backs anymore, we were free to acquire *stuff*. Lots of stuff. Stuff makes our lives easier, no doubt about it. "Staying put" has led to the comfortable, stuff-filled lives that so many of us lead today.

Comfort and stasis, however, can also be spirit-killers. *Stuff* has weight. It needs watching and maintenance and frequent oil changes and plenty of insurance. A comfortable life is good, a blessing; but sometimes, it's not enough. What else can account for that stirring in the gut, quiet but unrelenting, not to be denied? With our ancient ancestors, we share genetic material as yet unsatisfied by modern technology. (God bless it nonetheless for e-mail, ibuprofen, and peppermint ice cream with hot fudge syrup.)

We love our stuff, yet we want to break free of the restrictions imposed by it. A paradox. A long-distance hiker must embrace paradox from the start.

Thus, the stage is set for the rebirth of our inner adventurer.

That restless itch found a willing scratcher in me. Although I didn't know it at the time, I was a classic ordinary adventurer in the making. This was not immediately apparent though, for several reasons:

- I was a certain age (not young);
- I had binding commitments, time constraints, and financial obligations;
- My body was battered of foot and knee;
- I claimed a lifelong, and entirely understandable, aversion to serious exercise; and
- I possessed a comfort zone with a very narrow temperature range (68 to 72 degrees Fahrenheit works for me).

In short, I was your basic, ordinary, middle-aged wimp.

Hardly possessed of the skills to scale Everest or kayak the murderous Tsangpo Gorge, I happily abandoned those ultra-challenges to the ultra-fanatics. Silly me, I wanted to come home alive. My time for white-knuckled adventure—if there ever was such a time—was past. One look at the bank balance, and international yacht-racing was also ruled out. So walking seemed the ticket: walking for a substantial distance; making a journey.

I would need to lug certain basics with me: shelter; dried food and a means to cook it; sleeping bag; a few clothes; a guidebook; a headlamp; a raincoat; and sundries. Carrying these basics—instead of cramming them into the car trunk or canoe—would actually mean *backpacking*, an endeavor I'd never tried. In fact, for a thin-shouldered woman, backpacking seemed, well, *hard!* For most of my life, if anyone had asked me if I wanted to backpack at all, I'd have answered that I'd rather eat dirt. Get all sweaty? Carry all that heavy stuff? *Up* mountains? Snort! Go on …

Yet this inexplicable tramping bug did bite, and with it, I bravely faced the necessary evil of overloading my frame with unnatural weight. Obsession set in; I embarked on a self-styled crash-course in long-distance hiking. I bought backpacking and adventure books, haunted gear stores and hiking e-groups, visited long-distance trail festivals and seminars. I found backpacking mentors and sucked their memory banks dry. I took week-long excursions at every possible opportunity to figure out how to use all this new paraphernalia I had purchased on faith.

I bought lots of unnecessary gear. I learned to haul a backpack up a mountain. I acquired a raft of blisters and an ever-so-slight swagger.

Although my ultimate goal was to hike the Appalachian Trail in one fell swoop, a 2,000-mile pilgrimage was yet too epic. The timing was wrong for my horse-training business, my bank account, my customers, my commitments and, frankly, my courage.

I needed to do a genuine long-distance hike, though. I needed to gain confidence, test gear, learn how to re-supply from local sources. I also needed to prove something to myself: could I do it? Was this "living-in-the-woods" deal something I would like? I wanted to find out before I blew up my business and uprooted my settled life to attempt the entire A.T. in one go.

Why not start with a smaller bite?

On one of my test hikes, a group backpacking trip on the A.T. in north Georgia, I met Clyde Dodge. A landscaper from Jacksonville, Florida, Clyde had suffered a major heart attack in 1997. That icy tap on the shoulder inspired him to shape up (somewhat), quit smoking (sometimes), clean up (some of) his eating habits, exercise (a little), and lose (some, periodically) weight. He also decided to take up long-distance hiking. That week on the A.T., Clyde and I discovered we had a similar hiking pace, if dissimilar political views. We were also (gasp! wheeze!) stopping at the same rest points.

Originally Clyde had planned to hike the entire A.T. that year. So why was he in Georgia the fall of 2001, and not in Maine somewhere? Turns out a daughter had announced wedding plans, and Clyde had simply postponed his hike for a year. Clyde didn't know it at the time, but his landscape business would be booming that spring of 2002, and again he wouldn't be able to get away for a six-month hike.

Still, he had an urge to walk somewhere that year. So did I—but I wasn't ready for the A.T. Our lives were about to intersect again.

I was researching short trails when Clyde e-mailed me and asked if I wanted to hike the Long Trail of Vermont. "You need a long hike to prepare for the A.T.," he explained, "and I need to get away from my business for a while." He didn't know how much of Vermont he actually wanted to walk, but he would support me if I wanted to hike the entire trail. I considered the offer, found his logic sound, and agreed. We would hike the Long Trail.

Though in the world of hikers such agreements are common, it now seems necessary to point out that this was not a romantic arrangement. Clyde is happily married to Sandy, his wife of decades, and they have two daughters and a wide-ranging extended family. Clyde became my Long-Trail hiking partner because the timing was right and we were useful to each other's goals. My goal was to see if I, with my novice fear of the wild woods, could hike a long-distance trail. Clyde's was to see if he, with his weakened heart, could survive a challenging, multi-week hike. This was an alliance of convenience.

We would hike the Long Trail, then—a manageable, bite-sized chunk of a long-distance hike for the aspiring ordinary adventurer. A grand and challenging trail, it was the perfect training trail, really: spectacular scenery, and tough enough to show a body whether it could hack it on the A.T.

I got to work researching.

If you squint, the state of Vermont looks like a pants leg, rump and all. The Long Trail runs up the back of the thigh, from cuff to waistband. The nation's first long-distance recreational hiking trail, built between 1910 and 1930, the Long Trail is a remote and rocky beauty, especially in the northern portion. The southern portion—the first 100 miles—is co-joined with the longer Appalachian Trail. Both portions of the Long Trail are cared for by volunteer maintainers, members of the Green Mountain Club. About seventy people complete the end-to-end hike each year.

I hoped to be one of them.

Hiking the Long Trail would take less than a month, including travel to and from Vermont. Though the young and cartilaginous could hike this formidable trail in three weeks or less, Clyde and I both figured that, as mature, inexperienced long-distance hikers and baby adventurers, we would require more time. While we wanted to test our limits, we didn't want to overstep them.

A month in the woods would also satisfy that longing for nature, for simplicity, for freedom. I'd learn important things, like field-based foot care, re-supplying in unfamiliar areas, and out-running bears. I might even see a moose.

This book began as a collection of journal entries, written on the trail and posted online as I walked that August of 2002. Often I would take a break on a splendid, monstrous chunk of milky, moss-studded Vermont white quartz, or at the tops of the Green Mountains—some of the finest scenery this country has to offer—and jot a few lines to jog my memory later.

While I've cleaned up the grammar, I have tried to retain a sense of all the glee, freedom, and awe that hiking in wild places evokes. I also recorded the bumps, warts, and inevitable tensions that arose. Hiking is often extremely hard work, and fatigue makes equanimity difficult. Clyde and I were no exception to this truth. Our natures were quirky, wildly mismatched, and often at odds. Yet the expedition frog-marched us to an unlikely journey of adventure and friendship.

Day 1

"**I** feel like I got drunk last night," said Clyde.

I felt kind of shaky myself.

It was 8 A.M. Nearly eighteen hours before, we'd left my North Carolina home for the Vermont border. Driving all night, we'd arrived safely in Massachusetts, but at a cost.

We hunched over our coffees at the Moonlight Diner in Williamstown. We had been looking forward to meeting our friends Suz and Art that morning, but only our bodies had shown up. Our minds were sludge, our personalities non-existent.

By then, I'd been awake for twenty-four hours. Clyde bore the worst of the journey though, starting when his train wrecked en route from Jacksonville to North Carolina. Clyde was unhurt, but his trip was delayed by a half-day. Our road trip didn't even begin until the middle of the afternoon before—hours past our planned starting time.

The road trip itself further tore up our plans and rearranged them into unexpected adventures. We'd taken a wrong turn while driving through Washington, DC, the previous evening. I was negotiating the crowded freeway when we saw the late-afternoon August sun glinting off the Washington Monument. Clyde, who had never been to DC, pulled out his camera to snap a photo. To help him get a better shot of the monument, I maneuvered the unfamiliar lanes—and in a matter of seconds, somehow ended up off the interstate and on the National Mall. Both our speed and our thoughts slowed in the fading daylight.

It was then that Clyde said he would like to see The Wall someday. Both he and his brother, Darryl, had served in Vietnam, but only Clyde had come home. He wanted to see Darryl's name. I knew of the Vietnam Memorial, of course, but had never been either.

"No time like the present," I said. "It will never get easier." Within minutes, we had parked on Constitution Avenue. Clyde practically jogged the few blocks to the monument. It was twilight now; a pink skim hovered in the west, and a lovely coolness was settling after the day's brutal heat.

There it was: The Wall. Of dark polished granite, it started small and grew to well past head-height, stretching out for a vast distance. It was completely covered with tiny, engraved names—name after name after name. Fifty-eight thousand names, all listed by their casualty dates. Small flags and flowers, placed by so many unseen hands, dotted the base of the polished black stone,

A teenaged boy with paper and charcoal was rubbing an impression against a name. A woman passed, talking to the four lanky teens beside her, perhaps about her brother—their uncle, maybe? "He was six feet tall, born in '49, and loved to fly-fish ..."

It was impossible, in this reverent, hushed place, filled with quiet people in the dusk, to remain unmoved.

Clyde found a directory and looked up his brother: 22W, line 39. He turned on his heel without a word, and began walking very fast back the way we came. Unwilling to take his discovery away, I held back, letting him proceed with the search on his own.

He found the panel he wanted and began tracing the stone lines with his finger, counting. Then, a little higher than head-height, he found the name: Darryl G. Francisco.

"He was my half-brother," Clyde explained, still touching the name. "He was buried on his nineteenth birthday." I took a picture of Clyde pointing out his brother among the dark sea of names.

We walked back, more slowly now, my normally talkative partner quiet. I moved off the pavement to walk on the wide strip of grass, and Clyde did not follow, needing the space, I guess, walking a little ahead. I let him be with his thoughts. We didn't talk much again until we had been in the car awhile. Meanwhile, we got lost in the D.C. maze, and it took an Indian cabbie to steer me through the nation's capital back to the interstate. From there, we drove onward through the dark night to Massachusetts.

We arrived in Williamstown about six the next morning, pulled into a hotel parking lot, and fell asleep in our seats.

Two hours later, at the Moonlight Diner, I could tell that lack of sleep had made me purely stupid. For instance, after paying some last-minute bills in town that morning, I'd gone to the mailbox and had promptly posted my sunglasses.

The problem was, I didn't realize it until I'd later touched my letters to my brow.

Only coffee, OJ, and a monstrous, greasy corned beef hash could restore some semblance of spirit to either of us. Only then could we face Art and Suz, who arrived unbearably fresh and cheery, full of energy.

Art is great fun, very friendly, and talks to anyone. A retired high-school math teacher, Art and his high-school-sweetheart wife, Sue, now ran a few family-owned cabins on mountain-ringed Crystal Lake in New Hampshire. Sue liked the mountains but not hiking, so she willingly released Art to backpack with other hikers, including our friend Suz. Like me, Art was planning to thru-hike the Appalachian Trail, or A.T., in 2003. Art, who would later acquire the trail name of "Gabby," never lost breath as he chattered about the Long Trail's steep approach route, which we would be hiking within the hour.

Suz, from a nearby town, is an Episcopal priest—the fun kind. She was single then, and would joke, "Can you imagine how hard it is to get someone to hit on a *priest?*" Besides hiking, Suz and I shared a love of Hospice, an organization for which we'd both volunteered. Lots of heart and insight Suz has, with an upbeat attitude and a ready smile.

Before we drove to the trailhead, I parked my car at a local repair place for safekeeping. I'd gotten the suggestion from a guidebook. Clyde, who had over-packed, took several pounds of oatmeal out of his pack and tossed them into the back of my car. Art's truck was parked at a road crossing two days down the trail, so we piled into Suz's vehicle and headed for the hills. We arrived at a small gravel parking lot, unloaded our gear, and performed the anticipatory, pre-hike rituals: adjusting straps, hefting packs, lengthening hiking-sticks, consulting maps, filling water bottles. A buzz of excitement underlay our last-minute preparations. Clyde may have tossed even more oatmeal from his pack, and I may have added a breakfast or two to mine.

Finally ready for the adventure ahead, the four of us set off to hike the Long Trail.

However, as Suz immediately told us, "You can't get there from here." The start of the Long Trail was "up there," said Suz casually, as if it were no big deal, "on that mountain." She may have laughed at our expressions. To get "up there" and "on that mountain," we had to ascend the Pine Cobble Trail first, or else come in from the longer Appalachian Trail route. This, in my mentally compromised state, was *not* what I wanted to hear.

Nonetheless, we gamely started up the Pine Cobble Trail, which is two miles long, with an elevation gain of 1,380 feet—straight up. Not fair! It wasn't the Long Trail; it didn't even count! The trail offered no gentle switchbacks to break in these Baby Adventurers, either. An even ruder awakening was provided by the green state of Vermont: an unseasonably hot and humid day. Less than a mile under my boots, I was already sticky and struggling.

Well, why not? We, the unfit, were clambering up the side of a very steep mountain. Clyde and I soon fell silent, preoccupied with merely breathing, while mountain-dwellers Suz and Art chattered merrily.

We were very ordinary adventurers, Clyde and I. And our misty dreams of rugged adventure were meeting reality with a crash.

I was hanging in there, climbing, but barely. Just that morning, I had bragged about how light my backpack was, and my instant brag-karma was nailing me. A cruel weight now settled about my shoulders and hips, compressing my joints. *Why did I grab that extra oatmeal Clyde had chucked?* Experience had taught me that my shoulders would take several days to adjust to the strain of a pack. Today's pain was inevitable; brutally laden with water and five days of food, those shoulders weren't happy body parts, not at all. My feet, meanwhile, vied for my attention as the arches flattened out from the crush of oatmeal.

Admittedly, I began to entertain regrets. In fact, I felt panicky, claustrophobic.

"I can't do this for twenty-eight days!" I thought wildly, looking around. Mountains were everywhere. Beam me up, Scotty! Straight to Canada, please, and leave these climbs and this heat far behind me!

Later, when I was better-schooled in the gentle art of Ordinary Adventuring, I would recognize this same desperate early moment in every hike: *Hold it! Changed my mind! Kidding! Didn't really want to do this after all! Ha ha!* The desperation itself was an inevitable, whiny traveling companion to every brave beginning. As a baby adventurer and Long Trail aspirant, however, I didn't know that yet. And I was terrified.

The heat had us sweating like boiler stokers, and I stopped frequently to suck in the heavy air. This did little to offer relief. It was like breathing though a wet towel inside a greenhouse. The scenery looked a bit wavy, thanks to mental fatigue, and my feet felt leaden. Lactic-acid burn became a persistent presence in both calves.

"Finally ready for the adventure ahead ..."

But Suz and Art chugged up the hill like the seasoned hikers they were. They had hiked a lot in the nearby White Mountains, which explained their aerobic endurance and sheer calf strength.

"Somebody stuff my lungs back in my chest," Clyde gasped during our fiftieth or so pause on the Pine Cobble ascent. Suz and Art waited patiently, smiling. Hardly panting at all, I noticed. Clyde was panting and sweating enough for both of them; in fact, he seemed more soaked than me.

"Good," I thought meanly, in that misery-loves-company way people have when they realize they are being small but nonetheless don't care a bit because they are panicking too. "I'm not the only one freaking here."

It was clear then that Clyde couldn't outrun me. We were stuck with each other for the length of the Long Trail—all 270 miles and 28 days of it.

Despite the heat, fatigue, and desperation, Clyde and I fell into our usual trail banter, a standard behavior we'd begun back on our hike in Georgia. I called it "The Jan and Clyde Show," and it was quite entertaining for our companions. In resuming "the show," I felt optimistic about what I imagined would be the comfortable trail miles ahead. If we could kid around while miserable, overheated, and panicked, that was a good sign, right? I didn't realize then that my optimism was the result of being only *newly* miserable, overheated, and panicked. Once misery and panic became old hat in the muggy days ahead, we would learn to bare our fangs like siblings.

To the outsider, I suppose "The Jan and Clyde Show" would sound like bickering and complaining. That's because, to a degree, it was. But we were also showmen, putting it on for our audience. Naturally Suz and Art egged us on that afternoon; people just love a good car wreck.

The mercy of the top appeared, and Clyde and I slung our packs off with far too much gusto for prospective "End-to-Enders," the specific term for Long Trail thru-hikers. Lunchtime. We paused at the open rim of the Pine Cobble Trail, sweeping our gaze out over the Hoosic Valley to distant peaks of the Greylock Range, all blue and mysterious and glamorous. For lunch, we perched on a fantastic jumble of pink summit rocks. The stones appeared almost translucent. Granite? Surely not. In the hot noontime sun, the pink rocks, probably quartzite, looked lit from within.

The remainder of the Pine Cobble Trail was kinder after the summit—a fact that, while remaining unmentioned, did not go unnoticed by the two least fit members of the day's outing.

We stopped for pictures where the Pine Cobble Trail joined the A.T., walked another 1.2 miles on the A.T., and took pictures again at the Massachusetts state line, where Vermont—and our Long Trail hike—would officially begin. A few A.T. thru-hikers blew by us there.

Having begun the A.T. in Georgia back in the spring, they were sinewy and lean and moved with long, sweeping strides. They were confident. Graceful. Shaggy and very Jeremiah-Johnson-esque. We looked after them in wonder. Sure, we were adventurers on a lovely little thru-hike of our own; however, on Day 1 of that adventure, we were still a little star-struck.

Before long, we came to a simple sign and a head-high boulder at the Long Trail's southern terminus. Beside it stood a small register box with a protected notebook where A.T. thru-hikers and Long Trail aspirants alike could record their thoughts. In the register, I wrote, "The Jan and Clyde Show Does the Long Trail—Onward to Canada." Clyde wrote something about surviving the ride up to Massachusetts with "that mean ol' woman" at the wheel.

I felt better about life that afternoon—somewhat overheated, but definitely opting on the side of living. It was hot, though. My head was baking, my temples ready to explode. After the sweaty ascent up the Pine Cobble, we'd drunk recklessly at lunch and were all running low on water. A hiker needs to stay hydrated or bad things happen: one's joint cartilage turns to sawdust, and organs—useful ones like kidneys and brains—stop working optimally. Our guidebooks promised a spring ahead, and as we hiked closer, we passed an experienced-looking southbound hiker. He sneered at our upcoming water source: "I wouldn't drink it." Our spirits sank.

Yet, before long, we came across the lovely little spring, icy cold and sweet. Agua dulce! What was that fellow waiting for, a drinking fountain? After tanking up our thirsty selves, I offered my newly filled water bag to the others. Suz took it and dumped the ice water over her sweaty head. Great idea! I dumped a joltingly cold bag over mine too. *Yikes!* The action took my breath away. Suz and I shrieked and laughed like teenaged girls, shaking our wet locks like puppies and high-fiving each other while the men shook their heads and clucked in a superior manner. They really wanted to play too, I could tell.

After that, I got my groove back. Nothing like ice water to wake up a sluggish, overheated body. The Long Trail had just given me my first lesson on heat and hydration. Looking back, I should have it paid more attention, as the torrid humidity was to dog us for fully half of our trek to Canada. Ah, but some baby adventurers learn more slowly than others.

Near a stream where we'd paused to catch our breath, a young, polite A.T. thru-hiker named R-Kid paused briefly to speak with us. A man of few words, he informed us the shelter was close at hand—good news to at least two very tired hikers. When R-Kid left, he loped up the nearby slope. He made it look easy. We watched him in awe.

Clyde, who had thrown himself down beside the stream, spoke aloud my own thoughts, and the secret desire of all ordinary adventurers: "Before this trip is over," he vowed, "I will walk to the top of a mountain without stopping."

We hiked on to the Seth Warner Shelter, a rough, three-sided affair with a roof, our resting spot for the evening. Such simple shelters are spread all along the Long Trail, and maintained by the Green Mountain Club.

Clyde went to sleep within minutes of our arrival. Because of his train ride, on top of the car trip, he'd been up for sixty-one hours. He snored gently from the shelter as I wrote in my journal to unwind.

Not a bit sleepy, Art and Suz strung up their camping hammocks on the local hardwoods and commenced supper preparations on a nearby picnic table. I strung my hammock near theirs; we had a veritable pod of hammocks. I joined them at the picnic table and took in the scene.

To one side was a simple iron fire ring, blackened and empty. Romantic as a fire sounded, the evening was far too hot for pyro-play. To the other side was the brown-sided shelter, festooned with hooks for hikers to hang their food to protect it from the critters, mostly mice and raccoons. The surrounding earth was trod bare. I cooked my first trail meal of the hike, a simple packaged noodle dish I would not deign to eat at home. On the trail, the glop was ambrosia.

I met a dozen or more backpackers that night. It was exciting to be in the company of so many thru-hikers. Two young Long Trail End-to-Enders—later to be christened "Branch" and "Stick" by Clyde—hiked in late. Many A.T. thru-hikers camped here as well, including an astoundingly upholstered young woman with the trail name of "The Real McCoy." We just took her word for it. Everyone stared, even the women. She *was* an amazement. High, healthy collagen is a gravity-defying marvel, and everyone pays heed. She wore string tops.

"Stuffing ten pounds in a five-pound sack," Clyde would observe dryly the next day, after the life force had returned to him.

Despite all the excitement, when the evening's chill settled in, I retired willingly to my hammock, slithering in through a special opening in the bottom and wriggling around for several minutes until I worked myself into a comfortable position in my mummy sleeping bag. Finally settled, I surrendered to fatigue. After a day of preparation and a night of driving, I'd walked a full six miles uphill under pack, with only 2.8 of those miles "official" trail.

I remembered little after turning out my headlamp.

Day

2

The morning of our second day broke clear and hot. I stiffly lowered myself from my hammock, sleepy seeds in my eyes, and shuffled over to the shelter where I'd hung my food bag. I dug around for coffee. No fresh-roasted, brewed java this morning, alas. For this trip, I carried little "coffee bags," similar to teabags. They were rather unsavory, but the caffeine would prove useful.

Art was talking away, sitting at the picnic table in front of the shelter, exactly where I had left him the night before. It was as if he'd never slept. Clyde was awake too, looking only slightly better than I felt. It's not good to stay awake for more hours than you are years old. The men were talking to a slender, fragile-looking young woman who had introduced herself as Jeannie. Jeannie had started hiking at Delaware Water Gap, more than 300 miles south, so she apparently wasn't all that fragile.

We all packed up and were on the trail by eight. Workmanlike Clyde lit out first, just walking alone through the woods and enjoying the quiet. The three of us followed, chatting among ourselves. Vermont struck me as being very green. Make that very, *very* green. Since the name "Vermont" is derived from the French *les monts verts* for "the green mountains," this was definitely a case of truth in advertising.

Before long we came to a power line, and the open area provided the first real views of the trip. We weren't in the backcountry yet, just escaping the pull of town. The four of us sat on a rock slab for a rest, soaking up the sun, nibbling snacks to keep our strength up for the climbs. Although it was only our first full day of hiking, I could feel my internal furnace firing up as my hiking metabolism started to kick in. I was ready to burn some calories.

A soft breeze dried my back, damp with sweat from the pack. Already I was sticky and in need of a shower. Already I was starting to wonder when I would next have one. I put such pointless thoughts out of my mind as I cooled off and enjoyed the sheer leisure of just sitting around in the sun and talking to friends with seemingly nothing else to do.

A long-distance trail is a funny thing. It exerts a subtle pull. Often drifting unrecognized beneath the surface of awareness is an undercurrent of urgency to be *moving*. No matter how much we fantasize about lazing around a merry morning campfire and conversing over mugs of cowboy coffee, long-distance hiking is not about leisure; it's about *movement*. That pull comes from the next bend itself, and the one beyond that. To heed its call, we must keep moving.

I was still fighting that truth. I wanted to sit longer. Even out here, time moved too fast for me. Why didn't I linger? I could have chosen to do so. But I would have lost my companions to the pull of the trail. Truth be told, I still felt uneasy about being alone in the woods.

One by one, we picked up our packs and moved on. Suz and Art pulled ahead as Clyde and I struggled to climb, according to our guidebook, an "unnamed ridge."

"Something this hard should have a name," Clyde declared, panting, and suggested a few unrepeatable candidates.

As we four paused for various reasons—bathroom breaks, pack rearrangements, picture-taking—we would swap positions in the hiking order. Around lunchtime, I was leading. I came upon a beaver pond set like a gemstone in the mixed forest, with the Long Trail tracing its shore. I could see the rocky bottom of the pool, even though the water was stained dark like the acidic, blackwater rivers of eastern North Carolina.

The beaver pond, with its clear, cool water, was a tempting bathtub. It was only Day 2, but I was salty and drenched in sweat. My bangs dripped salt water into my eyes. Under my damp pack straps, my shoulders had pruned. I could hardly bear the hot press of the pack. I dropped it to the ground.

Only the second day, and I was already grossing myself out? What hope did I have for six months of this on the A.T.?

I considered the pond. I was a good five minutes in the lead. My clothes were of quick-dry material and could also use a good rinse. I was hot … so why not? I slipped into that stained water and swam away the salt crust.

Refreshed, I swam to a shoreline rock and was about to heave myself up onto its warm flatness when Suz showed up and snapped my picture. Art and Clyde arrived shortly after and found a flat spot near shore for lunch. Clyde dunked himself as well before we all settled down for lunch.

Later, while exploring the storybook setting, Suz and Art found a startlingly orange creature and called me over. It was like nothing I'd seen before: a little flame-colored salamander. "This is a red eft, the terrestrial stage of the red spotted newt," Suz explained. After two or three years, she and Art told me, the eft begins to transform into an olive-green aquatic adult. I looked it up months later, and they had been right; there was a *Notophthalmus viridescens,* in all its red-orange glory.

I remarked that the flamingly brilliant creature wasn't doing a very good job of hiding itself, lying there on the emerald Vermont moss. The contrast was startling, the hues opposites on the color scale. Maybe newts aren't good to eat, I thought, and don't need the camouflage that, say, pizza and fried chicken might require.

Pizza and fried chicken? Food! Now, why would I think of that? I had contentedly nibbled my crackers and pouch tuna for lunch, but now I was fantasizing about … oh, maybe a grilled filet, medium-rare, smothered in sautéed mushrooms with cheese-topped cottage fries on the side. Only Day 2, and already I was inserting food into the mental conversation. Already I craved "real" food.

Make that real food and a *milkshake.*

We hiked for a while longer, Suz and Art a few minutes ahead while Clyde and I chuffed in the distant rear. Around mid-afternoon the two of us came to stony Stamford Stream. The stream was overhung with trees, very Vermont in a rocky sort of way. We paused to admire it.

Yeah, that's it. We paused to admire it. Halted for a long moment, merely to appreciate the view.

About the time we'd caught our breath, er, the view, it started to sprinkle. The heavy, humid day was warm, and I debated whether to pull out my rain gear. If I wore it, I'd swelter, and I was already sweltering. Maybe yet another wash would be a good idea, I thought. Can a body be too clean while thrashing through primitive wilderness? I thought not. My raincoat stayed in the pack.

Mistake.

We trudged alongside the stream and within minutes, as Clyde put it, "we had a full-blown frog-strangler going on." Cold Vermont rain streamed through my hair and into my eyes, making it hard to see. We could do nothing but keep hiking. Minutes later, we rounded a bend in the trail, and there sat Congdon Shelter—snug, dry, and just two minutes away from our drenching. Who knew? Suz and Art, apparently.

The shelter was packed with damp, reeking hikers and even smellier gear, and we wedged ourselves in. The shelter offered bunks for eight; almost twice that many were jammed under its roof. In addition, one hiker's "partner" was a very wet black Lab who jumped into the rain and muck and back into the shelter, shaking muddy-dog water all over my new gear. I groaned inwardly and shot the dog's owner a look. I'm as much of a dog lover as anyone I know, but *some* owners need to be put on a leash, I thought darkly. Fido the Filthy was probably allowed to play in the springs—our water sources—too. Silently, I worked myself into a proper mental froth.

Despite the day's heat and my steamy thoughts, the late-afternoon storm blew cool. Soaked as I was, I began to chill off and shiver. I'm always cautious about chilling on the trail, and rightly so; I get cold very quickly. It didn't surprise me to learn a hiker could get hypothermic in the summer. I'd figured that out long ago. Far too late to prevent a soaking, I pulled my raincoat on, and it provided a small amount of warmth, just enough to slow the shivers.

When the rain abated, we resumed hiking and warmed up quickly. Suz and I fell in together, enjoying the cooler air and girl talk. Ripe raspberries grew on the bushes beside the trail, and we helped ourselves to nature's gifts as we passed. Soon we hiked into the shrubby, open meadows of Harmon Hill and looked down at the town of Bennington below. Bennington boasts a distinctive monument that commemorates a Revolutionary War battle. The post-rain mists had burned off, and we could identify the obelisk clearly in the distance.

Clyde and Art were already there, waiting for us. We took some pictures, both of the view and of ourselves, and had fun hamming it up for the camera. In one shot, Clyde and I stood side by side but leaned away from each other, holding our noses and making disgusted faces. After that bit of sport and rest, we hiked on and soon started to descend a seemingly endless series of stone steps constructed of native rock and stacked to blend in with their ancient mineral neighbors. The rockwork was marvelous, a testament to untold volunteer hours of trail labor. My knees, less impressed by the steep staircase, began to bark an alarm; the steps were not in sync with my natural stride, and my thigh muscles started to quiver with fatigue. I had heard experienced hikers speak of preferring climbing to descending. I wasn't there yet, but I was starting to understand.

Art seemed not to notice, chattering away the entire descent. He enjoyed telling us stories of math students he'd taken backpacking through his school's outing club. One girl lugged a small portable TV and was distressed to find no electrical outlets in camp. Over time, with a little coaching, she had turned out to be an avid and savvy backpacker, he reported. I took that as a sign that there was hope for me and Clyde. We'd already discarded the idea of a television.

The four of us emerged from the woods at Route 9, where Art had parked his grey truck in a small trailhead lot. The *Long Trail Guide* divides the Long Trail into twelve sections, or "divisions," and we had just completed Division One. Only eleven more to go! We all high-fived to celebrate a successful two days.

Clyde and I had planned to reenter the woods and continue hiking while Suz and Art drove home. But the threat of further rain and the lure of a hot meal and a shower proved too great. Thick, grey skies and the possibility of heavy rain made me feel uneasy. Vulnerable. I found my timidity disappointing. Here I had planned for nine long months to go play in the woods, and now I was diving for shelter, town food, and a telephone at the first sprinkle. Ah well, as the adage goes, plans are made to be broken.

We both craved town, and that craving was a wise instinct, we told ourselves. The weather took a turn for the worst at the trailhead. R-Kid, the hiker who'd blown past us the day before, caught up with us here and asked if we were heading to Bennington. We were, and Clyde, R-Kid, and I decided to split a motel room in town. All five of us piled into Art's truck for the ride to town, where we found Bennington's Autumn Inn reasonably priced. Suz and Art used our showers to wash off the trail dirt before bidding us good-bye and heading home.

After showers of our own and steak dinners at the Autumn Inn's next-door restaurant, we three went back to the room. We were conversing quietly, journaling, picking R-Kid's brain—after all, he'd just walked about 1,500 miles of the Appalachian Trail and was a walking god in our star-struck, baby-adventurer eyes—when the door blew open and a pure hurricane of plump, effusive femininity rolled in.

Two ebullient young women set upon R–Kid and covered him with hugs and kisses.

"Ooh, sweet brudda, you've lost so much weight! I can't believe it! You're so buff!"

"Oh, we just love you to pieces and are just so glad to see you!"

"Did you miss us? We know you did!"

"Of course he missed us, *to pieces,* he's our favorite brudda!"

This sisterly fussing-over went on for a while.

R-Kid's two sisters had tracked him down as he approached his home territory of Vermont. They were like large, lovable puppies, cute as hell and impossible to ignore; it was hard not to smile at their boisterous affection. In addition to their friendly racket, they had brought beer and an invitation to attend a party at a friend's house. R-Kid's eyebrows shot up at that. Within minutes, our room was emptied of the storm, and R-Kid with it. A quiet descended as the excited voices and trio of footsteps pounded down the stairs and away from the motel.

Clyde and I looked at each other with open mouths. Did that just happen?

That night, the rain sheeted down. A roof is a good thing.

Day

3

Saturday, August 3, 2002

Bennington
to Glastenbury Mountain

Today's Miles: 10.4
Trip Miles: 24.7

Before leaving the motel the next morning, I checked e-mail. I was using a Pocketmail device, which consisted of a small screen, a keyboard, and a rudimentary acoustic coupler-modem thingy that allowed me to send and receive text over the phone. I'd been looking forward to keeping up with my family and friends when I came into town, and Pocketmail allowed me to connect with many at once, as opposed to making expensive, time-consuming phone calls. I also journaled my adventure into the eight-ounce device each day.

The first e-mail I read was a delight—a note from Suz, identifying the hermit thrush, a little bird whose charming trill we'd been wondering about. I looked forward to hearing this birdsong again while hiking, cocking an ear to better appreciate the last sweet note and saying sagely to myself, "Ah yes, that's it. A hermit thrush."

The next e-mail came from a friend back home. When I read the heading—DIANA—my optimistic mood crashed. With the nudge of a few buttons, I learned that my friend, Diana, had died of pneumonia about the time we were sucking down air on Pine Cobble Trail. I was embarking on a new journey just as her life's journey came to its end. The chemo for her leukemia had so weakened her immune system that her lungs were unable to throw off the infection that later set in. Her funeral was to be that afternoon at 3:00.

Later, on the steep uphill trail leading out of Bennington, I kept waiting for the miracle of each breath, each leaf, each rock to manifest itself. It never did. I didn't have the energy for lofty thoughts or even the most mundane observations. The climb was hard, I was tired from not sleeping well in the hot room at the Autumn Inn, and the sobering news subdued the sparkle of my new adventure. I barely remembered our easy ride from town back to the trail.

I was fretting about some minor tension that had hung, mysteriously, between Diana and me in her last few healthy months before Christmas. The unresolved conflict would remain so. Now I would never know what I had done to chill our friendship. She had remained polite, but there was a subtle distance I hadn't understood or known how to bridge. It was frustrating to be walking the Long Trail that morning, Diana gone, and me not knowing, not being able to attend the funeral to bid my friend good-bye. Why didn't I broach the subject the moment I was aware of it? Such a minor tension between friends should never go unspoken for so long. Thank you, Diana, for that painful lesson.

Due to the immune-suppressing effect of the chemo and her doctor-mandated isolation, Diana and I were never able to speak in person after her illness set in; only immediate family was allowed any contact at all. That spring, I'd tried to think how best to reach out to her, and chose something we both loved: talks from a weekly meditation program we enjoyed. As I listened to each week's presentation, I taped it for Diana. The words were simple but powerful: about acceptance; about waking up and living life; about staying present.

The last time I dropped the weekly tapes off on her front porch, she was home, in her living room. I watched through the window as she stood up. It was a shock. The woman standing inside looked like a tiny grey husk of Diana, a thin, pale little wren. I waved at her through the window, held the tapes up before I set them down on her stoop, and blew her a kiss. She blew one back and rounded her arms, giving me an air-hug, which I returned. Sick as she was, she looked happy to see me. Radiant, even.

I remember the glow I felt from that. Maybe it was absolution after all.

Recalling this, I relaxed, and almost immediately I was present in these woods. Finally. I looked up to see a large beech tree, its tender bark scarred by claws, perhaps where some old bruin had scrambled up, years before, to harvest the nuts.

The old scars were healed over. I paused for breath, and ran my hands over the marks. They felt cool and smooth. I heard the breeze stir the treetops high above me.

I made a mental note to myself to "attend" Diana's funeral at 3 P.M., from afar, with some quiet time of connection and closure.

The A.T., with which the Long Trail is conjoined, is marked by single white blazes to guide the hiker along the path. Trail maintainers usually paint these six- by two-inch rectangular marks on trees, or on rocks or posts where trees are unavailable. Two blazes painted together are a signal of "Heads up! Pay attention!" for a hiker, and usually indicate a switchback, sharp turn, or other critical alteration in the path.

I could use this internal "double blaze," I realized, to help myself remember: to wake up; to look around; to pay attention. I didn't want to miss the Long Trail. I didn't want to miss my life. Stuck in my head as I was, I'd already missed a huge split rock I'd read about in the guidebook and wanted to see.

I hung back and let Clyde hike ahead for most of the day. The Long Trail continued up and up, and we stopped to rest, snack, and refill our water bottles at Melville Nauheim Shelter. An hour or so later, we stumbled across a magical, stony place with a jarring name: Hell Hollow Brook. Into the icy mountain water went our hot, reddened feet. I journaled from atop a smooth, broad rock in mid-creek.

A little spray danced from a mini-waterfall upstream. A sunbeam sliced through the hardwood canopy and threw dapples of light upon the scene. The reflections wavered on the dark underside of an overhanging shelf of rock. The play of spray and light and stone was strangely moving, and I teared up, letting the eye water slip down my face. I forgot about remembering to "attend" Diana's funeral from afar. No need.

Clyde was busy filtering water as I rose. "You ought to go sit on that rock," I told him. "It has a lot to say."

I continued to walk alone most of the afternoon. Inside, I was struggling. Peace doesn't come in sheets of relief; it comes in little breaths.

I'd spent as much as a week at a time on backpacking trips, and usually by the third day I'd established a rhythm. But I was still off-center on this one. I hadn't meant for the Long Trail to be such a somber and introspective hike. I had pictured something free and light-hearted.

The long, hard, hot grind to Goddard Shelter brought me back a bit. Life distilled to simple elements: trudging, breathing, sweating, pausing. I began noticing new trees as fir and spruce replaced the hardwoods of lower elevations. Chunks of white quartz appeared here and there in the rocks alongside the trail and beneath my feet. When I needed a break, I sat on one of the increasingly abundant boulders.

After a passage of steep log steps, about the time I was wondering when this uphill business was going to end, I crossed a clear little creek and a piped spring. Pausing to rest, I decided to fill up my water bottles. A few dozen yards farther, I found a clearing with a fine shelter, its porch overlooking a southern vista. Goddard Shelter was filled with hikers, but it didn't seem crowded. Clyde arrived long before me and had already eaten. Even though he looked tired and dug-in for the night, I mentioned something I had read in the guidebook; just three-tenths of a mile farther, atop Glastenbury Mountain, was perched an old tower that could still be climbed. Did he have another quarter-mile or so left in him?

Clyde perked up immediately, and we decided to push on the short distance and sleep on Glastenbury's summit. After a muffled and peaceful climb through the cool balsam woods, we found the old fire tower, shucked our packs, and scrambled up. At the top, we were met with stunning 360–degree views at 3,600 feet. Vermont's unbroken, rolling greenness stretched to the horizon. This was going to be pretty country to walk in. The breeze, which had been cool and mild down below, stiffened to a frigid wind on the platform and dried my sweaty back.

In fact, we were soon downright chilly—nice after a hot day. A few A.T. hikers joined us on the fire tower, including Dave, a weekender from Boston; Mo and Jeannie, the young couple that had started hiking in Georgia and West Virginia, respectively; and Branch and Stick, the two young guys from our first night at Seth Warner Shelter. Together we watched the lovely, soul-soothing sunset. The clarity of the air promised a nice sunrise.

Mo and Jeannie chose to sleep on the tower platform, despite the wind. The rest of us headed down the fire tower to the summit, where we set up our respective homes for the night. I walked around the mountaintop for a while, dog-tired but still restless. I examined the different types of lightweight tents that had sprung up like mushrooms on the mountaintop and chatted with their owners about the pros and cons of their gear selections. Finally unwound enough to retire, I pulled out my hammock and tied one end to a willing balsam, the other directly to the fire tower. It wasn't going anywhere and, given my fatigue, neither was I.

Day 4

U pon awakening, I took my hammock down. As I untied one end from the fire tower, I looked up the tower's steely length and got the early morning urge to climb up there again. I clambered back up the 80-foot structure, stepping gently over the sleeping bodies of Jeannie and Mo, whom I was amused to observe snoozing on a lower platform out of the wind. On top, I was rewarded with a worthwhile sunrise view; the fog hung low in the valleys that spread out before me in every direction. An eye feast. A nose feast, too; the balsam and spruce grew thick up here and smelled like Christmas, rich as chocolate.

The evening before, Dave, the weekend hiker from Boston, had climbed up the fire tower while I was up there taking in the Glastenbury vistas. I'd shifted, making room for him on the top level. In the instant accommodation that develops on a small platform among strangers in the wilderness, he joined me in the serious business of looking. After a requisite bit of polite conversation, and a subsequent period of silence, he pointed out a startling scene, one I'd missed completely.

"Look at the play of light out there," he said, pointing to the forest below, caught by the setting sun. "It looks almost 3-D."

"Well," he added, smiling. "I guess it *is* 3-D. But up here it looks even more so."

We had been looking down on the tall tops of the nearest dark balsams. Their pale, spring-green tips glowed in the slanting light, playing against the black of the mature needles. It was a chiaroscuro, a stunning play of light and dark, foreground, middle ground, up, down—kind of dreamlike, really. Very impressionistic. Very Van Gogh. I had been looking right at it, but I hadn't seen the 3-D effect until Dave mentioned it. Then it swam into focus. How could I have missed it before?

I looked for the phenomenon later that morning, but it was gone. The light was different.

Today, Day 4, was the day Clyde's pre-written schedule had us hiking to Stratton Mountain sixteen miles away. That wasn't likely to happen, given our weariness trudging up Glastenbury yesterday. Climbing big mountains in the late afternoon and early evening suddenly seemed less than wise. At 3,748 feet of elevation, Glastenbury had been our highest climb yet; Stratton Mountain was even higher, almost 4,000 feet. And we certainly wouldn't get there in time to fulfill one of Clyde's Long Trail dreams of riding Stratton's gondola down to the town of Stratton and back. Today was a Sunday—who knew?—and we'd discovered that on weekends, the ski lift ran only until 4:00 in the afternoon.

Even if we *did* manage to hike there in a single day, we figured, it would be close to dark by the time we arrived. Stratton was *sixteen* rugged miles away from us, and we were only four days into our hike. Sixteen miles was a ridiculous goal at this stage, on this terrain, in our middle-aged shape. We did not yet have our so-called "trail legs."

Call us fools …

The trail had offered us a useful lesson, but we were slow learners. We'd been keeping our mileage relatively low, yet we were already beat up. To be honest, most of our fatigue was internal; it was our Ordinary Adventure fantasy, not our knees, taking the biggest licking—although the knees protested, too. Our larger-than-life daydreams, entertained back at home as we pored over maps and guidebooks, had focused on gear and mountain vistas, not on the sweat, grit, and bone-deep weariness that comprised the day-to-day hiking life. Now discomfort was in our face, front and center. We had to wrap our minds around it and draw it into the total picture of our Vermont adventure—or else quit and go home.

There was plenty of external damage, too. Clyde was limping from a painful blister on his little toe, and I was nursing an instep blister of my own. In addition, I was feeling the pain of a toe that had been crushed by a horse two weeks before the hike. When we rose after a short break, our stiffened muscles caused us to hobble the first few steps. We'd laugh at our sorry condition; it seemed a better option than cursing or moaning in pain—although, I must admit, a therapeutic amount of such complaining may have occurred as well.

"Look at the play of light out there ..."

My lower back also ached. Whenever I stopped for a break, I would look for a smooth, flat rock. Lying down on it, I could draw my knees up to my chest in a relieving lumbar stretch. This, by the way, is how I discovered what I called "Vermont air conditioning." The rocks at high elevations are cool, cold even, and can act as a heat sink for a sweltering backpacker who craves respite from a long, uphill slog. The right Vermont rock can pull the heat right out of the weary hiker.

Minor physical damage, like whining, is probably inevitable. It's hard to add over 30 pounds to one's aging frame overnight and climb up and down mountains, over uneven, ankle-twisting rocky ground, without something giving way a little bit. I probably had known that. I just hadn't anticipated it.

On short backpacking trips, I usually consumed massive quantities of ibuprofen—dubbed "Vitamin I" by long-distance hikers—to keep me chugging through a few wilderness days. Now, I reasoned, I had to look at things differently for the long haul. I couldn't eat "Vitamin I" like candy anymore, or it would chew up my kidneys and liver. To minimize the inflammation that comes with hiking, I set a limit of only two tablets a day.

Even with my tower sightseeing, Clyde and I got an early start and were walking by 7:15. Vermont reminded me of Ireland; both are lush, green marvels. We traveled through verdant, park-like paper-birch glades that were carpeted with ferns of the most compelling spring green. We passed rock gardens padded with thick moss so inviting, I couldn't help but bounce a palm on the soft springiness. We encountered boxcar-sized rocks covered with lichen and moss, cleaved in half as if by a giant's hammer. We marveled at the many varieties of shelf fungi, each with a rubbery, resilient white under-skin.

I listened to a floating, musical trill that I now knew was a hermit thrush, Vermont's official state bird. The flute-like notes cut through the forest hush and dissolved back into the silence. The thrushes of Vermont sang to us frequently along the trail and never failed to lift my heart.

Things seemed to be working out pretty well for Clyde and me so far. Even the most beautiful hike can be marred by a poor hiking partner, and I did enjoy his company when hiking. When he wasn't delayed, overheated, inconvenienced, sleep-deprived, hungry, or walking uphill, he maintained an easy, "whatever-floats-your-boat" kind of energy. His wry take on life continually cracked me up. When hiking with other folks, we'd perform the "Jan and Clyde Show"; when hiking by ourselves, we mostly talked about our families.

Clyde had spent his life around strong women. His mother was the first woman sheriff in the state of Michigan—a job she held while raising eight kids. His two daughters are independent young ladies, and his wife, Sandy, is a take-charge nurse who "scares people," he told me fondly. As the owner of a large landscaping company, Clyde himself was no slouch in the taking-charge department. He talked about Sandy a lot; it was endearing. He also admitted that his female Vietnamese cardiologist "scares me too."

With all that gender preparation, he wasn't threatened by my hard-headed, independent self. In my short and happy exposure to backpacking, I'd discovered that some hikers "need" to be in front all the time. Clyde had no such need; he had no problem with my going ahead of him on the trail. Nor did he care if I hung back on a rock to journal. We'd found a pretty good balance of independence and cooperation, it seemed.

Even better, Clyde never offered helpful advice like "Be careful!" He just assumed I was being as careful as I could be (which I was, I was!), so he saw no point in stating the obvious. I appreciated his assumption of my competence, as I was still proving a few things to myself. It was a relief to not to have to defend my backpacking and climbing abilities before I was fully confident in them. He gave me the space to figure things out for myself.

Clyde also had about a billion nieces and nephews, and loved to tell their tales as we hiked. My favorites were the Pork Chop stories. Pork Chop was two years old, I learned, and was actually Clyde's great-nephew. Pork Chop liked to talk to Clyde on the telephone, even though "Hello" was just about the only word the tyke knew and spoke. But he said it *a lot,* and with enthusiasm, pouring his heart into his limited verbiage. Thus, Clyde and Pork Chop could engage in an enthusiastic five-minute phone conversation, exploring the infinite permutations of the greeting.

"I love that kid," said Clyde unabashedly. "I could run out my phone card just saying 'hello' to Pork Chop. He's the only kid that's ever cried when I left, including my own."

Or: "He's such a happy guy by nature. Like, when you give him Coke out of your glass, he shakes all over just like a puppy!"

We lunched that day at Kid Gore Shelter, a sunny spot with a view of a high mountain lake called Little Pond. I still don't know why New Englanders call their huge northeastern lakes "ponds," but they do. To me, a pond is a little thing, an intimate, human-scale puddle one could float a boat across in a minute or two. These northern watering holes were bona fide *bodies of water.*

After a hearty tuna-and-goldfish-cracker lunch, topped off by a cup of Clyde's coffee, I took a superb nap in Kid Gore's bunks, falling asleep to the view. This nap rated at least three stars—not quite a black-hole sleep, but just close enough to drift off to another reality. Finally! I was living out one Long Trail fantasy: leisure.

Rested and ready to hike, Clyde and I set off again, each setting our own pace this time. After four days, we had begun to fall into a rhythm of hiking together in the mornings then apart in the afternoons. I appreciated both the company and the solitude; it was a good mix.

Certain rhythms had begun to emerge in my own hiking as well. I hiked hard in the mornings, using Type-A Clyde as my driving wheel. Then, after lunch, I tended to slow down to journal, nap, sightsee, or stick my inflamed feet into a cold, flowing creek. I was more observant when alone, but it would be a lonelier trip without company. So the new rhythms worked.

We met up at Story Spring Shelter around three-thirty and held a conference. How much farther should we go? Seven hard uphill miles lay between us and Stratton's summit. That late in the afternoon, walking at a novice speed of less than 1.5 miles per hour, we didn't think we could make it before dark. Secretly, though, we both wanted to get to the telephone Stratton's warming hut would offer. Life back home was still pulling on us.

"Let's just go as far as we feel," I said, and Clyde agreed. So we hiked on, Clyde ahead of me. I wanted to be able to rest as needed without delaying him. My feet were heating up, and I stopped several times to soak them in the east branch of the Deerfield River.

Our main landmark was a dirt road at 12.5 miles from where we'd started that morning at Glastenbury. I caught up with Clyde shortly before the lonely gravel road, now empty of Stratton-going tourists at this late hour. When we got there, we found Mo sitting on a guard rail, eating a fast-food chicken sandwich. He greeted us pleasantly, as trail comrades. He'd hitchhiked into the town of Stratton to get the food, then brought it back to this road to eat. He seemed happy and unconcerned, just the way I'd imagined thru-hikers to be. When he finished his sandwich and started up the mountain, Clyde and I both felt the tug of the summit.

It was 6:00, and we decided to—what the heck—push on and climb, oh, the highest mountain in southern Vermont right before sunset, after the longest day yet of our trip, after eleven uphill hours of hard hiking already, with four more uphill miles and no reserves left. On Day 4 of our hike. Why not?

Such is the pull of a telephone on a baby adventurer.

That stumbly, grinding climb was intense, and we probably ought not to have tried it. Darkness fell, and still we climbed. We were too new to long-distance hiking to have hiked at night, and a deep, primal uneasiness took hold of us. We could hardly see the path after a while, though we stumbled among the rocks. Our muscles screamed from the lactic-acid burn, and our energy levels plummeted. We were running on fumes. Three-quarters of the way up, Clyde declared he could go no farther and was stopping for the night and camping right there on the slanting, narrow trail. He urged me to go on to the warming hut, on Stratton's north peak.

Alarm bells clanged in my mind. Something was very wrong with this picture. Clyde was afraid of the dark. He admitted this freely. All his friends knew it and enjoyed the incongruity of a tough, former Special Forces guy with night fears. Clyde would no sooner send me away on a black night than eat feta cheese (which also scares him).

My night-hiking uneasiness mushroomed into a full-blown sense of panicky helplessness. What were we doing, miles from nowhere in the dark, straining to the point of exhaustion—or heart attack?

Deeply worried that Clyde was on the verge of cardiac arrest, I flew up the stony path on a burst of adrenaline, found the summit caretakers' hut, and banged on the door. Two men and a woman were just sitting down inside the tiny shed to enjoy a meal. The two men rose from their dinner and, before long, were headed down the trail to help Clyde.

They hadn't gone far before they met him walking up. He'd changed his mind, he told them; a heart attack was preferable to staying alone in the dark. I smiled at this. What a goofball.

We were deeply fatigued. Summit caretakers Hugh and Jeanne Joudry and their guest kindly fed us tabouli with mint and directed us to the nearby warming hut, which had electricity—and that phone we'd been fantasizing about.

No longer under the strain of hiking upwards, Clyde seemed no worse for the wear, and swore he wasn't going to die on me that night. He admitted to complete and utter exhaustion, however, as we trekked the seven-tenths of a mile across the top of Stratton. To this day I can still recall my relief as our destination finally hove into view.

We made our calls—what a miracle a phone card is!—and I soon crawled onto the deck to sleep under the stars, where I found Mo and Jeannie were also camped. I returned their greeting wanly. I felt as if I had run over myself with a truck, and groaned as I stretched out on my thin air mattress. Sixteen miles was too much, too early. Still, we were glad we'd done it. Strange folks, hikers.

I could hear Mo and Jeannie giggling on the far side of the deck. It was a beautiful, clear night, the stars blazing above in the blackness, the lights of distant houses twinkling far below. I fell asleep too soon to appreciate much of the rare view. So this is how it was going to be on the Long Trail, I reflected in my remaining moments of consciousness: great beauty and even greater discomfort, punctuated by a few warming giggles before utter collapse. And the mix will be ever-changing.

Sometime in the night, it began to rain, and I scrambled back inside, dragging my damp bedding behind me.

Day 5

Monday, August 5, 2002

Stratton Mountain Warming Hut
to Prospect Rock

Today's Miles: 8.8
Trip Miles: 49.5

Forget what I said about avoiding ibuprofen. Massive quantities of "Vitamin I" were ingested in order to effect movement this morning. My feet had throbbed all night, letting me know I had demanded far too much of them the day before.

Mo and Jeannie hiked out well before Clyde and I were able to crawl. They didn't even limp. I wondered: Was that thru-hiker toughness, or merely youth?

Jeannie carried a little tin-and-plastic flute that she played very well. I'd first heard its high notes as they floated down from the fire tower on Glastenbury, then later across the deck at the Stratton warming hut. It was a joy to hear them. As with whistling, I reflected, fluting must surely be impossible to perform in an unhappy state. Jeannie was teaching Mo how to play the tiny instrument, which Clyde said was called a pennywhistle; the lessons were the cause of much merriment. As they hiked away, I hoped we'd have another chance to hear a performance.

The frigid early air up on Stratton's north peak looked smoky that morning. Chilly mist blew across the top of the mountain, filling the spaces between the hut, the ski gondola, and the outside john with its frigid moistness. But—hallelujah!—the nearby bathroom had running water. My joy was short lived; it was *cold* running water. Still, I took full advantage of the amenities, which also included paper towels and soap—sheer luxuries for this grimy hiker!

I wondered if I would ever be a *real* thru-hiker. I just couldn't get used to the inevitable "hiker stank," as we called it. Only a couple of days since my last shower, and already I could hardly stand my own odor—or Clyde's either, for that matter. He was ripening like a cheese. I made a mental note to stay upwind of my partner that day.

In the bathroom, I washed out my shirt, socks, and underwear, then gave myself a spit bath in the sink. I felt heaps better, but it helped the olfactory aspects only a little.

Taking advantage of the telephone, I whipped out my phone card and called my dad, who was 84 and still lived at home but no longer drove. Naps and *TV Guide* structured his life now; he watched television all day and into the night, sleeping whenever he felt like sleeping. He loved to watch baseball in particular. That morning, we spent most of our time talking about an exciting Braves game he'd seen. I mostly listened, content, as it was hard to get him to talk sometimes. He seemed pleased that I had called him from a mountaintop.

Stratton's warming hut had proved a boon to Clyde and me. After all, it offered a roof, a phone, *and* a bathroom with running water. Did it get any better than that?

Yes. We found that a potential problem had been solved for us. Before starting our hike, we'd each sent four maildrops to places along the Long Trail. Each maildrop contained several days' worth of food: basics such as instant noodle dishes, some foil-packaged tuna and chicken, breakfast bars, and of course, the all-important candy bars. I also tucked in some vitamins and some extra ibuprofen, "just in case." We'd both spent a small fortune on postage to ship these items and had sent our first set to the post office in the town of Stratton, far below ... but the gondola to town didn't run on weekends.

Therein lay the problem. I'd wondered all weekend how we would get our food before the gondola started running again on Monday. Much to our relief we learned on Sunday morning, that the hut's caretakers had already brought our packages up. We'd been too played out to notice this the night before.

It was clear to us as we hefted the weighty, self-sent packages, that we'd mailed ourselves too much food. Back when we baby adventurers were at home, dreaming of the rugged journey and packing our maildrops, we must have entertained some ancient survival instinct operating far below our surface of awareness: the blind impulse to ward off starvation in the vast wilderness. Now in the real world of trail life, we sorted our drops, discarded the unnecessary food and excess packaging, and loaded our packs. By now, we did not want to carry a single unnecessary ounce. The mountains were good teachers. Our excess food went into the warming hut's special box for the thru-hikers, who were always hungry.

A very tardy 10:45 A.M., and it was time to walk. No putting it off any longer.

"... the town of Stratton, far below ... but the gondola to town didn't run on weekends."

We dragged our weary bodies back toward the caretakers' hut on the south peak. We creaked down the rocky trail, dodging moose droppings and boulders, trudging up the 0.7 mile trail of "VER-mont flat" as Clyde pronounced it. The Joudrys, the caretakers I'd turned to for help the night before, had told us the trail to the hut was flat.

"It's a lie," said Clyde. "Don't ever believe it when a Vermonter says *anything* is flat! Their perspective is off."

31

We decided to make a special trip back to visit with the Joudrys to say goodbye and properly offer our thanks for their care the night before. We'd been close to played out, and these good people had helped us in critical ways. Even more than that, they had a unique "class" about them, something special, and I wanted to see them again.

Hugh and Jeanne Joudry had spent summers in a tiny ten- by twelve-foot wooden hut for the past 35 years, off and on. They'd been fire spotters on Stratton back in the sixties and seventies, when the fire tower next to their simple summer cabin was part of a mountaintop watch system. Now they kept an eye on things around the summit. They heated with wood, used a white gas lamp for light, and cooked on a propane stove. There was no electricity in their hut, and their cell phone had a weak charge and only worked "sometimes." What a grand way to spend summers, on top of the world.

Inside the wooden cabin—a shed, really—their few shelves bulged with bird- and plant-identification books, stones, bones, twisted bits of wood. They regularly saw storms savage the high lands and spied morning moose walking past their hut. They loved their simple mountaintop life, they said. Jeanne, the former art-department head for a major New-York publishing company, now painted landscapes; Hugh was a retired math teacher, just like Art. They both had a penchant for picking up the odd bit of gnarled wood, searching for the sculptural qualities locked inside. I felt a harmony with this gentle couple on their mountaintop, and I would miss it. We exchanged addresses before Clyde and I bade them goodbye and continued our painful walk north.

Though we felt pathetic and sluggish, we were actually moving right along. The climb up Stratton had put us firmly in Long Trail Division 3; Division 2 had ended on the forest road below, where we'd met Mo eating his snack the evening before. So, even though progress seemed slow, step by step we were making our way up the Long Trail to Canada.

It was hard to leave the peaceful top of Stratton. Our trip back to the actual Long Trail took us past the Stratton fire tower. Tired as I was, I wanted to climb it; the night before, we'd arrived too late for any view, even if we hadn't been too tired to enjoy one. From the fire tower, I could look back to Glastenbury Mountain, our home of the night before. They say the Long Trail was conceived up here in 1909 by Vermonter

James P. Taylor. On this same peak, planner and conservationist Benton MacKaye had first entertained his grand vision for a national footpath that would later become the Appalachian Trail. Stratton was clearly conducive to visionaries, even if our "grand vision" that morning was a bit fuzzy from fatigue.

Our bodies tired and our batteries drained, we nonetheless started hiking. The easy three and a half miles to Stratton Shelter were mostly downhill, but that downhill seemed endless. Our joints ached; every step was an effort. With great relief, we finally saw the fine new post-and-beam shelter come into view. Reaching it, Clyde sprawled on a bunk and fell immediately into a snoring sleep. I ate lunch before taking a few minutes to update my journal. The temperature at this lower elevation had grown uncomfortably hot, and the air was thick with humidity. My shirt stuck to my back. Eventually I found a bunk deep within the cooler darkness in this beautiful shelter, settled in for a nap, and promptly fell into dreamland.

I don't think either of us intended to hike any farther that day. Only three miles hiked! We'd never get to Canada this way. But we were exhausted. Everything hurt. We had done too much the day before, too many uphill miles when we were already too tired, and we were old enough to know better. We'd been dehydrated as well, and that only increased our joint pain.

Ah, the restorative power of sleep and food. Several hours later, we awoke—hot, creaky, and stiff, but not as worn out. We decided to go down to Stratton Pond itself and swim the stickiness off, to further perk up our still-weary selves. Knowing I needed to drink more water, I sought out a lakeside spring to refill my bottles. The small spring had tiny fish in it. I thought a moment, then proceeded to collect and treat my drinking water anyway, reasoning that fish were better than slime.

By the time I waded into Stratton Pond, Clyde had already dunked himself in the beautiful, clean lake—the largest on the Long Trail—and was off filtering his own water. A canoe rested lightly nearby. I had this stunning lake to myself.

The temperature was delicious and cool, an embrace. Fully clothed, I dove under, rinsing everything I could possibly reach. "There is *nothing* like flowing water!" I thought joyfully. I swam out toward the middle of the lake and floated on my back awhile, paddling just enough to stay afloat, and looking at the sky. Heaven!

When I came ashore, a black animal bounded into view. A bear! No, a Labrador retriever, of all things. I assumed the dog belonged to Green Mountain Club caretaker for Stratton Shelter. The Labbie greeted me wistfully with a blue ball. Of course, I tossed for a few minutes as I drip-dried in the sunshine. The caretaker lived in a large canvas tent on a wooden platform, safeguarding this fragile area for the summer. Ponds are natural gathering areas for campers, but heavy human activity—fire rings, tenting, and such—tramples protective vegetation and erodes thin soils.

Refreshed beyond expectation, Clyde and I decided to saddle up and ride. Yes, we were going to try hiking farther, a feat I'd not thought possible several hours earlier. We'd see just how far we could get, then quit when it stopped being fun. I struck out ahead of Clyde on the trail, setting a blistering pace. Where did this energy come from? I didn't stop to wonder. I felt reborn.

The next shelter was 4.2 miles away, a distance that hadn't seemed doable in the morning, but was now in our sights. Though my feet quickly heated up and began to scream, the old bod felt capable enough, so I pleaded with my overburdened footers to hang in there.

We took a pack-off break at the Winhall River, where I soaked my hot feet for about ten minutes, maybe longer. Then I crawled out mid-river on a tilted boulder, lay down on its flat, slanting surface, and listened to the endless music of river. Maybe I am not a backpacker at heart after all, I thought. Maybe I'm a river rat instead.

But I was a backpacker for the time being, and a tired, sore one at that. It felt good to get my back flat on that rock. I hugged my knees to my chest to further stretch out my lumbar region.

After a minute or two, it occurred to me to switch my position so my head was slanting downhill. It recalled a position my yoga teacher had encouraged us to do, one that caused the blood to flow to the head and was supposed to be highly energizing. I raised my feet up in the air and really got into the low-back stretch. Ah, that felt good.

Looking up from this position, I noticed the green-green of the river-birch leaves stippled with sunlight against the blue sky. Bright spring green. Bright primary blue. How long had it been since I'd lain back on a rock—or the ground, for that matter—and looked at leaves and sky? And *why* had it been so long?

The afternoon respite ended too soon for me. Reluctantly, I re-shod and left the lovely Winhall to continue the trek with Clyde. After that river rest, however, there was no stopping me. I had energy to burn. The shelter came up, and we passed it by. Our sights were now set on Prospect Rock.

The guidebook said this spot was merely a campsite, with no shelter structure nearby. What did it look like, though? As we hiked closer to our expected destination, we began scanning for a side trail.

We stopped at a likely candidate, and Clyde suddenly shouted, "Look! Mo and Jeannie!" He'd heard their pennywhistle playing below, on the cliffs. We peeked over the edge. There they sat, on an impossibly small ledge, legs dangling in the air, playing their happy tunes. This was Prospect Rock.

We had camped with this easygoing pair of A.T. thru-hikers for several nights already. After listening to our shelter banter, they had christened us "Bonnie and Clyde."

"See? We're keeping up with Mo and Jeannie," I pointed out to Clyde, who was always feeling behind the clock and restless to keep hiking. "We're making real thru-hiker miles."

"Yeah, but they're loafing and we're pushing full out," he noted wryly. True. We were operating at maximum effort—but, I argued, we'd been on the trail only four days and were *still* making thru-hiker miles. The work ethic persists, even out here.

Mo and Jeannie eventually mushed on for a few more miles; but for us, this was home for the evening. And an ideal home it was—good lord, what a reward for the day's labors was Prospect Rock!

The views unfolded below us as we prepared our suppers. We watched the sun set over Manchester Center far below. The bustling town, which one guidebook called "the yuppie Gatlinburg," hardly looked the six miles away that it was. To the west, the sky grew pinker by the second, backlighting the ring of mountains that framed Manchester Center.

We unpacked, and I strung my hammock and tarp from trees near the rock's edge. As the darkness crept in, the wind picked up to an alarming degree. Once I'd settled in for the night—a cumbersome ritual that involved wriggling into my silk liner, then scooching into my mummy bag, all while trying to keep my insulating foam pad underneath me—a powerful realization took hold: *I am vulnerable out here.* I hoped no wind-damaged limbs would fall on my hammock in the night.

Despite the physical energy of the afternoon, this had been my toughest day of backpacking ever, mentally. The adventure could have easily ended for me on Stratton Mountain. As I lay in my hammock, awaiting sleep, I made a mental note to drink more water, to cool off at every spring, and to no longer tackle big projects at the end of the day.

Of course, I would forget to take my own advice. I thought little of that, however, as I drifted into my second deep sleep of the day.

Day
6

Hikers sometimes find that the enjoyment of nature intertwines with the *call* of nature. I was no exception. The now-familiar song of the hermit thrush had sung me to wakefulness, its flute-like notes floating lightly on the cold air. Pure and clean and harmonic, its song lifted my heart. But my own inner voice nearly drowned out the birdsong: *Why did I have to pick last night to start drinking more water?*

I had to get out of my sleeping bag, fast! Emerging from a snug mummy bag—particularly when within a hammock that is enclosed by suspended netting—can be a production, even under the best of conditions. And these weren't what I'd call the best of conditions.

In desperation, I yanked clumsily at my bag's zipper; my silk liner jammed into it. I was trapped in my own silk cocoon like an inept moth. Neither love, nor money, nor teeth could loosen that zippered grip. Acute claustrophobia joined the bladder clamor. Crisis! Internal pressure was approaching critical mass as I fought down panic. I was forced to flop and dolphin and wriggle out of my warm, snug, suspended bag—*Yikes! Cold!*—then extricate my shoes, which I had tied to the line supporting the mosquito netting above me. Only then could I slither out of the special slit that is the bottom entrance/exit of the hammock. Whew! Reborn! Sockless, I jammed my stiff and swollen feet into unpleasantly cold trail shoes, and tensed to bolt for the nearest private bush.

But wait! Toilet paper! Where was it? I entertained the sudden, sickening possibility that I had no idea where my toilet paper was, though I had carefully laid it out the night before. There was no time to linger, no time to search—that is, if dignity were to be preserved, such as it had been so far this morning. So it became a mad, limping dash up the hill to a private spot, a few non-absorbent handfuls of green poplar leaves grabbed on the fly for assistance.

Then, in my sleepy desperation, I peed on my unlaced shoestrings. Damn!

Thus are gratitude and appreciation born. Such incidents make a warm bathroom with a waiting roll of soft double-ply seem like some sort of large miracle. Town was looking mighty good that morning.

Despite my self-induced frenzy, that morning at Prospect Rock was peaceful compared to the night before. The wind had blown hard all night, causing the tarp to make loud, snapping sounds for hours, keeping me awake. Then, the early-morning wind had settled into a sharpish breeze that cut across me. I'd cheated death again; no large limbs had come crashing down to crush me in my hammock.

A half-hour after awakening, I sat wrapped in my down bag against the chill wind, looking out with my back against the solid bulk of Prospect Rock. My legs dangled into space. Below me lay the long valley and the city of Manchester Center. Behind me, I heard Clyde stirring in his tent. As the life force percolated in, he sang—to use the word loosely—a few bars of "City of New Orleans." I smiled as I listened. "Good mornin' America, how are ya?" he croaked out with gusto between coughing fits.

The view below was almost prettier this morning, with the rising sun dappling the mountains behind Manchester Center. I noted clouds lurking in the background of this valley Eden and did the automatic mental calculus all hikers perform. Rain, coupled with this wind, could become hypothermically challenging. But let it rain, I thought magnanimously. We were going into Manchester Center today.

We cooked our breakfasts, watching as the clouds, pushed by the wind, rolled over the hills. At one point I dropped my Lexan spoon on the ground, but without thinking twice, wiped it off on my shirt and proceeded to stir. Green stuff, dehydrated bits from dinner the night before, floated in my hot cocoa water.

Clyde grabbed the spoon from my hand and held it at arm's length. He squinted at the hard-used utensil. "You know, if someone gave you this at a restaurant, you'd raise ten kinds of hell."

We laughed because he was right. One's perspective changes when living out in the woods.

After breakfast, I was sitting on my pack, trying to smush everything down to fit when Clyde called out from the lip of Prospect Rock: "Come look at the rainbow!" I went. There it gleamed, a pure beauty, stretching from the cloud ceiling all the way down to the town itself. It might have been the biggest rainbow I'd ever seen.

"I'll bet there's a phone for you at the bottom of it," Clyde teased, though he was no less phone-obsessed than I was. We *both* enjoyed phoning home.

Water was definitely in the air, and it started to sprinkle as I hiked alone down the trail toward Manchester Center that morning. Clyde had ranged ahead, looking for a good water source. Neither of us was drinking enough, though we seemed to go through many bottles of fluid each day. Hard work, hiking.

Later that morning, I met some southbounders coming towards me on the trail. Southbounders, called SOBOs on the A.T., are the bearers of news from the front for northbounders, or NOBOs. Similarly, we NOBOs could let SOBOs know who was ahead of them, whether the water source was just around the bend, and how much farther they needed to hike before reaching the top of the mountain.

This morning, the SOBO news was that Clyde was well ahead of me. This presented a dilemma, a difference in styles we were still sorting out. Clyde could hike faster bursts than I could, though at the end of the day we both arrived at the same place within thirty minutes of each other. A hard-working, hard-driving fellow by nature, Clyde was often impatient for movement and uncomfortable with pauses. This was a basic difference in our natures, as I am more willing to stop, relax, take side trails, and enjoy the quiet, still moments the trail offers. In fact, that slowed-down pace of foot travel is one reason I treasure it.

When I encountered a side trail to a view that morning, I hesitated a long minute. I didn't want Clyde to get so far ahead that he had to wait impatiently for me at the trailhead. But, looking up the side trail, I saw that the peak itself was a fantastic stack of rocks—the sort of boulder-filled climb that would set a ten-year-old boy a-quiver.

Truth be told, these were exactly the sorts of experiences I'd come for: rocky vistas and woodsy adventures. *Not* the town of Manchester Center. The lure of the little side trail was too great; I shucked my pack and headed toward Spruce Peak. I clambered up the precarious-looking rock pile—at times a petrifying experience, as the next handhold was not always evident.

I stepped on a shelf of rock and breathed it all in as I looked down on the valley. Manchester Center and the mountains beyond it spread out below me. Then I began to cry, just a little.

Damn! What was happening out here? I felt wide open. I didn't feel a bit sad; in fact, I felt great. Alive. Exhilarated!

My body felt like a million bucks, too—a machine that could go the distance. Even the feet had checked in as rested and restored. No "Vitamin I" needed yet. I thought I would see how long my body could go without it.

I returned to the trail, re-shouldered my pack, and soldiered on, still high from the side trip. Before long, I ran into Clyde—or rather, he ran into me. To my surprise, and his, he came up from behind me on the trail. He'd been at Spruce Peak Shelter, which I'd bypassed in my haste. He'd chatted with some A.T. thru-hikers, including Mo and Jeannie, who had stayed there the night before.

Together we descended to town, gobbling wild raspberries as we went. Before long, we crossed the Manchester-Peru Highway, the road to Manchester Center. Although we had no maildrops waiting for us there, Clyde needed to go to the local outfitter, The Mountain Goat, as his pack frame was digging a hole in his backside. The suspension on it hadn't worked since Day 1 of our hike.

We hitched a ride from a fellow hiker, a young woman who had worked at Nantahala Outdoor Center, a re-supply spot on the Appalachian Trail in North Carolina. I hadn't hitchhiked much in my life, having been strictly warned against it by my mother, so I re-evaluated a considerable amount of lifetime conditioning. Our driver didn't seem to mind the hiker stink, though I suspect she was only being kind. I was conscious of our woodsy odor and looked forward to a hot shower.

Our visit to Manchester Center became a flurry of activity: eating, phoning, drinking genuine brewed coffee, more eating, getting Clyde's pack fixed, and shopping at drugstores for supplies (blister dressing, batteries, stouter earplugs, adhesive bandages, "Vitamin I," reading glasses to replace lost ones, sunglasses to replace lost ones, etc.).

An A.T. thru-hiker named Foxfire, who hailed from Indianapolis, was taking a couple of days off from backpacking ("zero days," in hiker parlance) and had rented a car. She acted as a trail angel and drove us everywhere we needed to go. In the drugstore, she confided that she had lost fifty pounds while on the trail. Imagine, eating all manner of lovely things on town stops—pizza, fresh bagels, ice cream—and still losing weight. Backpacking up mountains is very healthy exercise, we agreed. And the views are great, too.

At the Laundromat, Clyde and I washed everything while wearing our rain gear—our only clean change of clothes. People glanced at us surreptitiously and quickly looked away, so I knew we were starting to look rough. Clyde had a good facial stubble going. My hair stuck out. We looked grubby and homeless.

Clyde was not used to being treated like a bum; back home, he is the go-to guy, the man who gets things done. He commands respect in his community. Several times, he commented ruefully on his downward shift in social status and in the changed public perception of him. He did not care for Manchester Center and thought it snooty; I, however, found its coffee shops and fresh bakery irresistible. Apparently my price was lower, and now I knew what it was: I could be bought with a hot sesame seed bagel, toasted and buttered, liberally spread with strawberry jam and cream cheese.

After laundry, Clyde was eager to leave town and head up the trail to the Bromley Mountain summit. I gave in reluctantly and bade a heartbroken goodbye to my dream of a hot shower. My second sink-spitbath of the hike was a poor substitute. If I didn't get a proper shower soon, I felt I would sit down in the middle of the trail and weep. I was still a baby adventurer, not yet accustomed to hard physical exercise combined with days of not showering.

After fixing Clyde's pack for free, a good fellow from The Mountain Goat drove us to the trailhead. These were acts of kindness beyond expectation. Touched, we thanked him several times. Back on the Long Trail, we resumed our labors. Enough luxurious living for one day!

The path started with a gentle uphill, passing some lovely tent sites not far from the road. It soon got steeper ... and steeper. The last half-mile seemed to climb straight up, or perhaps that was just an excess of jam-laden sesame-seed bagels clouding my perception. Dang. Only brave people must ski down this, I thought. We came out of the woods and onto the open ski slopes just in time to see a fabulous golden sunset.

On that final slope to the Bromley Mountain warming hut—our destination for the night—the remains of the day washed the ski runs with a beautiful, slanting golden light. The glow was mythic. Anything could happen in such a magical light. And, as it happened, "anything" did.

Clyde was ahead of me, alongside a mid-slope island of trees. His passing—or maybe it was his near-the-summit wheezing—flushed a bounding, brown creature into the open and across the slice of ski trail.

"A bobcat!" I called out, but the fat-rumped, bobtailed creature was gone in a flash.

Nonetheless, Clyde turned, magnanimous. "Well," he said, "now you've seen some shit."

The wind was screaming on the summit. When I saw the fire tower next to the warming hut, I couldn't resist; I immediately shucked my pack and raced to the top to see my second sunset of the day. The 360–degree view was the best of the hike so far. Mountains were everywhere. Stratton's fire tower, which was taller, had not offered such dramatic views. Yet we were still very close, geographically, to Stratton. Only 17 miles traveled, and what a difference in perspective.

Inside the warming hut, we made a discovery: another phone! The gods had smiled. As the evening progressed, it began to sprinkle, and soon the rains were slashing down. Many hikers holed up there that evening. Because the Appalachian and Long Trails are conjoined for 100 miles, we had an interesting mix of thru-hikers, with people walking in both directions on both trails. Because of the timing, with A.T. southbounders starting in Maine in early summer, Vermont is the place where most of the SOBOs and NOBOs meet. That night, we shared the hut with some Long Trail SOBOs and NOBOs, and several A.T. thru-hikers heading north, including a woman named Cous-Cous, a surly fellow named Rainbird, and an adorable, wild-haired young man named, improbably, Valley Girl.

Most A.T. thru-hikers had acquired a nickname on the trail, and used their "trail name" to sign their thoughts in the registers. Some brought to the trail a nickname already used at home—such as "Doc," "Chief," or "Sly." Others acquired a name on the trail, often a reference to a funny or embarrassing incident, hiker humor being more or less of the basic sort after living in the woods for a few weeks. Still others christened themselves something personally pleasing, fearing being tagged with something worse, like "Booger Belch" or "Privy Hog."

Assuming a trail name can even be a freeing act, I've observed—a personal declaration of liberation. Many who hike long distances on foot are undertaking internal journeys as well. In a sense, trail names offer a hiker the permission to try on new personas, or bring forth undiscovered aspects of the old. Colorful and fun, trail monikers also reflect the whimsical side of the trail culture. What sounds more playful and intriguing—walking a long-distance trail as a "Joe," "Fred," or "Linda"—or backpacking it as a "Felix J. McGillicuddy," an "eArThworm," or a "Waterfall"?

For my own trail name, I picked "LiteShoe"—a phonetic rendition of my Germanic surname, Leitschuh. It seemed slightly less imaginative than some of the other trail names, but it also freed me from having to explain, as I had so many times before, that "Leitschuh" is pronounced like a "light" and a "shoe."

By the time "LiteShoe" turned into her sleeping bag, the temperature had dropped to the mid-forties outside, and the rain was sheeting sideways. Summits could be rough places to camp. Before falling asleep, I breathed a quiet word of thanks for the luck of snoozing snugly in the dry, comfortable hut instead of in my hammock that night.

Day 7

Dawn brought with it a cold, roaring wind that shook the Bromley Mountain warming hut at intervals. I lay in my sleeping bag and gazed out a nearby window, watching as the sun's first angled rays caught the fire tower outside. Emerging quietly from my bag, I pulled on my raincoat, tiptoed over the sleeping bodies strewn about the floor, and slipped outside into a breath-stealing wind. After pulling the raincoat's hood over my ears, I started the climb up the tower. The icy wind tore past. About halfway up, I had second thoughts about my early-morning climb.

The sun was up, just. It drew a thin band of light across the mountains to the west. The low cloud ceiling blocked the light from reaching the tops of those western peaks, so an unusual, horizontal streak gleamed across the mountainside. Spellbound by this uncommon view, I forgot my uneasiness in the cold and climbed up to see more.

At the top I found Valley Girl hunkered down in his sleeping bag to shield himself from the wind's onslaught as he watched the sunrise. He shot me an astonishment of a white smile, welcoming me to share his vista. The most memorable thru-hikers, I observed, were the inclusive ones like Valley Girl and Mo, who treated new hikers as comrades and fellow travelers.

A likable fellow, Valley Girl was so named for his exquisite command of the words "like" and "as if." His hair had grown long on the many months of his A.T. thru-hike; he now possessed a gorgeous mop of golden curls that would, indeed, be the envy of any real-life Valley Girl worth her lipstick. This Valley Girl, however, was a muscular young man, six feet tall and weighing around 180 pounds. He was unperturbed by the gender confusion of his name; in fact, he thought it hilarious. Ambitious young men had hiked twenty-mile days to catch up with "Valley Girl," only to learn that the hiker signing the shelter registers was not a potential dating partner.

That morning on the Bromley fire tower, Valley Girl pointed out Stratton Mountain to me. The peak that had wrung us out two nights ago was mere backdrop now, slumbering in the far distance. I was amazed.

"I walked that far in one day?" I exclaimed. "Get out!" It looked, as we say in the South, "a far piece."

We were soon joined by Clyde. Once he had clambered up and caught his breath from the climb and the wind, I showed him Stratton.

"We walked from there," I told him.

It didn't seem possible.

"Well, kiss my ass," he said wonderingly, to no one in particular.

That morning, I realized that, somewhere out here, I had lost a very important thread: I no longer knew what day of the week it was. Nor did this realization trouble me.

I knew we'd started the hike on a Thursday, and I could do the necessary calculations, but I lacked the mental will to follow it forward. I didn't care. The constant awareness of time, always lurking in the background of my civilized life, was absent here. The persistent restlessness that had driven me to walk this trail in the first place was stilled by the general motion of hiking—of progressing, step by weary step, up the narrow, white-blazed path to Canada. On the Long Trail, I was somewhat at peace with Time. The simplicity of my daily routine had rendered so much of my usual mental activity moot.

Clyde and I got an early start that morning. The trail down Bromley Mountain pitched steeply down rock at first. Once we descended into the trees, the air felt warmer and the wind softened. A short uphill stint warmed me further before we dropped down again into Mad Tom Notch. There, at a Forest Service road, we bade good-bye to Division 3 of the Long Trail and began the fourth section of twelve. Could we actually be one-quarter finished?

Near the dirt road stood an old pump, where we found a handful of thru-hikers gathered for water. For about three seconds, I considered using that pump to wash the sweat-deposited salt out of my hair, but the water was too cold even for the Shower Princess.

Water bottles filled, we continued hiking. I walked part of the morning with two former Peace Corps workers, a woman named Detour and her partner, He-man. By coincidence, we'd met before, earlier in the year in Georgia. I'd been on the A.T. for a weeklong hike to see what the weather was like there in March, and they had just started their long trek to Maine. Now, some 1,600 miles north of Springer, here we all were in Vermont. They remembered my coming up Georgia's grueling Albert Mountain wearing a large grin—the vertical Albert had been such a kick for me—and a red bandanna tied around my knee. My knees had been killing me then; Detour and He-man were happy to learn that, thanks to a new knee brace, my knees had held firm so far on the Long Trail. We now laughed at our earlier perception of little Albert as "grueling."

We stopped for a snack at Styles Peak and were rewarded with a fine vista from that rocky outlook. Cous-Cous, one of the thru-hikers we'd met at Bromley the night before, was also there. Because she was carrying a brand of backpack I'd contemplated, I spent some time comparing backpacks with her. Cous-Cous wasn't happy with hers—no small thing when you live with your pack day in and day out. I was thankful to have chosen a pack that worked for me.

Cous-Cous was a petite woman and all muscle. "She must have near-zero body fat," I thought, marveling at the effects of long-distance travel on the human body. We talked about weight (and weight-loss) on the trail; she said that when she swims now, she sinks like a rock.

"Why is that?" I asked, and she explained that fat is buoyant, and she had little—despite her bottomless thru-hiker appetite.

My own appetite, light at the start of the hike, had come roaring back as the days progressed. I indulged it, of course, because I could. I'd hauled my most recent meals up from Manchester Center the night before: a smoked-turkey-and-avocado sandwich on a salt-encrusted bagel for dinner, and a raspberry-studded bagel spread with honey-nut cream cheese for breakfast that morning.

We rejoined Clyde and a half-dozen other hikers at Peru Peak Shelter. Shelters, I was learning, are natural collection points; hikers linger there, some longer than others. I sat at the picnic table in front of the shelter. My sore feet and I were ready for some serious lingering.

Lunch was first on the agenda. Since I was planning for a long break, I decided to cook and proceeded to make a more typical trail meal than I'd had for breakfast or dinner the night before. I used a chili-flavored Ramen noodle soup as a base and spooned in some refried bean flakes and home-dehydrated sweet corn. The dried corn was so tasty I sometimes ate it like candy—right out of the bag. When I finished lunch, I washed my pot as a bona fide thru-hiker would: after pouring some filtered water in, I stirred the leavings around with my spoon, scraping as much free as I could, and I drank the pot liquor.

Why not? Calories were hard to come by in the woods.

Thus continued my slide from civilization.

In the old days of camping, hikers would just wash their pots in the creek, soap and all. The impact was small, it seemed. Nevertheless, it added up. These days, as more people find their way into the woods, a "Leave No Trace" ethic is being promoted by hiking groups across the country. Their aim—and ours—is to keep the wilderness from being loved to death. All leftover food is either ingested or packed out; all trash is also packed out, of course.

Clyde, always wanting to be on the move, had trouble sitting still after lunch. Since he wasn't in a mood to linger, I sent him on his way and settled down to take that most time-defying of activities: a nap. Before Clyde left, we agreed to meet up at Lost Pond Shelter, 4.7 miles ahead. We had originally thought of ending our day at Big Branch Shelter, two miles beyond Lost Pond, but the other thru-hikers were planning to stop at Lost Pond, which was only a campsite since the shelter had burned down. We didn't feel ready to hike farther than the thru-hikers in a single day, so we made Lost Pond our destination as well.

Clyde hiked away, and I felt a small sense of relief. He'd been especially grumpy that morning. He couldn't find his sock. Nor could he find his special bandanna, the one his mother-in-law had sewed for him, the blue one that looked like a biker doo-rag. Also, "someone" had moved his gear around in the Bromley Mountain hut. The topographic maps had lied about the climbs, and the guidebooks had lied about the miles, and the hills were *hard* and never-ending. And so on. His implication was that I'd somehow had a hand in all this misery.

So I was deliberately giving my partner space today. I was in a good place mentally and didn't want to get sucked into any sock drama, doo-rag drama, or other tension at all with Clyde. The missing items weren't in my pack, nor had we left them in the warming hut; I'd helped him look that morning. I secretly suspected the missing items were somewhere in his pack, but of course, now was not the time to say so. Wouldn't be prudent.

As for the uphills, I couldn't do a thing about them either. That's one reason I didn't look at the maps that often. It was better for me, on such a well-marked trail, to just put one foot in front of the other and march, taking what came. Or maybe it had more to do with the fact I needed to fish my reading glasses out of my pack to read the map.

I was distressed, though. My partner and I weren't getting along so well. We were both worn out. Fatigue brought on an edginess when we were together. I found myself enchanted with long-distance hiking and was reluctant to surrender my delight, despite the grueling heat and hard work; Clyde dealt with the challenges by grousing. Two different energies. Neither of us minded hiking apart that day.

After I woke from my nap, Mo and Jeanie walked in. I greeted them happily and learned they planned to stay at Lost Pond as well. They took a lot of time off in the woods to play the flute, swim, nap on peaks, climb fire towers, or hang out in a river. The two young hikers sucked up the experience and flowed with the trail. They didn't appear to worry about much.

"When I hike the A.T. next year," I thought as I hiked away, "I want to be like them."

Perhaps because I didn't look at the map, Baker Peak came as a stunning surprise.

Earlier, Clyde had told me the rock face we went down after Bromley was a 10/12 pitch, a very steep slant with 10 inches of drop per foot. Baker Peak, in comparison, was a fascinating shelf of granite and quartz standing on its side; it beat Bromley's pitch all to hell. What pitch is greater than a 45–degree angle? I looked up the bare slab in awe, then dug in for the ascent.

I crawled to the top of the peak, panting. As I dropped my pack and flopped down, exhausted and satisfied, I saw a hiker emerging from the woods in the opposite direction. Richard was an A.T. southbounder and had just hiked Maine and the rugged White Mountains of New Hampshire. This seasoned hiker, who had seen some treacherous climbs in the past month and a half, looked down the rock I had just ascended.

His comment: "Oh, WOW!"

"What pitch is 'Oh, WOW!'?"

After we'd introduced ourselves, Richard informed me that "a woman from your Internet women's hiking list is waiting at Big Branch Shelter with a six-pack of beer for you. It's cooling in the river right now. Your friend gave me one."

Beer? For me? Really? Who?

He couldn't remember her name, but said she had been keeping track of me on the Internet. Thanks to the wonders of Pocketmail, my transcriber, Kahley, was posting the journals every time I passed a phone, and others were reading them as fast as she could post them.

I'm not a big beer drinker, but living in the woods changes one's perspectives. I could taste that crisp amber bite already. Calories! Carbonation!

As I neared Lost Pond, Clyde walked up the trail to meet me. I stiffened a little. Was he still grumpy? On his head was his special bandanna. So, I thought, he'd found it. Of course, I said nothing. My partner looked much happier.

"You know how yesterday when you saw that bobcat and I said 'Now you've seen shit?'" he began, grinning.

I nodded, cautiously.

"Well I've seen shit today!"

"No!" I said. "Not … a moose?"

"Yup," he answered, proudly, "at Griffith Pond. And I got the pictures to prove it."

A *moose*. We were a long way from Old Dixie. We were in the *North*.

Glad to see Clyde happier, I told him about Big Branch Shelter. He agreed that I should hike the two additional miles that day. He wanted to stay at Lost Pond, though. This was a good thing, I figured, a chance for us to be apart and have some breathing space. When I left him, he was happily telling stories to the thru-hikers camped there.

The walk north rolled pleasantly downhill, and thoughts of trail magic hurried my stride. I walked beside the Big Branch, a river I could easily fall in love with. Huge, round boulders studded the channel, and the cold water was perfectly clear. I could see every round rock on the bottom.

When I pulled into the shelter, I met an older man. "Is my beer still here?"

The man's smile faded. He said that the last hiker through there had read the note in the register about the beer. "He went down to the river and drank the last three."

"What?" I was dumbfounded. "All three? *All* three?" My jaw sagged. I couldn't believe it.

In the register was a bragging note from the unpleasant Rainbird, another hiker we'd met at Bromley. He had crowed, in block printing: *I LOVE beer!*

How inconsiderate, to take someone's last beer. "I mean, take *one*," I thought darkly. "But all *three?*" A civil person wouldn't take the last beer out of another's refrigerator, would they? Why drink all of them?

Bad form, bad form …

I read the register note above Rainbird's and discovered that my trail angel was a former A.T. thru-hiker named Mrs. Gorp. She and I had met through the Internet and later at hiker gatherings. Like me, she'd also been hiking in Georgia that spring. I knew she lived in this area, but had forgotten.

Mrs. Gorp had delivered Fritos for me, too—also gone. But not all was lost. Next to her phone number, she'd written, "Call if you want a shower."

My eyes widened. A shower!

Hot water! Now all I needed to do was find a phone …

I left the phone puzzle for the next day. After laying out my bed roll, I walked out of sight of the lean-to and found a sheltered spot among the river boulders. Luxuriously, I slipped into a clean, crystal pool of the beautiful Big Branch for a soapless wash. The cold water pulled out the day's hiking heat nicely. Refreshed, I waded downstream to explore the lovely, playful river. Someone had set up whimsical cairns—long, thin

"What pitch is 'Oh, WOW!'?"

stacks of rounded river rocks standing impossibly on end—on mid-river boulders. The cairns suggested the work of mountain faeries and elves—the little people. I couldn't help but smile. I would snap a few pictures later on.

After dressing in my camp clothes, I wrung out my hiking clothes, then dried them at the little campfire three young men had built in the fire ring in front of the shelter. They were all related to the older gentleman who had first welcomed me to the shelter, and we five enjoyed a quiet, pleasant hour around the small campfire.

"... long, thin stacks of rounded river rocks
standing impossibly on end ..."

The next morning, I would note that the campfire smoke had much improved the odor of my hiking shirt.

The weather that day had been cool, reminiscent of late fall in North Carolina. It made for great hiking weather, actually. The clouds disappeared in time for sunset, and the wind died to a whisper. I felt very peaceful that night. I'd spent one solid week in the woods.

I thought back over the week's memories: the view of Stratton from the fire tower; Clyde's moose; my Bromley bobcat; the spare rock outcrop of Baker Peak with its sun-washed western view.

"Oh yeah," I thought as I later snuggled into my down bag. "Now I remember. *That's* why I lug cruel weights up unforgiving climbs, suffer culinary indignities, and undergo serious hygiene degradation."

I fell asleep hard.

Day

8

Thursday, August 8, 2002

Big Branch Shelter
to Little Rock Pond Shelter

Today's Miles: 3.7
Trip Miles: 74.3

D ay 8 on the Long Trail broke with the music of birdsong and the rhythmic rushing of the rocky Big Branch outside the shelter. The first hiker awake, I lay quietly for a while among the others, just listening. At some point, I realized this was my longest stretch of time on a long-distance hike yet. Though I had been out in the woods longer while horse-packing, I hadn't been the one carrying the groceries. I didn't get as stinky on horseback, either.

My stomach growled. I was always hungry on this Long Trail. A second thought followed as I rolled over and looked down at my smoky, grimy clothes: It's shower day!

Within hours of that thought, Clyde and I would have laid waste to a massive sausage-and-mushroom pizza before swilling down cups of freshly brewed coffee while our laundry swished clean in a washer. Relaxing inside Mrs. Gorp's stylish post-and-beam Vermont saltbox, we would lounge around her cozy dining table in air-conditioned comfort, looking out at her swimming pool. Surrounding the turquoise water of the pool we would see lush and colorful perennial beds, the yellows, pinks, reds, peaches of the riotous daylilies competing for our attention. Several regal Siamese cats would look down their noses at us, then casually relenting, grace us with the barest of surreptitious leg rubs. Best of all, I would be squeaky clean, having stood in Mrs. Gorp's hot shower until my entire body turned beet red and pruned.

This miracle of teleportation began that morning, after I rose and started packing. Clyde, ever the early bird, soon arrived. I tossed him the shelter register. Specifically, Mrs. Gorp had written next to her phone number: *Jan: If you and your sidekick Clyde want a shower, give me a call.*

I'd found the term "Sidekick Clyde" pretty funny. I made sure Clyde noticed that part. I might have even repeated the phrase a few times in his presence that day, for emphasis.

Truth was, Clyde was no sidekick. Although we each pretended to be independent operators, hiking our own hikes, this improbable venture was a team effort. As somewhat experienced backpackers but novice long-distance adventurers, we were both still figuring our way down the Long Trail. We'd come pretty far, but we had a long way to go. We had not yet mastered the dynamics of hiking with a partner; when it came time to make decisions on the trail, we still struggled. We did, however, make decisions jointly—after a fashion.

Despite the challenges of hiking with each other, Clyde and I both drew an unspoken comfort from having the other at our backs—not that either of us would have admitted it then. Our nerves frayed with the heat, the dehydration, the fatigue, and the sheer immensity of the project. After all, when each day's walking grinds you to a pulp and spits you out, it's hard to imagine an additional twenty days just as hard—or harder. We were also both proud and independent-minded, though "opinionated" and "hard-headed" are perhaps more accurate descriptions. We were aware of our weaknesses; I knew full well I didn't have the courage to hitchhike alone, and Clyde still didn't completely trust his heart to stand up to the climbs. In fact, he had yet to commit to going all the way to Canada. We needed each other out there.

As my hiking partner pored over Mrs. Gorp's note in the Big Branch Shelter register, a gleam of interest came into his eye. Of course, he pretended otherwise; mountain man Jeremiah "Clyde" Johnson didn't need no stinkin' shower or pizza. He heaved a magnanimous sigh of acquiescence. I hid my smile.

"I guess we're going to town," he said. "My mind's made up."

A wandering journey takes many unforeseen turns. What emerges often confounds expectation. This upwelling of possibility is impossible to predict with any certainty. The paradox is that we long for the possibility while craving the certainty. It's why we over-plan an adventure.

We would have to learn this lesson again and again on the Long Trail. More often than not, we labored mightily to shoehorn the way things *were* into our idea of how things *needed* to be. The trail often had other plans. An honest adventurer knows this.

Yet there's no denying that unexpected changes in plans, at first resisted, can be delightful. Many long-distance hikers speak of feeling plugged into a certain "flow" while on the trail. Need a pen? Find one in the next shelter. Run out of toilet paper? Discover a half-roll in the privy. Crave a hot, soapy shower with all your heart, mind, body and soul, crave it to the point of distraction? Surprise! The longed-for shower is offered by the trail angel in the next town. Quite remarkable, really; simple abundance, appreciated.

My trusty sidekick and I hiked through the Big Branch Wilderness and emerged from the pizza-less wilds onto USFS 10, a dirt service road with a primitive parking lot. Both were deserted. The sun beat down, our feet hurt, we smelled like bears, and we were without a ride, without the *potential* of a ride to town—or a phone. Our hopes sagged.

In addition, while we were eager to hook up with Mrs. Gorp, we couldn't be sure she would be at her house. The guidebook claimed that a three-mile walk to the west would take us to the town of Danby, where we could find a phone. Clyde and I dawdled a few moments, indecisive, then began to trudge, our feet compelled by the lure of pizza and a shower. Without knowing if Mrs. Gorp was home, or if we could even find a phone, we tried not to think about having to turn around and trudge three miles back. If only we could call her *now*.

All of a sudden, a car, tossing up dust, hove into view. It slowed when we threw ourselves bodily in front of it. Well, perhaps we just waved. But what waves we waved. We waved vigorous waves. Heartfelt waves. We put our very souls into our waves.

The driver's-side window rolled down and a blonde woman bravely looked us over. Mustering into our eyes all the pleading desperation we had at our command, we asked where the nearest phone was.

"Do you need a phone?" she asked innocently. "Here."

Trail magic! She clicked on her cell. The microphone in her car was affixed near the top of the door. "You'll have to lean in to speak," she said.

I leaned as close as stinky self-consciousness would allow, and—zing!—in came Mrs. Gorp, as loud and as clear as mountain cell reception would permit. She was home. She'd pick us up in ten minutes.

And so she did. Blessed be. So she did.

In town, our first stop was, of course, the pizza joint. There we ran into our curly-headed buddy, Valley Girl. Pizza in tow, the three of us gave Valley Girl a ride back to the trailhead, the hot-pizza fragrance tantalizing me as I held it on my lap. As we rode, we chattered on about the trail, specifically Baker Peak. Mrs. Gorp smiled and told us that Baker Peak was nothing compared to what we would see farther north on the Long Trail.

The ditches along this Vermont roadside brimmed with wildflowers: purple loosestrife, Queen Anne's lace, sky-blue chicory, buttercups, and oxeye daises, to name just a few. I watched them fly past me from the car window. After eight days of hiking, I wasn't used to moving so fast, and it was a little jarring to see flowers racing by me at forty miles an hour.

Our stay with Mrs. Gorp was short but unspeakably sweet. It was the ideal break for a weary hiker. A woman who'd walked the Appalachian *and* Long Trails, Mrs. Gorp was a freckle-faced strawberry blonde "trail angel" who understood the value of a respite. Her husband Larry, resigned to a parade of unshaven, grimy backpackers, was equally inclusive. Their glacial-valley land looked up at a stony cliff formation named White Rocks, and newly mown hayfields surrounded her country home. In another lifetime, I decided as I sipped coffee and listened to my clothes drying, I would live in Vermont. In August, anyway.

Mere hours after our wilderness intervention, Mrs. Gorp dumped us back at the trailhead and bade us good-bye. She looked wistful, as if she'd really rather go to Canada with us. I couldn't blame her; it was a gorgeous day for hiking. Under the trees, out of the hot sun, we hiked with renewed strength and enthusiasm. The weather felt like fall—sunny, crisp, dry, breezy.

The climb to Little Rock Pond was easy walking, despite the recent pack-upload of bananas and Snickers bars. Before long, we'd rounded the corner for our first view of the impressive, lake-sized "pond." The sun sparkled off the clear water, and a large, white rock outcropping on the far side caught my eye. Some very brave children were leaping off that tall cliff, daring each other to jump into the water.

We followed the trail around the "pond," soaking in the visual oasis. Mrs. Gorp had warned us that this beauty harbored a lovely crop of leeches. Nonetheless, the temptation to swim here was strong. At the nearby shelter, Clyde and I dumped our packs and looked at each other. There was no doubt about it. Newly showered or not, we were going swimming. We grabbed our cameras and camp towels and scurried back to Little Rock Pond.

Not far from shore sat an island that had been hiking legend Earl Shaffer's favorite campsite. Earl had been the Appalachian Trail's first official thru-hiker, back in 1948. A bridge had once spanned the distance to the island campsite but was removed to protect the fragile island environment from overuse. All that was left were a few sunken pilings. I kicked off my shoes and paused. Dawdling, really. I dipped a toe in the water. Ice-cold. The breeze was chilly, too. It was "do or die" time. Not ready to die, I waded in. The temperature shock left me gasping. But the life force kicked in, strongly.

I churned across to the island. After I got my breath back, I checked my legs for leeches.

Safe! Yes! Cheated the predatory little bloodsuckers on the first pass!

As I explored the island, Clyde took the plunge to join me. A father and son were fishing on the other side, but that's about all the island excitement I could see. It was too cold to sit and contemplate; I'd goose-pimpled right up in the chill breeze. I didn't linger. After a quick tour, I jumped back in, gasping anew.

Much to my delight and relief, I dodged the sucking parasites on the trip back, too.

Just call me "Dances With Leeches."

Back at Little Rock Pond Shelter, I realized Clyde had found himself a trail name. Atop Bromley fire tower during the previous day's sunrise (a time that now seemed impossibly distant), when Valley Girl had pointed out Stratton to show us how far we had walked, Clyde had actually said, "Well, kiss my ass! Not bad for a middle-aged fat man."

Valley Girl had laughed and observed that "Middle-Aged Fat Man" was a fine trail name. I agreed, especially considering how often Clyde referred to the "235 pounds of chiseled fat" he'd started the trail with.

Upon hearing the story, Mrs. Gorp had said she thought the name workable with a little shortening: "MAF Man." Now, at Little Rock Pond Shelter, Excalibur, a Long Trail thru-hiker, was calling Clyde "MAF Man," and Clyde had signed the register thusly. The moniker appeared to be official.

"... we christened ourselves Little Rock Pond End-to-Enders ..."

I felt terrific that evening. High-calorie pizza, rest, a hot shower, clean clothes, and a cold swim could do that to a body. My hiking partner and I felt so good after our swim that we even hiked the entire Little Pond Loop Trail, just because we could. The extra miles didn't count a bit toward our Long Trail thru-hike. They were an accomplishment nonetheless, and we christened ourselves Little Rock Pond End-to-Enders for successfully completing our lake tour. This night, we were full of ourselves.

That was a good thing, too, because the trail would turn uphill the next day. It was bound to happen.

Day
9

On the morning of our ninth day, Clyde put his finger on it: "What I like about this trail is not having to get up and go to work." One more day, according to him, and it would be the longest he'd ever gone without working. He would be treading new ground, and not just physically, as we trudged north on the Long Trail.

As we shelter rats lounged around in our sleeping bags, reluctant to leave the relative comfort of our plank-floor beds, Clyde mentioned another milestone: Today, he said, we would walk off the third page of the twelve-page Long Trail map. He planned a page-burning ceremony to celebrate the occasion.

Clyde was feeling friskier. He'd been a little testy of late, as the extreme heat and hard physical work flayed our sensibilities. Now he wanted to play. Tongue firmly in cheek, Clyde offered me a deal: "You carry my pack this month, I'll carry your pack next month."

"The Jan-and-Clyde Show" was back. I was delighted to see my hiking partner having fun again. We performed for the benefit of our shelter-mates, Newsman and Excalibur. The "show" had started first thing that morning.

"Jan?" Clyde had called out from his sleeping bag.

"Yes?" I answered. Everyone was awake, but barely; it was nearing six-thirty, and we were all still lying rather stunned in our bags.

"Be glad it's not raining today and you don't have to follow me holding that little umbrella over my head."

I never knew what would come out of that man's mouth. I attempted to rise to the production, though it was rather early for onstage improvisation.

"It's not even the fanning and grape-feeding that goes along with it that I mind so much," I replied, rapidly searching the mental data banks for comic material, and added, "It's the damn *peeling* of the little bleeders that slows me down."

Yes, it's likely one of those routines best experienced in the moment. But at the time, we brought the shelter down.

It was good to have my partner back.

Finally up and moving, we set our sights on the day's goal: Minerva Hinchey Shelter. In between, as had become our custom, we carved out smaller goals: White Rocks Cliff at 3.9 miles, Greenwall Shelter at 4.4 miles, and Roaring Brook at 5.9. If we felt strong, we'd push on to hamburgers and milkshakes at the famous Whistle Stop Restaurant, which sat close enough to where Route 103 crossed the trail at 12.2 miles.

Although the day promised to be another steamer, the early walking unfolded easily for us, and we were soon ascending White Rocks Mountain. Small, gentle breezes helped lower the humidity as we gained elevation. Clyde pulled ahead.

In time, I gained the ridge and entered a muted, open forest. Instead of the brushy chaotic green of undergrowth, I now trod upon a soft, brown mat, a needled duff that muffled my steps and covered the abundant cracked Vermont stone like a blanket. I was in a forest of large spruce and fir; little else seemed to grow in this brown layer, other than the mature trees. I could peer quite a distance through the army of black trunks on either side of me. Such evergreen forests were becoming common on the high ground of the Long Trail.

In these dark woods, sound no longer behaved in expected ways. Swallowed by the high, needled canopy and skeletal lower limbs, it played tricks with the ear. The empty hush felt like a physical pressure on my eardrums. The hum of the silence was unnerving. I found myself listening for the smallest hint of a noise. When a hermit thrush finally trilled nearby, the purity of the notes knifed through the thick mantle of dead air. Startled, I jumped. It was like leaning on a heavy door and having it swing open easily: not an unexpected shift, but disquieting in its suddenness.

Near White Rocks Cliff, I caught up with Clyde, who was staring thoughtfully at a large group of stone cairns. They were a veritable small forest of piled rock columns, reminiscent of Stonehenge in their mute solemnity. Rocks of all shapes and sizes stood in tall, impossible-looking columns, stalagmites of stone. Some reached higher than my hip. One past traveler had even stacked rocks into a cunning stone arch. The scene projected the same earthy, pagan whimsy as the river cairns I'd seen near Big Branch.

The stones themselves were varying shades of white and grey and included chunks of what looked to be milky-white quartz. I later learned that this was white schist, a metamorphic rock that contains quartz and other minerals.

In the silence, I waited for Clyde to say something snarky about someone having too much time on their hands.

Instead, he glanced around at the hushed forest and said, "You kind of expect to catch little hobbits out of the corner of your eye, running from tree to tree, you know?" He'd felt it too.

We decided to head down the White Rocks Cliff side trail to catch a view. Clyde went first and, after a pit stop, I followed. The pale rocks overlooked Mrs. Gorp's picturesque valley; in fact, she'd pointed out the cliff formation to us from her property. We guessed which house was hers, but it could have been any number of the small, pastoral dots below.

Back on the Long Trail, we reached the spur trail to Greenwall Shelter. Since it was nearly a half-mile off the trail, we declined to visit it. I still had plenty of water, and my feet hurt, so it wouldn't do to make the long side trip out and back. So goes the thought process of the hiker with a load.

Shortly after crossing Roaring Brook, we began climbing again. The humidity had flooded back, and sweat was dripping off my nose. We eventually overtook my friends from Big Branch Shelter, the elderly father with the three young men in tow. Today he sat on a hill, red-faced and sweating. Exhausted. Observing his heft, I wondered about heart trouble and was relieved to see the three young men standing watch. Clyde told me later that when the old man wasn't looking, they had quietly taken some heavier items out of his pack and loaded them into their own.

Clyde later wrote in his journal, "When he shouldered his pack, you could tell he knew what they had done. He said nothing, but he hiked out with an obvious look of pride on his face."

About midday, we rolled into Minerva Hinchey Shelter, our original destination for the day. This shelter was Mrs. Gorp's baby; as a Green Mountain Club maintainer, she keeps the area clean and in repair, packs out trash, clears trail, and reports any problems that need addressing.

It was early and we felt strong, so we decided to push on. We did stop briefly at the shelter for a snack—despite our plans to do a trencherman number at the Whistle Stop Restaurant in the very near future. First, however, I left Mrs. Gorp a note in the register. Also, because I needed to make a pit stop before we hiked on, I rummaged around in my backpack for toilet paper. I then made a discovery no hiker welcomes: my toilet paper was gone. I had left it in the bushes near the White Rocks Cliff side trail. My face darkened and I cursed under my breath.

Well, adventurers must be flexible, I told myself. So I shrugged and set out to find some non-toxic leaves that could serve as a substitute.

But Clyde called me back.

"Yes?" I said sourly.

He handed me some paper. Not toilet paper, but paper nonetheless. I was appreciative. Paper would work better than leaves.

"Thank you." I started to walk away, but I stopped suddenly, peering closely at the paper. He'd given me the first few pages of the Long Trail maps—the maps we'd used since Day 1, which covered all of the ground we'd just finished walking. I looked back at Clyde. He was grinning like a monkey.

"That's the proper end for those!" he hooted. "Better than a map burning!" I grinned, too. He was right.

By the way, did I mention that MAF Man Clyde found his missing sock? In his very own pack? I didn't? That's probably just as well.

Eventually we descended the deep Clarendon Gorge. I looked longingly at the clear water rushing over the rock ledges far below, where a few sunbathers were stretched out, half in, half out of the cool stream. The Gorge's snaky suspension bridge shivered as we crossed it. On the paved Route 103 that followed, out of the shady trees, the August sun blasted. Walking became a sweaty irritation. Even though we stuck our thumbs out like old hands, no one wanted our smelly bodies in their nice cars. Who could blame them? So we hiked the blazing half-mile to the Whistle Stop.

It was an ideal stop for me; I had an excellent milkshake and a burger, and the staff later let me use their phone. Clyde fared less well, however. He felt a server had pointedly ignored him; maybe it was that "bum" thing again. This sort of treatment steamed Clyde, a proud man, and he devised a scheme to get his message across. After he'd hauled his scruffy self out of there, he confided to me that he'd left behind a very large tip.

"I could tell she was embarrassed to pick it up," he said, and added mischievously, "You don't have to be rude to get even."

The blast-furnace heat of the sun had eased by the time we finally caught a ride back to the trail: a taxi driver delivering some other hikers a much farther distance. We expected to pay a couple of dollars for the six-block shared ride and had our wallets out, but when we exited, we learned the half-mile trip, all sixty seconds of it, cost $10. We paid, but I can't recall that we tipped.

Our bellies straining to the point of bursting, Clyde and I labored up a steep, rock-strewn ravine. The dramatic stone walls dripped with mosses and ferns, and despite the incline and our extreme fullness of gut, we both commented on how enjoyable these extra "free" miles were. We'd planned a shorter day and now, thanks to café food, the Long Trail could lure us effortlessly farther down its white-blazed path, making miles that, according to our pre-set schedule, we didn't "have" to make that day.

"I like the 'don't hafta' part," said Clyde, continuing the conversation we'd started earlier that day. The work ethic still preyed upon his mind.

New freedoms emerge on a long walk, but so do new tyrannies. Hiking with a pre-set deadline entails a certain obligation to cover a calculated daily distance, and our situation was no exception to this rule. Like children distracted by a lollipop, we loved making the "free miles" that pushed us past the required daily distances. Throughout our hike, we strived for "free miles" when we could; such lofty goals helped to ease us along and often spared us from our own internal grumblings.

After a leisurely climb through the steep, rocky cleft, we cooled off at Clarendon Lookout, which quieted us with its views of the slanting sun. We still had a bit farther to hike, but it didn't seem to take any effort; we soon strolled into Clarendon Shelter and unpacked for the evening.

The shelter gleamed, as well-swept and as neat and clean as Minerva Hinchey had been. Curiously, someone had laid out cut wood in the fire ring. It was just waiting for a match.

Not long after we arrived, I heard the faint whine of an engine. Ten minutes later, an old fellow on a noisy four-wheeler emerged from an obscure, brushy two-track trail into the shelter clearing. At first, we thought he must be a site manager for the Green Mountain Club. No, the fellow said over the chugging of his engine, he was retired and just liked to "keep an eye on things, haul up wood, haul out trash, things like that." That accounted for the plentiful supply of wood for the fire ring.

The fellow finally cut the engine but remained sitting on his vehicle. His name was Poor Boy, he said, and he ran a local trash route during the day. He had no teeth in his head, real or false. Regardless, he engaged us in conversation, plied a ready laugh, and had an ample belly that jiggled with every guffaw. Before long a fire was lit, and the voluble fellow settled in for a chat.

Characters can delight, and I hung out until the evening's weariness overtook me. Clyde, who was less tired, stayed up. He and Poor Boy had hit it off; likable and talkative, Poor Boy had found a kindred spirit in Clyde. Both were enthusiastic storytellers well versed in the art, and they commenced to chew the fat around the fire.

I lay in my sleeping bag in the shelter and listened to their conversation a while before falling asleep. After the obligatory dissection of politics men seem to need in order to take each other's measure, Poor Boy had mentioned that he would be driving to the nearby town of Rutland the next day. Now, Clyde possesses an unparalleled "opportunity radar" and can whip up a scheme faster than any person I know. He started negotiating with Poor Boy: Could Poor Boy take our packs to the Inn at Long Trail, seventeen miles up the trail? It would be right on the way to Rutland. This delivery, I knew, would allow us the chance to cram in some more "free miles." It would also be our first chance to "slack-pack," hiker slang for hiking a section of a long-distance trail without a full pack.

Dozing off, I imagined how Poor Boy must be twinkling as he deftly sidestepped Clyde's parrying. Good-humored Poor Boy played Clyde like a fish on a line, avoiding a direct answer, yet not saying "no" either, drawing the evening out.

I never did hear the deal struck, but it was well after dark when Clyde shook me awake to say we would be slack-packing seventeen miles come morning, and that I needed to get a good night's sleep.

Yes. He woke me up to tell me to get a good night's sleep.

I was insensible, mostly in dreamland, my somnolent stupor stripping me of either personality or opinion.

"Snzzz … uh, huh? Okay … whatever … snzzzz …."

The reality of an impending seventeen-mile day, without packs, would have to wait until morning to sink in.

Day

10

Clarendon Shelter
to The Inn at Long Trail

Today's Miles: 16.4
Trip Miles: 103.6

S ince I hadn't participated in the previous evening's measure-
taking and negotiations, I think it understandable that I awoke
in a skeptical frame of mind. Would Clyde's fireside buddy
really return? Were we really going to slack-pack?

My questions were soon answered by the rumble of an engine from
somewhere beyond the trees. Clyde's judgment of Poor Boy, so far, was
apparently well placed. Up trundled Poor Boy, returning by the same
obscure two-track trail, but this time in a massive one-ton garbage truck.
He'd painted his name in bold letters across the front. Our toothless
friend was grinning as he drove up; he appeared to be in the same good
humor as the evening before.

He greeted us cheerfully before tossing our packs into the back of his
big rig. As I handed him money for gas, I felt another twinge of doubt. I
was a little nervous about handing my pack to a near-total stranger. Was
this wise? Without my gear, I knew, my adventure would be over.

Poor Boy remounted his truck with a jolly and confident wave that
inspired optimism even in a skeptic. Thus, I allowed hope to triumph
over good sense and waved goodbye. Off the truck rumbled to a
destination seventeen trail miles ahead. Anchors aweigh!

Clyde and I thought we would fly down those seventeen miles
without our packs. We *were* able to go faster, farther, but fly up the hills
we did not. Thru-hikers still outpaced us, easily, sweatlessly, lopingly—
and toting their full packs. Perhaps our pace would have been faster if

we hadn't had famous Killington Mountain—Vermont's second-highest peak at 4,235 feet in elevation—to ascend that day.

Early in the climb, we came upon a lovely bit of creek. To our delight, we found sodas chilling in a little wire corral in the water. I selected a cola and thumbed through the nearby register, digging out a pen to record my gratitude to whoever had left the trail magic. As we enjoyed this free glucose bonus, up walked our benefactor, who introduced himself as The Outhouse Repair Guy. He was packing in twenty-four more sodas. He said, so far this year, he'd spent $169 alone on pop. We left him with our genuine thanks.

Clyde and I grabbed a lunch break at the notorious Governor Clement Shelter, a stone hut that drunken locals were said to frequent on weekend evenings. Its proximity to a road crossing encouraged rowdy beer parties; aggressive confrontations between locals and hikers were commonplace. It was a lovely setting, but guidebooks cautioned hikers to avoid it.

All appeared quiet, however, when we hiked into the shelter's cool, cavernous depths at noon. There we found a stone fireplace with a crafted, cobbled arch crowning it. A great deal of love and care had clearly gone into the construction, I remarked. Guidebook warnings aside, we found the shelter an ideal spot for a much-needed break.

After ten days on the trail, my body had grown efficient, demanding rest every at every opportunity. I snatched a quick power nap in the shelter, feet upon the upper bunks. Elevating my feet helped relieve their soreness, I was discovering. My angle also revealed every manner of interesting shelter graffiti, which was abundant. Clyde spotted a few of his own.

"Hey," he said. "God was here and wrote his name in charcoal on the roof." Minutes later, he read aloud a register entry from a female thru-hiker named Buddha: "Why would God do that?" she had written.

Rested by the break, we headed back to the trail, where the terrain kicked strongly upward toward Killington. Even unburdened of our heavy packs, Clyde and I slogged and slogged and slogged up the mountain. Killington was the highest mountain we'd climbed on this hike, and it felt like it at every step.

Finally, as trails are wont to do, the path crested. We paused, panting. A spur trail ran directly up to the actual summit, Killington Peak, where

French explorer Samuel de Champlain is said to have coined the name "Verd Mont," from the French "vert mont," meaning "green mountain." Friends had been encouraging me to make the rugged hike to the top; it was only two-tenths of a mile from the trail, and there I could visit the ski lodge and take in the fine views. These sorts of suggestions seem like excellent ideas at the time; however, jellied calves and inadequate lung power always trump ambition. After a brief break, we started down.

The lovely stone Cooper Lodge, a four-walled shelter, beamed its friendly "take-your-pack-off" vibe at us on the start of the Killington descent. How could we resist? We settled there for a longer respite than we'd had at the trail's crest. I was well into my second power nap of the day when I heard two hikers enter, talking in excited tones. I looked up sleepily.

Blocking the doorway was a massive fellow, a tattooed giant built like a brick privy. He had arms larger than my thighs and an impressive pectoral development. He introduced himself as Bramble and said that he had been an Army Ranger. He looked intimidating. I shifted, alert now, and watched as the large man moved from window to door, exclaiming appreciatively in every direction he looked: "Wow, look at this!" and "Man, this is gorgeous!" I smiled. The guy was a cream puff.

I sat up, and Bramble soon engaged me in conversation as if I were his long-lost sister. He was day-hiking and commented with enthusiasm on our Long Trail journey and my A.T. plans for the following year. His introduction to the Green Mountains had proved eye-opening, he said. He declared, on the spot, his plans to return to Vermont and backpack a trail. His childlike pleasure charmed both Clyde and me; the juxtaposition of massive bulk and puppyish enthusiasm was engaging. On top of that, Bramble and his slighter buddy, who introduced himself as Squirrel, shared some of their crackers and cheese with us. I'd grown fond of the two by the time we packed out a half-hour later.

As I started hiking again, I realized that Bramble's obvious excitement had reawakened my own weary enthusiasm for the privilege of being on these green and stony peaks. Yes, magic and awe lived in these mountains; one needed only to receive it. It was a good frame of mind for hiking, and the remaining six miles of the day's trek went smoothly.

It was late that afternoon when Clyde and I descended to pass Pico Camp Shelter, the victim of hyperactive porcupines that had chewed up the boards of the shed. Four miles later, we reached U.S. Route 4. A mile to our right was our destination for the night, and it wasn't long before we got our first glimpse of it: the Inn at Long Trail.

I quickened my pace and soon ran inside. I immediately saw our packs. Relief! Poor Boy had come through, bless his heart. Good man. I thanked him silently.

I'd sent my second maildrop to the delightful inn. Along with that heavy carton from home, the desk clerk handed me a package I wasn't expecting. It was from my fellow prospective Class of '03 A.T. hiker, Ted Anderson ("Soleman") of Florida. Ted planned to hike as a fundraiser for Hospice, so we'd struck up an Internet correspondence. He'd sent his gift of breakfast bars in a box from Amazon.com. Ted, fond of mischief, had waggishly sub-labeled the return address in large, look-at-me block print: "ADULT PORN DEPARTMENT." The desk clerk eyed me curiously as I ripped open the box.

Clyde opened his packages to discover he'd hit the carbohydrate jackpot. Various family members had mailed homemade treats, including chocolate chip cookies and a solid pound of fudge. He generously urged his bounty on everyone within earshot. And why not? As we surveyed our maildrops, we saw at a glance what we hadn't known back home: we'd sent ourselves far too much food to carry. The fear of starvation lurks deep in our human psyches, but the truth was, there was always plenty to eat.

Still, we were happy to put dehydrated meals behind us for a day. Once laundered and showered, we hit McGrath's Irish Pub, located inside the Inn. A large, stewy bowl soon steamed before me. With thick chunks of homemade, fresh-baked, thickly buttered Irish soda bread on the side, the pub's signature Guinness Irish stew was a lip-smacking change from the four basic hiker food groups—Ramen noodles, filtered water, Snickers bars, and Vitamin I.

With bellies full of stew and shepherd's pie, Clyde and I raised a mug of Guinness in homage to our friends and families. Neither of us was particularly fond of beer, but "when in Rome," one must do as the locals, and this was an Irish bar. The Guinness was on tap, and the golden foam lay thick upon the dark brew.

This rustic Inn at Long Trail cost my budget dearly, but I felt cosseted by the hot shower, the hearty meal, and the amiable company. We sat in the pub and chatted with several of the A.T. thru-hikers we'd been keeping pace with, including Cous-Cous and Foxfire. My heart warmed to see them, and surprisingly so, given our short acquaintance. I was beginning to glimpse how fellow travelers could bond so strongly in a short time. The "linear grapevine" of the trail offered news of people ahead and behind us. In talking with our fellow hikers, we caught up on the trail gossip, and I was struck by how many trail names I recognized.

Meanwhile, in the background, a cheeky two-man Irish band had set up for Saturday night. Before they switched on, Clyde said he needed to call home and turned in for the night. I lingered, as the pub was stuffed with hikers and locals who were there for the music and draft brew. The playful musicians soon stirred the willing crowd to croak out a few verses of "Cockles and mussels, alive, alive-O!"

It wasn't long before the weight of the day fell upon me like a stone, and I pushed my chair back to retire. Before returning to my room, I walked outside and lay on the clipped lawn to check the skies. The time for an annual Perseid meteor shower was upon us, and I spent a few of my final moments of wakefulness that night scanning the stars for the fallen.

Day 11

We had hiked ten full days, covering more than a hundred miles. No longer did we think of ourselves as Baby Adventurers. Certainly, we had more to learn, but we were keeping pace. The facts were these: with the first hundred miles well under our pack belts, we counted the Long Trail as more than one-third done. In the next few days, we would pass the halfway mark. That was serious progress. We may have *felt* slower than tar on pavement, but we were inching forward to Canada—even though Clyde still hadn't fully committed to that goal.

The A.T. thru-hikers, with 1,500 miles behind them, strode these brazen mountains with ease, unleashing graceful, long strides up the steepest slopes. Clyde and I were still grinding out the uphills in trudge mode. But trudge we did. In fact, I was impressed with the genuine progress an ordinary, out-of-shape trudger could claim. "Step-by-step" *was* getting the job done.

Besides us, seven Long Trail hikers had stayed at The Inn at Long Trail that night. Every one of us had begun walking on the first of August. Clyde and I were pleased to be among "the norm," whatever *that* was, given the pleasantly off-center bent of the folks we were meeting. The world of "civilization," I predicted, would have some serious work on its hands when we all reached the northern U.S. border.

Before we started hiking that day, I was disappointed to witness a Long Trail casualty: the speedy young Excalibur had learned of a beloved grandfather's serious illness and was leaving the trail.

"You've got to take care of your family," he said to me when I extended condolences. "The trail will always be there." His situation reminded me that, despite the heat, drought, and discomfort, this long-distance hike was a gift, not a given. I resolved, again, to savor this gift.

Speaking of savoring, what an utter pleasure it was to suck down true percolated coffee at the Inn's restaurant that morning! I'd finally given up trying to brew a cup while on the trail. Tea-bag coffees just didn't cut it for me; they were a great idea but a cardboard-tasting hassle. On the trail, it was easier to abstain. My first real cup in too many days was downright luxurious. Brewed just minutes before, the bean oils curled up my nostrils and exploded in my head. Marvelous!

Clyde joined me as I was basking in java heaven and waiting for breakfast. After ordering himself a cup, he told me a funny coffee story. It seems he'd been snacking on his chocolate chip cookies earlier that morning and wished for a cup of joe. He'd descended to the lobby to find a pot with a stack of cups, so he poured himself a cup.

"A lady coming downstairs asked me, in the most acerbic tone possible, whether I was a guest," he said.

"What did you say to her?" I asked, ever the dutiful straight woman.

"What *could* I say?" He paused, relishing his punch line: "I replied, with as much calm as I could muster, 'No, you charged me a hundred bucks! I'm a *renter*, not a guest!'"

We laughed. Clyde had a knack for turning potential conflict situations into tales he could tell for years. But we agreed the lady likely had a point. There was a free camping spot across the street, and many hikers opted to stay there rather than pay for a room. We could imagine how the Inn at Long Trail might have a problem with penny-pinching hikers sneaking in for freebies.

Here at the Inn, we shared our last breakfast with the A.T. thru-hikers who had become our traveling companions. We Long Trailers would split from our A.T. brethren that morning, just a few miles north, at an intersection called Maine Junction. The Long Trail would head northerly, up the spine of the Green Mountains, while the Appalachian

Trail went east to the formidable White Mountains of New Hampshire. I would be sorry to see the thru-hikers go; besides providing playful and inclusive company, they had become a valuable source of information for me in planning my own A.T. thru-hike.

I observed an interesting contrast between us Long Trailers, ten days in, and these A.T. hikers, who were well into their fourth month on the trail. We of the Long Trail were fresh, unfit, and starry-eyed. Most of the A.T. northbounders, by the time they had reached Vermont, were somewhat burned out. The stars had dimmed in their eyes, their spirits dampened by the sheer, grinding rigors of the trail—injury, chronic joint pain, teeth-gritting endurance, generally poor nutrition, and the day-in, day-out pattern of walking mile after mile after mile, up and down hills, through the endless "green tunnel" of the Appalachian Trail. They freely admitted that their enthusiasm had abated over the months and the miles.

On the other hand, they were the toughest of the tough: the survivors. Many of their comrades had dropped out weeks or months before. Each year, only some ten to twenty percent of A.T. hopefuls manage to walk the entire 2,000-plus miles in a single stretch.

I wanted to know why. I wanted to be one of them.

I quizzed as many NOBOs as I could. Four sources of motivation, I discovered, had kept them moving through Vermont. First was a burning desire not to quit, now that they were little more than a month from their goal. After all, they'd already endured so much, and they really didn't have that much farther to go.

Another factor was anticipation: they were excited about the upcoming White Mountains to the east, and Maine after that. They hoped the stunning beauty ahead would restore their sense of wonder in the woods—something else they admitted had staled a bit.

The third factor was a no-brainer: if they went home, they would have to return to work. No small thing, as a hard-earned six months of freedom had proved attractive.

Finally, many of these thru-hikers enjoyed deep support from home. Family and friends, amazed that their Couch-Potato Beloved had actually walked more than 1,500 miles, lovingly sent treats, letters of encouragement, and phone cards to them at the Inn at Long Trail and elsewhere. Even those onlookers who had been skeptical at first had become proud, impressed, and enthused well-wishers by the time their thru-hikers had reached Vermont.

While most A.T. thru-hikers treated us Long Trail "End-to-Enders" as kindred spirits, some demonstrated a less-pleasant attitude toward "outsiders." I could understand their attitudes, to a degree; after 1,500 miles, only the grittiest—and the luckiest of those to escape injury, illness, bankruptcy, and family recall—get this far. A hiker feels proud, and justifiably so.

Sometimes, though, pride can bleed into the indulgence of arrogance. Particularly in trail towns, I had observed a certain "better-than-thou" air about some of the A.T. hikers, though none was as blatant as that of the beer-glutton Rainbird. I watched this attitude, however subtle, put shopkeepers and hoteliers on edge. This arrogance, combined with the hikers' innocent, natural bonds of having gone through many trials together, gave some A.T. hikers—and observers—a sense of "us versus them," creating situations that appeared ripe for conflict.

Mo, the laid-back thru-hiker we'd met early in our hike, had once mentioned a smug NOBO whose attitude had rankled a later-starting SOBO. Mo found this ridiculous, as the southbounder, who had started his thru-hike in June, had just traversed the toughest portion of the A.T.: Maine and the White Mountains.

"Some NOBOs act like, 'Well, I've just walked 1,500 miles and you've only walked 500, so I'm better and can give you all kinds of unsolicited advice,'" said Mo. "As if a SOBO's 500 miles don't count for much. You can tell it really pisses off some of them." With a smile, he added that the low-mileage folks—overburdened day hikers, work-weary weekenders, and persevering section hikers—had been his greatest source of trail magic along the trek. I smiled back; Clyde and I had donated our share. In town, we'd offered our excess bounty to all hikers in the vicinity.

Mo seemed happy to see everyone, accepting them no matter how much (or little) time they'd spent on the Appalachian Trail. I felt certain this his lively, pleasant attitude was a big reason he attracted all that trail magic—the rides, free phone calls, and extra pack goodies—provided by less-ambitious hikers. Happily, most thru-hikers I met were more like Mo and less like Rainbird.

The night before, Clyde and I had kicked around the possibility of taking a day off, called a "zero day," at the Inn at Long Trail, but we had never come to a firm conclusion. Instead, we spent a leisurely morning doing laundry, eating Clyde's fudge, and hanging out with fellow hikers in a sunny room off the main lounge. At least I was in leisure mode. Clyde, who could only stand so much inactivity, had begun to pace.

Cous-Cous looked up from her book. Observing my Type A partner, only five years distant from his heart attack, she suggested he might benefit from unwinding that tight internal spring of his a bit.

"Like, CHILL, man," she counseled. Then she curled her forefingers to touch her thumbs, extending her arms like the Buddha. "You know," she said. "Ommmmmm."

The thought of Clyde sitting still for thirty minutes and meditating on his breath tickled me to no end. I laughed and laughed.

About mid-afternoon, after a pleasant day of rest, the lure of adventure returned—or perhaps it was the inclination to save a hundred bucks on a room that prevailed. In any case, we decided to sleep in the woods. The next shelter was a mere mile and a half north.

We shucked out of the rustic Inn at Long Trail, with its slab tables, twig furniture, 40-year-old Irish pub, and rock cliff wall. (The building's unusual restaurant incorporated some massive slabs of bedrock; it was a mountain inn anchored to the mountain.) We were reluctant to leave this place we had come to love, but we had miles to go. The rugged north awaited us. In that rugged north, I thought excitedly, *moose* awaited us. *Canada* awaited us! It was time to move on.

Our re-supplied packs were so heavy that we caught a bus to avoid walking to the trailhead in the blazing sun. I scanned the sky. So far, we'd been blessed with weather, getting our rain early in the hike to toughen us and increase our appreciation of the grand, sunny days we'd had recently. With any luck, it would remain clear.

As we lumbered up the trail, the paranoid part of my brain insisted that a mischievous "someone" had hidden five-pound river rocks in my pack. I eyed my partner suspiciously. Like children, hikers love sophomoric pranks; I'd even heard of one unlucky thru-hiker whose friends had installed a dead woodchuck in his pack. Surely these six days of *food* I was carrying wouldn't weigh me down so cruelly, smashing flat my poor, abused feet. But no, I learned later, neither river rocks, mischief, nor Clyde were to blame; my overloaded food bag was the culprit. Though we ordinary adventurers had gained much experience already, clearly we still had a lot to learn.

Clyde had mailed his tent ahead to our next re-supply point six days ahead, keeping only his tent's light outer cover, a fly-tarp, for emergency shelter. By saving weight on his tent, he'd made room for all that homemade fudge, no doubt. Space in the shelters would not be at such a premium from now on, we figured, since we Long Trailers were about to leave the A.T. behind. Clyde could be fairly certain of gaining a dry bunk in the small six- to ten-person shelters.

We groaned and griped our way to Maine Junction, the actual crossroads where the Long Trail and the Appalachian Trail part company. Here an amiable day-hiking couple took our picture for us. Before we moved on from this decision point, I stared hard at the place where the A.T. split off to the east toward the steep and rugged Whites. I felt the tug.

"Next year," I thought. Next year, I would begin hiking 1,500 miles south of Maine Junction, in the hills of north Georgia, where the A.T. began at Springer Mountain. Next year, I hoped to make it at least this far and rank among "the survivors." I turned away from the A.T. and hiked north.

The Long Trail immediately looked different to us. Where the A.T. was a cleared, worn path, the less-traveled Long Trail was overgrown with thick nettles and a yellow flower I thought might be Jerusalem artichoke. The Long Trail seemed lonelier, almost deserted. Not a soul chanced by during our whole afternoon trek.

We soon reached Tucker-Johnson Shelter, aired out our feet, and did a spot-damage assessment. We felt good and decided to keep chugging another 3.6 miles to Rolston Rest Shelter. Before we knew it, we were at Rolston Rest and five "free" miles had unfolded on our intended "zero day." We'd tucked in some unplanned mileage with a minimum of strain and difficulty. Hikers call such a restful, low-mileage hiking day a near-zero, or a "nero."

Though he had meticulously prepared and insisted that we stick to the schedule that was slave-driving our adventure, Clyde loved those "free" miles. He repeated his freedom mantra: "That's the part I like: the 'don't hafta' part!"

I agreed. Such is the power of the mind on attitude.

The mosquitoes were lusty and fierce at the shelter, singing for blood. The drinking source proved to be an icy blast of mountain-cold water, a charming pool with a tiny waterfall tumbling down a slab of mossy rock. I sat on another rock, soaking my hot, sore feet in the bowl, typing my journal. For some reason the mosquitoes, who had whipped themselves into a biting frenzy at the shelter, had no interest in following me to this sitting-rock. A squirrel joined me, though, nipping a drink and then scurrying off.

What a peaceful way to end a day of needed rest, easy hiking, and free miles. Heaven at last had proved to be a magical little watering hole, a deep, frigid, clear pool hidden far in the tranquil Vermont woods.

The night promised to showcase the peak of the August Perseid meteor shower. I very much wanted to fall asleep watching falling stars zinging across the dark heavens. Thus, no buggy shelter for this hiker. I had a problem, though: If I hung my hammock, the supporting trees would block my view. I quickly found a solution and set up my rig directly on the ground, as a sort of groundcloth, and left the tarp off. I used my hiking poles as "tent poles" to lift the attached ridgeline, allowing the mesh screening to repel the bugs. Now I could sleep out under the stars—away from the bugs, far from town lights—and catch a few stars to wish upon.

The setup took some work. Clyde observed my bustle of activity and predicted I would most likely see little more than the back of my eyelids that night.

Before turning in, we perused the shelter register, which reported recent sightings of bear and moose. Excellent! Now I would see a moose. Once I settled in my tiny "tent," though, my enthusiasm wavered. The register's mention of large wildlife started to work on my mind. I felt vulnerable, lying on the ground, in a virtual trail crossroads. How would Clyde tell my aging father that his only daughter, his fine baby girl, had been moose-trodden?

The battered register, stained and edges curling from the damp, had offered another nugget for the spirit: a poem, a familiar old verse. Yet having just stood at Maine Junction and seen—and almost felt, viscerally—the two paths splitting, the poem took on a fresh light for me. The possibilities—both for this journey and for the much larger one I would attempt the next year—hung in the air. Why, if I did *this* trail, then I could do *that* one! And if I did *that* one, who *knows* where the next "trail" would lead?

I felt inspired, my decisions for adventure validated. It seemed so much easier to be sentimentally optimistic in the woods. Why was that? I'd sleep on it.

The poem was "The Road Not Taken" by Robert Frost, and it read:

> *Two roads diverged in a yellow wood,*
> *And sorry I could not travel both*
> *And be one traveler, long I stood*
> *And looked down one as far as I could*
> *To where it bent in the undergrowth;*
>
> *Then took the other, as just as fair,*
> *And having perhaps the better claim,*
> *Because it was grassy and wanted wear;*
> *Though as for that, the passing there*
> *Had worn them really about the same,*
>
> *And both that morning equally lay*
> *In leaves no step had trodden black.*
> *Oh, I kept the first for another day!*
> *Yet knowing how way leads on to way,*
> *I doubted if I should ever come back.*
>
> *I shall be telling this with a sigh*
> *Somewhere ages and ages hence:*
> *Two roads diverged in a wood, and I—*
> *I took the one less traveled by,*
> *And that has made all the difference.*

Yes, I knew how "way leads on to way."

In my case, however, I had the solid, growing certainty that while I, too, "kept the first for another day," I would indeed "come back" and walk it in 2003.

No burning meteorites streaked across the sky that night as far as I knew. Maybe this was one of those rare instances when Clyde was right—I just couldn't keep my eyes open for long.

Restfulness did not come easy, though.

I hadn't slept well the past couple of nights and awoke dog-tired each morning. Clyde would pop a few Tylenol PM caplets each evening to combat insomnia, but his solution didn't appeal to me. I didn't want to combine acetaminophen with the ibuprofen I was gulping down almost daily for my aches and pains. I'd read the combination was rough on the liver, and I believed a liver might be a useful organ to keep around.

I attributed the night's lack of rest to circumstance. Initially, my little hammock-tent, comfy and bug-free, had worked well. I'd set up in a tiny clearing in front of the shelter and could look up through the mesh and see a patch of sky through the trees—perfect for meteor-spotting. My small campsite, set as it was in the open intersection between the paths to the trail and to the water hole, allowed me to hear the spring's tiny waterfall tinkling musically all night.

The flowing water hadn't been the only sound affecting my dreams, though. All night long, that register entry about large, wild beasts worked on my mind. My ears, now ultra-sensitive to animal sounds, had picked up an entire parade of critters traveling to the watering hole just fifty yards away. I could hear their little wild tongues lapping, or so I thought.

To make matters worse, I would sometimes hear heavier footsteps (a moose, surely!) approaching my ground-level bivouac, pausing—just about the time I rose to full wakefulness—then retreating. I was never unnerved enough to get up, probably because *that* would have been too much work for my bone-tired body. Some primitive part of my awareness remained on high alert, though. I never did drop down into a black-hole sleep.

Early that morning, Clyde proposed shooting for Sunrise Shelter, more than fourteen miles away. I balked. Fourteen miles was too much! It was then that Clyde explained the situation: the distances to the shelters were awkward. David Logan Shelter lay only eight miles ahead, too little mileage for a full day's hike, even for an ordinary, half-fit adventurer. Sunrise Shelter, on the other hand, was six and a half miles beyond David Logan. We agreed that a hike to Sunrise was an ambitious goal, considering our fitness, the growing heat of the day, and our overstuffed backpacks. We considered camping somewhere between the two shelters and finally agreed to meet in eight miles for lunch. Once we got to David Logan, we would know how much farther we wanted to hike that day.

Clyde was packed and ready to go at 6:45 that morning; for him, the workday had begun. He slung on his backpack and hiked out in his workmanlike way. I remained behind. Unlike Clyde, I hadn't fully grasped a major strategy of long-distance backpacking: that of walking early to avoid hiking in the worst of the day's heat. I much preferred the camping, socializing, and eating parts of backpacking—the stationary bits. I would soon learn the cost of my early-morning, pack-shouldering reluctance.

So I procrastinated, lingering at Rolston Rest's beautiful water hole, tracing the sweet, cold water upstream, looking for the source. I never did find it. The lively trickle bobbed and weaved, appeared and then went missing beneath the cracked jumble of mossy rock.

Finally, thirty minutes later, my latent work ethic surfaced. It was time to strap heavy weights on my body and start walking. I sighed and shrugged on the pack. Better get moving.

The day grew hot enough to melt the Snickers bars I'd hidden deep in my pack. Abundant, chest-high nettles blocked the breeze, with few trees directly shading the trail. The ridge forest beside the trail seemed to have been logged in the last ten years; the spindly trees did little to block the sun as it bore down. I might as well have been hiking a North Carolina power-line clearing, I thought.

The path nosed slightly upwards all day and offered no obvious break spots. I seemed to be ascending an inclined plane; it wasn't exactly a serious slope, but it was just slanted enough that a body couldn't get a head of steam up. To further aggravate the struggle, deer flies buzzed and tangled in my damp curls all morning. I'd raise my hand to free them, and they would churlishly bite my scalp before whizzing off in a huff.

The temperature rose rapidly and was well into the steamy nineties by mid-morning. August was definitely here, and in full force. I could catch no views through the high weeds and young trees. Merely breathing in the cloying jungle humidity was like trying to suck air through a damp washcloth. On this airless and uninspiring stretch, my recent sweet-smelling cleanliness vaporized.

The worst smell of all was the one emitted by my synthetic poly shirt, which, even when clean, offended me. It had raised a stink before I ever left the lobby of the Inn at Long Trail. Not for the first time that morning, I longed for a cotton tank top to walk in. "Cotton kills!" is the rallying cry of the mountain hiker; unlike synthetics, cotton dries slowly, making it a potentially dangerous covering in the cold, wet conditions that can spring up even in summer at high elevations. I snorted. Even trail rules could have their exceptions. It seemed to me that, in the summer, a slow-drying fabric like cotton could prove useful, if used judiciously. I resolved to try it for myself sometime.

Whenever I passed one of the trail's numerous tiny brooks and found privacy, I pulled off my rank shirt and rinsed it out. I'd developed a primitive little routine of rinsing, squeezing, and agitating. I even carried a stout zip-locked plastic bag labeled "WASH" for this purpose. Wash cycle over, I pitched the rinse water well away from the water source, in keeping with the Leave-No-Trace ethic.

The constant wetting of my shirt in icy waters kept a total meltdown at bay. It was a good thing, too; the sun blistered down on large stretches of today's relentlessly uphill and often shadeless trail. I found myself measuring my breaks to coincide with shade patches. After climbing to a meager scrap of shade, I'd pause, gasp the muggy air until my heart rate dropped, and then soldier resolutely through the sun-broiled stretches.

The trail's logged-over openness also favored thorny, leg-ripping brambles. Now and again, the chest-high raspberry bushes yielded a few precious berries: rare, red drops of sweetness hanging in the sea of abundant green. Is there any finer fruit to find ripe in the forest? What sweet taste explosions were contained in such a little bit of seeded stuff! Abundance!

I was struck by how quickly my mood could shift as I walked—from irritation to enchantment, from resistance to acceptance, and then from peacefulness back to annoyance again. I nibbled ripe berries when I could, swore at the tearing brambles when I couldn't. Simplicity and a certain spareness were working their way into my journey. My absurd delight at finding one ripe berry was a measure of that process. It didn't matter that a whole pint of raspberries cost just a few dollars at the grocery store in town. Nothing compared to the joy of finding the berries free and unexpected in the woods.

I walked alone all morning. It was no hardship; I enjoyed my own company. One reason for taking this journey was to see what surfaced when I hiked by myself. A long walk can settle a person down, can sharpen one's focus, even on difficult days—or maybe especially on difficult days. Early in the hike, I'd discovered that I observed more when alone: birds, clouds, plant life, animal tracks, weather. As the days progressed, an unaccountable happiness would often bubble up as I studied the green and rocky world around me, though it sometimes took me hours to wind down enough to notice the details. Luckily, the mindless exercise of walking helped the unwinding.

With no billboards, television, traffic congestion, ringing phones, road rage, strip malls, car parks, loud music, ads, or other attention-demanding distractions, I had begun to let down, day by day, and to focus on one thing at a time. The inclination towards multi-tasking diminished, and an unbidden process of reflection began. I often found myself pondering, in many different ways, the same question: How did I want to live the second half of my life?

That question shaped itself into a number of forms: What does it mean to live a life without fear? Where is the "juice"? How could I trust that inner voice more surely than the surrounding sea of conflicting voices? How could I structure life to be productive, yet remain flexible enough to cultivate "a sensitivity to the impulses of grace in our lives," as Benedictine Sister Joan Chittister so eloquently put it?

While I reaped benefits from this solitude, I was also finding that I genuinely liked people. The life of a recluse was not for me. Those few of us in the woods were kindred spirits, each of us challenging something in our lives, all of us testing the boundaries of this novel, wandering freedom. Fellow hikers could appreciate both the big sweep of cloudless sky at an overlook and the bright pebbles in a brook. In the evenings, we would gather at a shelter, talking, telling jokes and tall tales, taking comfort in the presence of others.

I was in no mood for the presence of others that hot morning, however, and instead embraced the task of hiking alone. The trail traced a narrow ridge for much of the steamy day. The mountain-ringed Chittenden Reservoir sparkled far below, and I entertained myself with fantasies of leaping off the ridge like a sweaty super-heroine, landing in the water, backpack and all, with an enormous *kerplunk!* The wild backcountry lake appeared largely undeveloped from my vantage point, with forest trees growing right down to the shoreline. Wouldn't a swim there be fine? Without the bugs, without the heat, and without an albatross of an overloaded pack, why, this might actually be a fine walk, I thought.

A small fog of mosquitoes brushed my arms and brow all morning, but as long as I kept walking and ignored their dentist-drill whine in my ear canal, I suffered only a minimum of mental mayhem. The mosquitoes buzzed incessantly, but they didn't seem to be biting. I wondered if this was due to the B-vitamin complex I was taking each day. I'd read somewhere that it could repel the biting bugs.

The water sources, so plentiful earlier, vanished on the late-morning stretch. Before I realized it, I was rationing water during the hottest part of a scorching day. I generally carried three twenty-ounce wide-mouth plastic bottles, but that morning, with a heavy pack-load of food, I had foolishly lightened my burden by leaving one bottle empty, thinking I could get by with two bottles. Wrong. I ran out of water well before noon and soon began to feel the effects of dehydration.

The day's trail seemed endless. The eight miles to the shelter should have taken no more than four hours, yet well over five hours later, I was still fighting my way uphill. "Should" counted for little out here. This simple, uninspiring path was kicking my butt. Visions of long, cool drinks of water danced in my head. I fretted uselessly about missed opportunities, about the morning's crystalline, cold spring. Why hadn't I filled my last bottle?

About one o'clock, the trail dropped into Telephone Gap. Of course there was no phone there, just some snowmobile trails. I hadn't expected a phone booth, but Clyde had had some fun with the idea nonetheless. He later wrote in his journal, "What a cruel joke to play on Jan. The Green Mountain Club has no compassion for a phone-starved woman."

I felt very much like a trail-weenie that last hour before reaching the shelter. The farther I trudged, the harder I pushed, the "hurrieder" I went, the "behinder" I seemed to fall. My mental noise cranked into overdrive. I imagined Clyde waiting at David Logan Shelter, tapping his foot with impatience to march six more miles. I grew resentful of the image. I couldn't just grab a snack and go, either; my bacteria-killing water treatment alone took thirty minutes, and I needed to tank up. Didn't he know I was seriously dehydrated? Couldn't he just *chill?* I regretted tarrying at the lovely spring that morning.

But I could go no faster. My exhausted feet began to tangle up in themselves. At this hot, sweaty and stumble-footed point, I knew I didn't have another six miles in me. How would I convey this to Clyde? Every rock of seat-height I passed called out to have a sit: "Jan, park your weary butt here, and rest a spell." Often I did just that. This dragging and dehydrated death-march wasn't quite the adventure I'd had in mind. Where was the bliss, the transcendence? Where were the windswept peaks, the blazing sunsets? *Where were the moose?*

After an eternity of exhausted trudging, I saw a greying sign: David Logan Shelter was a mere two-tenths of a mile off the trail. I took the side trail, hoping the shelter spring was running strongly; even so, with my water treatment, relief would have to be postponed for at least a half-hour. I might just have to lie down and lap it directly from the pool, I thought feverishly—treatment be damned! As I shuffled down to the shelter clearing, I spotted Clyde sitting by the piped water source, filtering away. I thought to apologize for my late start, and for keeping him waiting. I thought to give him hell for wanting to push on further and make my life a living misery.

Instead, I held out my water bottle, mutely. It was all I could do. Bless his heart, the man filled it up with filtered water. If he never did another good thing in his life, surely Clyde's karma that day had tipped strongly to the positive. I drank forty cold ounces at that sitting, and another twenty after lunch. I was dry.

Clyde then uttered words that gladdened my heart.

"Man," he said. "I sure hope you don't want to go on to the next shelter. I can't do it today."

Yes!

"Well," I ventured generously, "if you *really* would rather stay here …"

Later, in the register, we read that others had struggled with that same perplexedly simple stretch of trail. Some of the most profane comments were from Long-Trail hikers who had *already* thru-hiked the A.T. If accomplished thru-hikers had struggled, well then, we were in good company, we figured. At this point in the hike, we were still sifting and judging our performance, secretly unsure of how we were "measuring up" to some ill-defined ideal.

Clyde and I picked listlessly at our lunches, knowing we needed to replenish muscles exhausted by heat and effort. Long naps followed. I slept a good two hours, then rose, overheated. I ached all over—probably the residual effects of dehydration. I felt even hotter after my nap, if that was possible, so I walked downstream for a cool rinse-off. Though I'd pared my base pack weight down to sixteen pounds before food and water, I still carried one luxury item: a thin, blue washcloth. Rough like a mother cat's tongue, the washcloth delivered a satisfying scrub and rendered, for a moment, the splendid illusion of spa-like cleanliness.

After the wash, I journaled on a rock near the water, my feet cooling in the stream. Fiddling with the Pocketmail device, I discovered a few new functions, resetting the date and time, and setting the alarm for the reasonable hour of six. As a wake-up time, it seemed a good compromise between efficiency and leisure. I was embracing my lesson about procrastination and late starts on stifling days.

Toward the end of the steamy afternoon, Branch and Stick, whom we'd first met at Glastenbury Mountain, dragged in. Branch tossed down a good thirty ounces of cold spring water right away. I later learned that he, too, had misjudged his water on this stretch and, like me, had run out. Storyteller Clyde, meanwhile, looked delighted to have the masculine company.

The two young men set up camp in the shelter, and the now-familiar pattern of a shelter evening on the Long Trail began. We all built a fire eventually, and a communal spirit settled over our group; we were Long-Trail End-to-Enders, on our own long-distance quest. Awash in good feelings and recalling that childhood fable about sharing, we invented the hiker's version of "stone soup." Clyde broke out a dehydrated apple-cobbler mix his niece had given him for Christmas, and I donated some oil for the baking, a granola bar for topping crumbles, and some pecan pieces as a capstone. Branch and Stick contributed some extra pans and their white-gas stove.

Together, we created a fine campfire cobbler, all the sweeter for the hardship of the day. Adventuring was proving to be an unending series of lessons, struggles, and rewards. My day had begun in sweet solitude, had moved through lonely challenges, and had ended with the restful camaraderie of my fellow long-distance hikers. Drained by the full day, I selected a top bunk in the shelter for my sleeping bag and promptly fell asleep.

Day

13

Tuesday, August 13, 2002

David Long Shelter
to Sucker Brook Shelter

Today's Miles: 12.6
Trip Miles: 128.9

Rare are those nights when true, deep, black-hole sleep blesses the bone-weary supplicant. Such profound slumber does much to restore a ragged body and mind, and following the previous day's heat exhaustion, I finally slept hard. So hard, in fact, that I snoozed right through the Pocketmail alarm.

Despite my careful, expert programming the evening before, my Pocketmail had fired off its cheerful wake-up call in the middle of the night. I never heard it. Clyde said later he'd called out to me. No response. I was gone. The device had beeped for about fifteen minutes, my unhappy shelter-mates claimed. At some point, young Branch had climbed down from his top bunk to look for the source, purportedly to pitch the appliance deep into the woods, but he couldn't find it. Being in another dimension, I slept through the lengthy search-drama, too.

Finally, Branch shook me awake so I could find the unit. Groggily, I rose from the slumberous depths and fumbled for my reading glasses; by some miracle I found them, despite the dark and my stupor. Stiff, unyielding muscles slowed my arthritic descent from a top bunk. I found my pack and located the faithfully peeping unit by ear and turned it on, the bright LED screen instantly blinding me. I tried to focus through scrunched eyes and scrolled madly, searching the screen for the programming directions—the pressure, you might say, was on—and eventually managed to shut the blasted thing off.

In the dreadful silence that followed, I glanced at the time. It was—gasp!—only 3:30 A.M. Oh no! I had joined the ranks of Obnoxious Shelter Beepers. I had earned my bunk in the Hiker Hall of Shame.

Such annoying, insomnia-inducing noise, always on the part of *other* hikers, was one reason I used earplugs. Communal living in a rough eight-by-ten-foot shed posed a number of challenges: raucous snoring, unsubtle early risers, foraging rodents, beeping watch alarms. No matter that I set the Pocketmail alarm by accident; an obnoxious beep is an obnoxious beep. What an ignominious fall from grace! With the flick of an electronic button, I'd tumbled from an entertaining, stone-soup–making fireside colleague to shelter *persona non grata*. In the morning, after a few more hours of sleep—none, I might add, as fabulously delicious as the previous slumber—I disabled the alarm function for good.

Scattered showers were predicted for the day. While ordinary adventurers might give the weather casual attention at home, out here we had all become acutely attuned to the forces of nature. Our little hiker-antennae quivered and probed the atmosphere many times during a day. Lacking a waterproof carapace, our vulnerable hiker bodies would scuttle from ridge to shelter, eyes on the skies. I'd begun to note where the sun set and where it would rise. I would watch clouds to see if they billowed into thunderheads, or fluffed off into wispy cirrus clouds. Subconsciously, I would gauge the strength of the wind.

Light clouds cruised across the sky that morning. The air was again thick with humidity, but nothing looked too watery yet. I'd stay tuned in; muggy, hot days often meant afternoon thunderstorms. As I emerged from my sleeping bag for the second time in four hours, however, I tuned in to another sort of climate: the emotional weather of camp.

The David Logan Shelter boys woke up a tad grumpy. Oops. Certainly the sleep-shattering beeps had made me no friends there. *Mea culpa, mea culpa.* I apologized yet again for my technical ineptness. But we were also mentally wearied by the hard hiking of late, and no one minded admitting it. At that point, we all hurt. Everyone had blisters, and everyone felt worn down by the previous day's heat, dehydration, and uninspiring trail. This I knew.

No meteorologist was needed to sniff the wind and smell the major grump tide that was a-comin' in. I was still the shelter goat; time to skedaddle. I packed up early and headed out first, not wanting to be an easy target for the general spewing of anger. Hiking was hard enough without having to carry the added weight of "head stuff."

The first twenty minutes out of camp led straight uphill, making me doubly glad to be alone. I knew tempers would fray on this early climb. My own mental noise fired up immediately: "Why is the trail always uphill right out of camp, when I'm at my stiffest? Good Lord, I'm tired. I could go right back to sleep. It's going to be hot again today. I bet it rains too. I don't think I can do this for another two weeks. This is *hard.*"

Naturally, my internal chorus was the most clamorous for the first half-mile or so. As the joints loosened up and the birds sang of their boundaries, the voice of calm and reason prevailed: "Don't … think … about … that. Just … put … one foot … in front of … another." Trudge mode always prevails, like water on stone. A rhythm opened up.

Clyde had reminded me to keep my camera handy in case I stumbled upon a moose in my early walking; the first hiker out of camp usually saw the most wildlife, including spiders in their webs, built overnight across the trail. Clyde had claimed that he, MAF Man the Ultra-observant, had already seen a moose on this trip and had pictures in the bag. Was he having me on? The thought occurred to me. One of us needed to come home with a photo, though. I loosened the zipper on my camera case and swung it to the front of my hip-belt. I would be ready when I saw my first wild, cloven-hoofed beast.

The initial signs of moose were promising. I saw enough acorn-sized scat on the ridges to open a compost boutique. Peering about me as I walked, I amused myself with ridiculous wordplay ("Say *that* fast three times: moose scat, moose cat, muscat …").

Before hitting the trail that morning, I'd tied a fabric-softener sheet to the back of my ponytail. Hikers claimed it would help repel the eye-diving gnats that had become annoyingly prevalent. Hiking poles in hand, I'd practically knocked myself out swatting them over the last few days. I secretly hoped my new gnat repellent would stave off those ultra-soprano, ear-whining mosquitoes as well.

It seemed to work. Even though the sheet was affixed to the back of my head, it seemed to be helping up front. The gnats attempted fewer kamikaze runs at my eyeballs. No maddening mosquito whined its irritating *nnnnnnnnnn* in my ears. Even the deer flies avoided tangling in my hair today. I'd read that A.T. pioneer Grandma Gatewood, who first thru-hiked the trail in 1958, had used a sprig of sassafras branch for the same purpose. I'd seen none of those shrubs on the Long Trail yet, so fabric-softener sheets would have to do the trick for me.

Happily bug-free, I hiked alone for most of the morning, eyes scanning my surroundings for moose. Evidence of their passage peppered the trail, causing me to skip in spots, but no moose was to pose for me that morning. On a quiet uphill slog, however, I was stopped in my tracks, heart banging, by a sudden explosion of feathers from a log roost about shoulder-height. Grouse!

Well, that sure gets the old adrenaline surging for a climb. I stepped lightly because—sure enough!—three more of the beautiful, fat birds exploded from the other side of the trail. Like great blue herons on a river, the grouse flew directly up-trail, so we repeated this exciting dance several times. They eventually realized they could cut away from the trail and swing behind me to complete their morning in peace—that is, until the David Logan Shelter boys arrived. I chuckled, imagining *that* scene, again glad that, as today's goat, I was out of snarling range.

Mid-morning, while crossing a small bridge that spanned a steep gorge, I paused for what should have been a brief water break. My system needed hydrating. Again.

My body awareness had heightened in more ways than one. My feet, for example, had developed a messaging system that could penetrate my normal cloud of oblivion. By alerting me to early hot spots and potential rubs, the feet gave me a chance to improve their circumstances by airing them out, changing socks, or taping a spot.

The stomach had an effective messaging system, too. On the small bridge that morning, I cleverly deciphered its persistent rumbling and got the clear message that the old bod was craving lunch: pouch tuna and salty goldfish crackers, my ultimate summer power meal.

"Lunch?" I argued. "Already? You've had plenty of fuel!" All morning long, snacks had supplemented my breakfast of a granola bar topped with peanut butter. Surely I'd consumed enough calories to sustain movement. But no, this highly tuned hiking instrument wanted *protein! Now!*

I tried to reason with the Beast of Burden that was my body. "Come on! Buck up! It's still two hours until lunch. You know, lunch hour? As in, when one sits and eats?"

WANT ... PROTEIN ... NOW! growled the Beast stubbornly.

We had a tense standoff, the Beast and I, there on the bridge. Necessity won, as it always does in the end. The Beast had the last word.

I shrugged off my pack, sat, my legs dangling off the bridge, and dug out my tuna and goldfish crackers. The meal proved meaty and lip-smacking, swilled down by icy filtered water. I topped off this wholly satisfying feast with a sugar indulgence, my second-to-last Snickers bar.

Thus are the bounds of civilized life loosed, I philosophized. Eating when hungry, and not by the clock? How anarchistic could one get? Somehow, I knew that two more weeks in the woods would offer further insight on the subject.

Refreshed and pacified, the Beast carried me to Sunrise Shelter, where two friendly Long-Trail southbounders fiddled with a white gas stove that was dribbling fuel. Lighting it in the shelter, they'd been caught off guard when the thing had flamed up dramatically, so an outside repair seemed wise. Temporarily ensconced in the clearing in front of the shelter, they persisted, wanting to cook pancakes. I couldn't blame them; they'd packed an entire quart of real Vermont syrup. Clearly, these long-distance backpackers had struck their perfect balance between hiking hard and eating well.

It wasn't long before Clyde joined us. As the official scheduler, he checked his maps and reported his findings to me. About midday, he said, we would cross VT 73 at Brandon Gap. Then he surprised me: Did I want to hitch into town and find a phone so I could send and receive my Pocketmail e-mails?

I was suspicious. Clyde, suggesting a phone? I pondered this change of heart. Usually, I was the one pushing for town and a phone, while Clyde argued for the extra mile. Then I smiled, remembering that he'd given his family my e-mail address when we were at the Inn at Long Trail. Now that *he* was expecting e-mail, he regarded my Pocketmail device differently.

We chatted awhile with the southbounders. One of the best things about meeting hikers going the opposite direction is that everyone can exchange useful information on the miles ahead. The southbounders told us the next twelve miles were dry and that we would be wise to load up on water there at Sunrise Shelter. I thought about chancing it, going light on the water, since we were planning to hitch to civilization from the upcoming road only a mile away. But a potential hitch was not a sure thing. In a process hikers call "cameling up," I tanked up at the creek, drinking as much water as I could hold. Next, I filled all my bottles to the rim. I groaned at the extra eight pounds dragging on my shoulders. Unbeknownst to me, more weight was to come.

As we were preparing to hike out, Branch arrived with a gift. Out of his pack he pulled out my entire gallon-bag of suppers—all six days' worth. Mentally, I hadn't had it together that morning at the shelter. In my early haste to pack and run, I'd left the meals behind. Rather than leave me without a meal, Branch had packed my food all morning, all six and a half miles, on top of all his gear. My hero!

I was truly moved. Hauling someone else's gear is an act beyond expectation. Hikers must prepare to be self-sufficient and remain vigilant about their packs, and I was embarrassed by my careless mental lapse. I'd have to do better if I was going to tackle the A.T. I also felt a little chastened; Branch had literally carried my weight after being rudely awakened by my Pocketmail in the middle of the night. His game decision to return my meals touched me. His was a large act of kindness or, at the very least, of responsibility.

We all shared a laugh at my expense. Luckily, everyone seemed more cheerful after lunch, to my genuine relief.

Clyde and I soon limped out of Sunrise Shelter, hoping to catch a hitch at Brandon Gap and find Clyde his phone. Truth be told, I wouldn't have minded a phone, either. At the country crossing, however, no one stopped for two disheveled, scary-looking hikers. After nearly two weeks in the woods, Clyde had acquired the "hiker look," sporting a grizzled, fourteen-day beard. His special bandanna was wound on his head pirate-style, and his shirt was grubby and sweat-stained. I knew I must appear equally frazzled: sunburned, wild hair, no makeup, scruffy attire. I was having a rash of bad-hair days, as my comb had disappeared well before Clarendon Shelter. Fingers just didn't do the job.

The strange thing was, I *felt* beautiful on the trail: fit, strong, graceful, adventurous, curious, healthy, and competent. Alive. After an extended time on a long-distance trail, "stuff" starts to drop away, and a certain serenity reflects outward. This glorious internal image is fostered by the distinct lack of mirrors in the wild. I also loved the feel of new muscles forming, hardening, lines leaning out, and of my increasingly sinewy frame as the "baby fat" melted off. On a good day, I imagined I saw the shadow of an abdominal "six-pack," its first visitation in some time. I was even able to take my pack's hip-belt in a notch.

But later, in "civilization," the mirror told a different tale. Sometimes it's best not to know. Yikes! Hairs standing on end like I'm Krusty the Clown. Sunburned nose and cheekbones. Dirt-smeared legs and face. No makeup. Rumpled, stained clothing. Bosom melting away.

But there would be no mirror, and no phone, that day. No one gave us a ride. The roadside sun pressed down like a heavy hand, so scorching that we couldn't stand in it for long without getting dizzy. We bagged the idea of further thumbing while baking beneath the sun and began the long, hard trudge up the face of Mount Horrid as thunder rumbled in the distance.

Though seemingly unshackled two weeks into the hike, we remained well aware of time. We were still keeping score with the clock. We were still fighting these mountains. Hiking uphill made for slower times, though, and the uphill out of Brandon Gap showed no mercy. Clyde felt it, too. "That sonofagun went on for a while, especially after seven miles already," he grumbled later that evening.

We eventually gained a lovely rock ridge lined with red spruce. Despite the rocks underfoot, our stride kicked into gear on the flatter trail. The day's predicted showers blew our way, the spruce bending, the sky darkening, the thunder booming closer. A ridge top is hardly the optimal place from which to protrude in a thunderstorm, so we hustled as fast as rock and pack would allow.

When I stopped to put on rain gear and stow my camera deep inside the pack, Clyde pulled ahead of me. Meanwhile, the wind picked up and the thunder crashed even closer. Then, in a single moment, the heavy skies cracked open, and I was suddenly pelted by cold, sideways rain. Water dripped from my eyelashes, and stray hair plastered itself to my cheeks. My heart raced. My skin tingled with awareness of my vulnerability. I was unnerved. There was no clear way to descend the knife ridge, so I did the only thing I could: I kept hiking. I didn't want to be a potential lightning rod, but I didn't know what else to do.

Eventually, inspiration struck. With single-minded resolve, I stopped and did what any red-blooded long-distance hiker would: I dug out my last Snickers bar and ate it. No sense in being vaporized with an uneaten candy bar in the pack. *Eat dessert first!*

The terrain was slick and treacherous. Rocks were greasy with sodden moss, and crumbling humus turned into grip-less mud. I fell hard on my rump twice, cursing my first falls of the hike and lamenting my cold, soaked backside. Parts of the rocky trail became a rushing watercourse, and sometimes I literally waded through a roiling river of trail. Traction was not a given. My shoes and socks sloshed with every step.

After inflicting a satisfactory amount of discomfort, the storm left as quickly as it had come. The sun soon emerged, just in time to begin its slow setting. The slanting rays cut through the spruce bows and highlighted every crystal drop. The mini-prisms shivered as I passed by, fracturing the light. A joy came over me, balancing the heart-stopping anxiety I'd suffered during the storm.

The smell of the forest after rain is a glorious scent—part piney compost, part mineral steam, part good earth. Part moose scat too, to tell the truth. Why were there so many moose so high up on a ridge? I wondered. I understood they were pond browsers, but the scat on high was plentiful. Clearly, like hikers, they enjoyed a good trail.

Six o'clock passed, and I figured I had missed the shelter; you can imagine the nervous chorus in my head. At 6:39, I stumbled, relieved, upon Sucker Brook Shelter. I was all done in. The heat had baked us, and the rains had drenched us.

We had hiked almost thirteen miles—an impressive distance for an ordinary adventurer. But A.T. thru-hikers in Vermont considered fifteen miles an easy day, I knew, and we were still short of that. On the other hand, I reasoned to myself, we were only two weeks into our journey, and they were four months into theirs.

No matter how hard I tried, I couldn't stop this mental obsession with miles, this "measuring" of my capabilities. I suppose I was always seeking to answer the underlying unknown: Did I have what it took to backpack more than 2,000 uncomfortable A.T. miles?

At the shelter, Clyde sat listlessly and declared he was too tired to cook. I believed him. He looked ready to pass out. Eventually, though, he mustered the energy to eat; his Vietnamese cardiologist—the one he was afraid of—had read him the riot act before the hike, warning that his damaged heart muscle required attentive refueling. Looking at our schedule, he promised that, given the heat and terrain, the next day would bring a shorter, easier hike.

Good thing. The Beast's position was non-negotiable.

Day
14

Wednesday, August 14, 2002

Sucker Brook Shelter
to Skyline Lodge

Today's Miles: 9.6
Trip Miles: 138.5

"More days out behind us than in front of us!" I announced in a rousing voice from my sleeping bag.

Clyde grunted, groggy. He'd taken a sleeping pill the night before, no doubt as insurance against wayward alarm beeps.

I was eager to hike, even if my aching body wasn't. Clyde and I had another milestone day ahead of us. At Brandon Gap, the site of our unsuccessful hitch, we'd walked off Map Six of our twelve-map series. Today we would reach our halfway point, mileage-wise. And although we often felt slow and inadequate to the task, we were keeping pace with a few other Long-Trail hikers, such as Branch and Stick, who had hiked in at dark the night before.

Sluggish and slow-moving, hikers groaned as they rose from their bags and lowered themselves gingerly from the shelter platform. Everyone had baked in the sun the previous day, and we all felt fried and ground up this morning. The chronic stiffness of the long-distance backpacker is so common it even has a name—hiker hobble. Clyde's "hiker hobble" was the result of the usual sore muscles and unyielding joints; dehydration was also taking its toll. Plus, he was nursing a blistered toe. I pitied him as he limped gingerly toward the privy.

Three other hikers had stayed in the shelter that night. Corey and Joe were a pleasant couple on a shorter adventure, hiking north from Brandon Gap. Colin was a friendly young fellow who chatted with us that morning as we creakily prepared our breakfasts and organized our kits. He, meanwhile, pulled on a complete suit of mesh—pants, shirt, hood. It would keep the aggressive northern bugs at bay, he said. Though sparse at the end of their season, black flies could draw blood, and Vermont mosquitoes inflicted their own special brand of misery. I was curious about the suit though. Other than the gnats, the bugs had not been that bothersome for us this late in the summer.

Colin, we learned, had established a base camp at Sucker Brook Shelter two days before and was planning to sleep here one more night. Such an extended stay at a shelter is rare; ordinary backpackers almost never spend more than a single night in one place. Colin, however, was no ordinary backpacker. He had an official mission: forest inventory for the U.S. Forest Service. His job, he explained, was to assess the area's mature trees for lumber. That morning he sat on the shelter platform and pointed out the primary northern hardwoods he was searching for: yellow birch; sugar maple; American beech. Nearby, one magnificent yellow birch, far larger than the ordinary, was split into two trunks.

"That one we'd call 'overmature,'" he said. So it was too old to be cut down. I was glad; it looked born to rule over this forest fiefdom.

I'd begun to perk up at his conversation. As I pulled myself out of my sleeping bag, I described for Colin a local, low-growing plant I'd seen lately that brought back memories of flora from my northern Wisconsin childhood visits. Did he know the name of it? The plant resembled a substantial lily of the valley and had a whorl of thick leaves—broad, flat and wide—that gave rise to a single thin stem. On this stem were three to five striking blue-black berries about the size of blueberries, but harder and far glossier. My mystery plant grew abundantly in the acidic forest duff here. I'd also seen it in the Boundary Waters area of Michigan and Canada. Colin the forester shook his head sadly and confessed that he was hopeless with non-woody plants.

Returning from the privy after a long absence, Clyde announced that he'd run out of toilet paper. Everyone looked sympathetic—"There but for the grace of God go I," and all that. He looked directly at me, his faithful hiking partner. I thought his situation might make for some amusing leverage. Of *course* I would share what I had with my partner— but not without a spot of fun first! But before I could start, Joe offered his roll to MAF Man, eliminating a fine opportunity for mischief. Clyde,

I could tell, actually had the makings of a great "yogi"—a trail term for a hiker who is able to receive something without actually asking for it, a behavior recalling cartoon icon Yogi Bear. "Yogiing" is the act of achieving an unsolicited treat, and Clyde had just "yogied" his first bit of toilet paper.

As I packed, Clyde pinpointed our day's destination as Skyline Lodge, a shelter scarcely more than ten miles away. The lethargic shelter crowd finally broke up and began hiking at a shockingly late 8:45. Industrious A.T. thru-hikers would have been appalled at us laggard Long-Trail End-to-Enders, who still resisted the start of the morning. So much for the work ethic.

The Long Trail led, as always, uphill. We struggled up Mount Worth, which I quickly dubbed Mount Unworthy. While the younger hikers never seemed to need a warm-up to hit their rhythm in the morning, this is not the case for the "overmature" among us. Weeds obscured the trail, snatching at our legs and clothes and immediately drenching us with their dew. What a mess! This was the worst overgrowth yet. Our hiking sticks were rendered nearly useless as they snagged in the tangle of raspberry and nettles. The sticks' only function at that point was to steer the worst of the brambles away from our tender flesh.

Finally, we crested a ridge. Here the high-elevation red spruce and balsam fir took over, shading out the thorny underbrush. This boreal forest, fragrant with coniferous trees and seasoned with moose droppings, concealed mysterious northern denizens such as fisher cats and pine marten. This new environment fascinated us southeastern hikers to no end, as our most exotic southern mountaintop tree was the beleaguered Fraser fir, our most unusual creature the least weasel.

Here, we were seeing a forest similar to the woods of northern Russia. "Taiga" is the Russian word for these tough, needled northern forests that scratch out a living in the thin soils of formerly glaciated areas. Every peak we climbed in northern Vermont rewarded us with a little island of taiga.

Clyde later wrote, "One good thing about going up is that an increase in elevation always changes the plants growing near the trail. As we get to the top of the mountains, the bushes give way to conifers. You can smell them before you see them. It gives you energy to make it to the top."

Near the summit of the newly christened Mount Unworthy, I noticed about three dozen spruces blown over by some fierce, funneled gale. Their crowns pointed one direction, and their roots dangled nakedly above the sheer rock from which they were torn. Northern Vermont's ridge-top forests rest not in deep, rich loams, but on the solid native stone of the mountain. Tree roots wedge themselves into cracks, digging in against the forces of the elements, drawing spare nourishment from acidic duff and decomposing stone. The conical shapes of the trees themselves shed snow, and their height is kept pruned by the bitter, high-elevation conditions. Life stakes a claim on the peaks, no doubt. But it's a tenuous hold on the rocky pinnacles of Vermont, in the Kingdom of Weather, where the powers of the wind and ice are sovereign.

The trail eventually left the wind-tossed conifers and descended back to the steamy realms of the deciduous. We'd been looking forward to Lake Pleiad, where the guidebook promised good swimming. On our third brutally hot and humid day in a row, I was craving a fully clothed jump into the water. Water would cool and refresh. It would rinse off the thin blanket of dried salt, formed from my own sweat, that now covered my body and clothes.

Six of us from the Sucker Brook Shelter—Clyde, Branch and Stick, Corey and Joe, and I—ended up hiking the late morning together. We lunched early, high upon the ridge top, spreading out on the handy wooden deck of the Middlebury Snow Bowl gondola platform, drying in the cooling breezes, and peering down to Route 125 far below. Clyde kept us laughing with his jokes and told us of his desire to ride the gondola. He stood for a moment to eye the cables; strung from matchstick poles, they seemed to tumble precipitously down the steep slope. "Whoa, dude!" he said, and the rest of us cracked up laughing. He'd picked up the "dude!" habit from his college-aged summer landscape crew, and it sounded funny to hear the MAF Man say it.

The lunchtime atmosphere grew downright social. We were a cheerful company of kindred spirits, all very different, yet sharing the same journey. I wondered: Was this how the A.T. would feel next year?

We soon set off as a group, but the merry mood evaporated immediately in the unbearable heat. Sweat dripped off my nose as we descended through the stifling forest, and I drank most of my water, which was warm and did little to refresh. Conversation died down to grunts and oaths; generous natures turned cranky and short-tempered. We spread out along the trail, the others forging ahead of Clyde and me.

Only the promise of a swim, six-tenths of a mile past our lunch spot, cheered us that afternoon, but somehow Clyde and I missed the side trail to Lake Pleiad. We cursed, but there was no question about it: we would not be walking back uphill to find it. We hiked on, and shortly after noon, we reached the hot pavement of Middlebury Gap and Route 125. Out came the thumbs. We held them like old pros now, but for twenty minutes, car after car passed us, blowing hot wind in their wake. Well, who could blame them? We looked like sweaty bums. We looked like we'd smell. We *did* smell.

Finally, a young Indian couple slowed, looked us over, and then rolled to a stop not far ahead. We ran over and climbed into their clean backseat. The young woman, petite and feminine, kindly offered us cold bottled water. I attempted to sip politely, but ladylike sips turned into noisy gulps as I guzzled nearly a liter right there. They raised their eyebrows, expressing surprise at my thirst. All of us laughed. They had just witnessed, in action, my sincere appreciation of their kindness. The couple never once mentioned our "woodsy" odor either, which must have been considerable, and dropped us off at the door to Middlebury College's Bread Loaf campus, where we could scout out a phone and a bathroom with a sink, soap, and flush toilets. I didn't dare voice my hopes of scaring up a cafeteria or hot shower.

Another of those "hiking paradoxes" was shaping up for me. Clyde and I adventured daily on Vermont's backcountry trails and peaks, yet we made a run for the luxuries of civilization every chance we got. The irony of our situation did not escape us, and we kept a good humor about our inconsistent habits. Simple things, such as toilet paper, soap, and hot running water, acquired an elevated status, and we no longer took them for granted. Vending machines, so under-appreciated by us in our pre-trail lives, now held precious carbohydrate treasure. As this paradox emerged, we did not try to fight it. We freely relished these dashes into the margins of "civilization"; they felt like provisional raids and evoked great glee.

We found a couple of indoor telephones at the college. Feet up, thirst somewhat quenched, we made our respective calls in air-conditioned comfort. I was on my last call when Clyde burst into my booth. "We got us a ride back to the trailhead," he announced. "Come on!"

Whoa, dude, indeed! My larger plan—complete with dreams of a hot shower—was immediately eclipsed by the excitement of so effortlessly scoring a return ride. Every time I hitchhiked, I felt the deep, lurking uneasiness of the foot traveler—that barely conscious fear of hitching into to town miles away and becoming trapped there, a stranger in a strange land, with no one willing to lug us back out. The offer of a ride back to the trailhead was not to be taken lightly.

There was no time to nose out a vending machine. I dashed into the nearby restroom, threw water on my face (no soap, no time), skipped the luxury rinse, and scooped up my pack on my way to the car. So much for my fantasy of slipping into a dorm for a shower and finding a co-ed to cover for me in exchange for a few tall tales of the trail.

Our trail angels were nineteen-year-old Damon and his father, Wingnut. Damon had hiked a good chunk of the Camino Santiago in Spain and France the previous year. A kindred spirit, he had clearly recognized the look of foot travelers in need of a ride. Or perhaps Clyde *was* a born expert at yogiing. Whatever the reason, Damon and Wingnut were happy to drive us to the trail in their van, chattering cheerfully about hiking as they fed us fresh-picked cherry tomatoes. We thanked them profusely for the ride and the veggie snack. Such simple acts of kindness mean much when one is afoot.

Back on the Long Trail, we hiked into the Breadloaf Wilderness. Naturally, the land rose steeply from the road, as civilization tends to settle into the low spots. No question about it: we were back in the mountains. Halfway up sun-baked Burnt Hill, Clyde paused ahead of me to lower his racing pulse. With the heat and elevation, my heart was banging right along, too.

Never one to leave an effort undocumented, Clyde was formulating his commentary. I could see it in his face.

"Damn," he said, starting up again as breath returned. "It's a damn hard mountain and it ain't even got a proper name! Burnt Hill! *Hill?* What kind of name is that for a damn hard mountain? It's a *mountain,* it's not a *hill!*"

I reached for a drink and realized that, in my haste, I'd failed to fill my water bottles. On such a hot, dry stretch of trail, my mistake was a foolish and forgetful one. While hiking, especially in the heat, water is even more important than food.

But there was no going back. Clyde and I never went backward. It just was not something we did. It wasn't because we were stubborn. We simply had little interest in revisiting the sheer physical effort needed to get from here to there with weight on our backs—particularly when mountains lay between "here" and "there."

We passed the halfway point of the Long Trail on our chug to Boyce Shelter. This merited celebration. We were, after all, officially half-done with the Long Trail of Vermont. Hurray! We had walked in two weeks what my four-cylinder Subaru could do in two hours. Brilliant. I could only shake my head at that thought.

We found Branch, Stick, Corey, and Joe resting at Boyce Shelter. The spring was dry, they said, and they were going to push two and a half more miles to the shelter at Skylight Pond, where there was supposed to be another spring. The heat had done me in for the moment. "Go ahead," I said to Clyde as the others started to hike out. "I need to eat something first. I'll catch up with you at the next shelter." He followed them out, leaving me alone at Boyce.

I sat alone on the shelter platform and exhaled deeply in the silence. Immediately I felt the freedom of being accountable only to myself. Here was another paradox: as a budding adventurer, I still didn't feel brave enough to travel fully alone. Indeed, the Long Trail experience would have been less satisfying if I'd hiked it solo. To decipher a map and point at distant pinprick mountains ("we're going *there*") and then actually walk *there*, with all the shared experiences of the journey, was proving to be big fun—in a twisted, dehydrated sort of way.

I used the last of my water to cook a tasty mélange of dried mashed potatoes, refried bean flakes, home-dehydrated Vidalia onions, textured vegetable protein, hamburger gravel, and what I called "soylent green," a home-dehydrated kale, chard, spinach, and broccoli mix, ground to a vegetable powder. The finishing touch was a seasoning of cheddar-cheese powder. While it sounds like a concoction guaranteed to send someone running to the outhouse, it actually tasted fantastic that evening.

After supper, I set off for the next shelter, Skyline Lodge. The walk through the high Vermont woods unnerved me. I knew I was on the correct trail, but I never saw a white blaze between Boyce Shelter and

Skyline Lodge. Only later did I learn that trails in designated wilderness areas are very lightly blazed. At the time, walking alone, I felt acutely the vulnerability that accompanies solitude. Later in my hiking adventures, I would learn to tolerate, and even relish, such trail uncertainties, but at that juncture, I felt poorly prepared. Plus, I was very, very thirsty. The thought of spending the night out there—lost, alone, and out of water—began to prey on my mind. The unpleasant internal dialog had just cranked up to full throttle when, near sunset, I finally reached the shelter turnoff.

Weary, scorched, and desperately thirsty, I scuffed down the side trail and into the shelter area. Visions of crystalline waters were dancing in my head, so I was horrified when Clyde told me that the spring had long since dried up in the summer's drought. The only fluid at Skyline Lodge was from the putrid, shallow mudflat out front—the so-called Skylight Pond, which offered slime rather than water. One word floated to mind as I looked at our water source for the night: *eutrophic.*

Re-hydrated and lounging on the shady shelter porch, Clyde had long since come to accept the situation. He tossed me his water filter. "You'll want this."

My sluggish, dried-out mind worked slowly. I must have looked shocked. I stared at the dying pond. It was choked with scum, frogs, lily-pads, and decaying matter. Its level was half what it should have been, exposing bare mud flats dotted with dragonflies. A massive beaver lodge enclosed the far side. I wasn't keen on drinking beaver-water, since beavers were one carrier of the intestinal parasite *giardia lamblia.* I voiced my concerns.

"No worries. Even the beaver left," said a man standing nearby, who I later learned was Jay, the Green Mountain Club caretaker. "And in this dry year, even the moose don't come anymore."

Hiker creed dictates that one come prepared with all the necessary gear and not have to borrow from others. When a true situation arises, however, one's fellow hikers can be generous. Clyde was loaning his filter to anyone who needed it, and several hikers had already accepted his offer. I took the filter gratefully and stared toward the pond. After filtering, I figured I could treat the strained brew with the chlorine dioxide mix I used for water purification.

To get past the shoreline mud and to the actual retreating waters, I crawled out onto a slimy log, flushing a few frogs back into the thick, stagnant water. Balancing on the narrow, slippery surface, I held my bottle between my knees and worked the pump with my hands. The filter, already clogged with green slime, was difficult to pump. I used all my strength to filter what little water I could and only managed to extract fifteen ounces of warm, smelly liquid before the filter and I both gave up. That left me forty-five ounces short. Fifteen ounces of filtered scum would not even hydrate me for the night, much less for the next day. Still, I had water. Life would go on.

I backed off the log carefully, clutching my equipment. A fall into this foul-smelling mud must be avoided at all costs, I thought. If I slopped in up to a haunch, how would I manage at bedtime—slimed, with no means to wash myself, and a sleeping bag to crawl into?

Eutrophic. I didn't want to be eutrophic.

I shuddered. Why was I doing this to myself?

At the same time, surrounded by dragonflies and birds settling in for the night and frogs plopping into the fat waters, I straightened up and noticed the last rays of the sun glancing off the pond. The distant mountains reflected some of that pink light. I swiveled, taking in the full view for the first time. For no obvious reason, an ease began to settle about me.

When I returned, I explored the amenities at Skyline Lodge. I liked what I saw: a roomy cabin with a porch, a view, and space for a good many hikers, a dozen or more. A few hikers, all of them new to me, were cooking and talking on the porch. Joe, Corey, Branch, and Stick had apparently set up camp somewhere south of the shelter. I took in the view from the roomy porch. Barring the water situation, I thought, this could be someone's mountaintop Shangri-La.

The Green Mountain Club provided for a seasonal caretaker at Skyline Lodge to ensure minimal impact to the sensitive ridge top and to perform routine maintenance, such as hauling in wood chips for the compost privy. Our caretaker, Jay, collected a small GMC fee from each hiker, and I was glad I'd remembered to stash a few dollar bills in my pack. Mostly I relied on my debit or credit card while hiking.

Clyde and I discussed our options. Although he had more water than I did, his would not last through the next morning. We would eventually hike to Battell Shelter, fourteen miles away and the site of a running brook. But we needed some relief *now,* not in fourteen miles. Jay explained that an unusual drought and heat wave was sweeping the state, and that even higher temperatures were predicted for the next day. I groaned at the news. The extreme heat had made the last several days a particularly unpleasant trial of patience and endurance. In crisper weather, we might have sailed forward, rather than grinding painfully through this half-baked adventure.

It was a trial all right, but we were still hiking. Clyde and I were still on the Long Trail, and we were still moving slowly north toward Canada. When I finally settled into my sleeping bag and glanced around at the hikers, the shelter walls, and the view outside, life looked just fine to me—sweat, blisters, irritations, dehydration, and all.

Day

15

No doubt about it. We were dragging.
Clyde spoke first. "I don't feel like walking today."
There. He said it.

I didn't feel like walking, either. The heat had cored and dried us out from the inside, leaving us drained, dehydrated, and dispirited. In addition, issues from home were tugging me mentally out of the present, away from the hike. I tried to ignore the unwelcome thoughts that crowded into my brain, but I couldn't get my mind to chill.

Then there was the sheer physical factor. Everything hurt. The Beast that was my overworked body found great comfort in the simple act of sitting still, of just doing nothing. Get up and move? Shoulder a heavy pack and *walk* up those mountains? In *this* heat? The Beast wasn't so sure about that. It was a case of simple, basic physics: An object at rest prefers to stay at rest until something annoys it enough to make it move.

We did move, though. After all, what was the alternative? Drink the slime water of Skylight Pond another day? Not an option, even with a working filter, which we lacked. Part of living this simple life meant being blessed, or perhaps cursed, with few choices. Our choice that morning was to keep hiking north.

We shuffled into forward motion and headed down the trail. Soon our rigid knees, backs, feet, and attitudes started to loosen up. As happened every day on the trail, the act of putting our bodies into motion made it easier for us to remain in motion; another law of backpacking physics.

A mile or so down the trail, hiking always ceased to seem like such an unpleasant chore and just became the thing we were doing.

That morning at Skyline Lodge, our reluctance to hike seemed like only one of dozens of daily challenges to our goal. Such routine decisions about inertia are significant on a long-distance trail, especially in the creaky mornings. They comprise, frankly, make-or-break moments. It often seems flat-out easier to throw in the old pack towel and retreat to the land of recliners, frosty glasses, and ample, thoughtless horsepower. Such moments are critical junctures; before you know it, you've checked the map, shot down a side trail, and are sticking your thumb out beside some road crossing before day's end.

I didn't realize it at the time, but in those simple acts—of rising from the shelter, of packing, of setting foot back on the trail that day—Clyde and I both passed an important test of resilience. Long after our hike was over, Clyde would tell me, speaking of that morning at Skyline Lodge, "I would have gone home if you hadn't been there. I'd had enough."

What shifted us onward? I wasn't sure about Clyde. Pride, maybe? Plus, he was a doer, never one to sit still if he could help it. As for myself? What had motivated *me* that morning? I desperately wanted to find good water, certainly; the warm slime of Skylight Pond just wasn't doing the job of re-hydration. But water was merely an immediate, physical desire. Truthfully, that was only a small part of what urged me on that morning.

The bottom line, I believe, was that "inner call" thing. I wanted to walk to Canada. I had something to prove to myself. I didn't know what that "something" was; all I knew was that it was prompting me, day after sweltering day, to put one foot in front of the other and trudge north.

As I trudged, I was also keen to see what would appear around the next crook in the path. While that constant anticipation could not diminish the journey's annoyances and discomforts, it did shift my focus from them. The rough stuff was there, certainly, and I griped with the best of them, but that "rough stuff" was part of a much larger context. Even though the aches, pains, and mental noise loomed large and loud, an important part of me remained detached from them and was perpetually excited by the adventure at hand. More often than not, annoyances were background rather than foreground—even when they were in the foreground. Funny how the mind works.

Once we were in motion, treats and benefits always appeared as if to reward us for our recommitment. The sunrise over Skylight Pond, for instance, stabbed my heart with its beauty while the White Mountains smoldered darkly to the east. Couch and television just couldn't provide that kind of soul-grab. Sparkling and lovely, Skylight Pond proved worthy of its name that morning. I snapped a picture. When folks back home see *this* shot, I thought, they'll never believe such a pristine view was, up close, a scummy, stagnant frog hole.

To the beauty at Skylight Pond, I said goodbye with sadness. To its mucky scum, I bade good riddance. Clyde and I would fill our water bottles elsewhere.

As we hiked, we fantasized about the benefits a cool, clear water source would bestow. With good water, we declared, our scrawny, desiccated cells would plump right out. Good water would lubricate our creaky, complaining joints. With good water, the cushions on the bottom of our feet would return. And then, in some future golden moment, we would stride out, loose-limbed and powerful, like the toughened fitness gods we were becoming. We wouldn't ache at all! Once we found good water, life on the Long Trail would be great!

Life *was* great, actually. I had a candy bar in my pack for lunch, which I had traded for a spare supper—and it wasn't long until lunch. Soon I would be able to sit, rest, and consume calories. *Chocolate* calories.

Such is the unaccountable optimism of the long-distance hiker.

Two miles later, at Emily Proctor Shelter, we found the next water hole. It was active, but just barely. The weak spring was a mere trickle. The water, however, was crystalline, fresh, and icy, with a deeper pool for dipping. We drank to the point of bursting. The unexpected watery bounty cheered us enormously.

While snacking at the shelter site, we were joined by a confident young woman with two fat, black braids and a heavy gemstone around her neck. Self-assured, lovely, and braless, she was hiking southbound solo. Had I decided to hike alone for weeks at a time (braless, no less), my mother would have had a meltdown.

Women seem to possess a primal, near-constant awareness of their vulnerability. It's a program that always runs in the background, affecting much of how we behave. I was amazed whenever I met women like this one on a trail, who shucked society's rules and set off on solo long-distance hikes. Where, I wondered, did these young women get the courage to set aside their conditioning and head out alone? Would I find that same sort of confidence, initiative, and guts before tackling the Appalachian Trail?

Leaving Emily Proctor Shelter, we encountered several trails that spidered out. Not knowing the true exit, we picked a route and started walking. Our chosen path led us up rocky, cracked washes, and we wondered aloud, "Is this really the Long Trail?" Yes, it was. We finally spied a blaze, long after the stony point of no return.

The morning had dawned slightly cooler, despite predictions to the contrary. The weather, combined with proper hydration, put some spring back into our steps, and we walked over two mountains—Wilson (a butt-kicker) and Roosevelt—before lunchtime. The White Mountains over in New Hampshire to the east had *nothing* on Vermont, we declared; we had our *own* Presidential Range!

Some of the rocks in this range glinted with a coppery, eye-catching sheen. They looked (but didn't feel) like what I would call soapstone back home in North Carolina. These rocks tended to shatter into flat plates, and their glitter dusted everything. "I have sparkles," Clyde said that night, looking down at the toes of his boots.

On the way to Cooley Glen Shelter, about seven and a half miles from the day's starting point, I overtook and chatted with a friendly family from Massachusetts. The boys, I learned, were getting their Backpacking 101 course from Mom and Dad. Experienced hikers, the parents were wisely taking it at the boys' pace, resting often. I thought they were smart to choose such pretty and interesting terrain for the boys' initiation to backpacking. They would have sparkles, too.

Walking on, I eventually hooked up with Clyde at Cooley Glen Shelter and dropped my pack on the wooden platform with relief. Thud! Day's end. On the trail, an end-of-the-day pack-drop is an event to celebrate. Again, it's that "simple-life" thing: with a flip in perspective, the ordinary becomes extraordinary.

After a breather, I wandered down to the marginal water source to stock up. The drought was taking its toll on the springs, the heat parching the thin, rocky earth. Still, with patience, I was able to find life-sustaining water and eventually filled all three bottles from its little puddle. I shifted over to a private clearing to have my cat bath with a bottle of the spring's water and a bandanna, and to avoid fouling the only water source for miles around.

Dried sweat had left salt crystals all over my body. Dumping a bottle over my head, I rinsed the salt from my hair. I used a dab of soap to wash my stinky shirt and salt-encrusted sports bra in a plastic bag—my portable clothes washer. Behind good drinking water on a hot day, a rinse-off in the woods must be the second of life's supreme pleasures. The bath was only bark water, but I felt heaps better.

When I got back, horse-trader Clyde had arranged a slack-pack with the Armstrong-McGuire family who, it transpired, were the hikers I had passed earlier. Terrific! I marveled at Clyde's well-timed ingenuity. It seemed he was always scheming to make things a little easier for us. My admiring grin vanished, however, at his next words.

All we had to do, he said casually (too casually, I thought), was walk five more miles.

Five more miles?

"This evening," he added in the silence that followed.

My mouth opened, but no words came out. Did he mean *tonight*, as in *this* night?

He tried again, laying out the plan. As he spoke, a disbelieving internal conversation played in my head.

"Here's the plan," he said. "This evening (*Tonight?*) we'll hike our packs down to Lincoln-Warren Highway below (*Um, Clyde, that's five miles from here.*), where this family has parked their Subaru. (*Tonight. You're not kidding. It will be* dark *before we get there.*) We can camp there for the night (*He really* means *this!*), then stash our packs under their car before hiking out in the morning."

The family was heading down in the morning anyway and would be driving right past our next stop, the Hyde Away Inn and Restaurant. They would be happy to drop our packs there, Clyde said. I looked at the parents curiously. They nodded. I thanked them for their easy kindness. I never could account for the unexpected openness and generosity I found among hikers in the backcountry.

Tomorrow, Clyde emphasized, we could walk freely, unencumbered, and upright—like the evolved human beings we were. Plus, we could kick out some major miles quickly, as befitting the fitness gods we were becoming.

They'd hammered out a good plan. I had to admit that. All I could hear of it, though, was *five more miles. In the dark.*

In truth, after I had some time to absorb the initial shock of walking yet farther on tired, sore feet, the idea sounded better to me. Inspired, even. Clyde was something, always working an angle.

We spent a pleasant two hours resting, eating, napping, and socializing at Cooley Glen Shelter. More hikers drifted in for the evening. A young man, Amos, bunked down, as did two other hikers who introduced themselves as Carob and SBD (Silent But Deadly). Branch and Stick blew in and then out again as thunder muttered in the distance. The thunder set me on edge. Would we get hammered by a lightning storm? Should we abandon our idea? Inertia, always a powerful force, breeds endless rationalization.

About six o'clock, we decided to risk the weather and hike what I had begun to think of as "those damn five miles" down to Lincoln Gap. One of the items on Clyde's wish list was to night-hike. The man was about to get his wish.

From the start, the hike went splendidly. The air had cooled, and the slanting, setting sun made magic for the first hour. Its lingering rays struck a paper birch glen with a startling golden light; the sideways sunlight splashed across the stark white tree-soldiers, their trunks underlain by a forest of bright green fern.

"Monet would have killed for a paintbrush out here," I said.

As dusk fell, we crested the scoured stone of Grant's rocky summit. Clyde took in a quick view and walked on. I paused a moment, my sweat evaporating in the dry air. Standing with crossed arms, taking in the deep, dusky view, I caught a powerful sense of what it must have been like in a more primitive time. Green mountain after green mountain rolled away from the summit, with not a single airplane, electric wire, or cell tower to spoil the view. To the east, a stunning golden half-moon lifted over the mountaintops, lighting the scene. All that was missing was the call of a wolf.

An overwhelming sense of space enveloped me. The vastness and beauty of the rolling scenery overpowered the pettiness of my buzzing thoughts. Silence has a sound; I heard it. There on the crest of Grant, I felt the most peace of any single moment on the hike. That respite from troubled thoughts was a like cooling draft.

What followed became Jan and Clyde's Excellent Night-Hike Adventure. We switched on our headlamps around nine and proceeded gently into that dark night down the stony, unforgiving trail. The blackness threatened to swallow the weak cones of our pitiful lights, and we lost the path several times. We sometimes found ourselves at the black edge of a drop-off and felt the quick spurt of adrenaline as we backpedaled like the Two Stooges. She was a bloody-minded old dog, that dark bit of trail. But Clyde and I were working as a team now, and we always managed to bring her to heel.

We clambered down a fair number of sheer rock faces that left us incredulous: "What kind of person would put a trail *there?* Those GMC trail maintainers are crazy!" The trail was challenging. Truth be told, it was a bit frightening, too. And it was ... terrific! Thrilling! Successful long-distance hiking, as I was learning, required the willingness to be subjected to such paradoxes.

We were bone-tired but emotionally energized—another paradox. The day's freshness had acted as a tonic on both of us. After a morning of soreness, discouragement, and uncertainty about continuing the hike, we had successfully tucked Cleveland's and Grant's summit scalps into our pack belts. The next day, Lincoln Peak and Mount Abraham would be ours.

We finally found the parking lot and made camp by the side of the gravel lot, switching off our headlamps to avoid unwanted attention from any cars that passed. Although we craved "civilization," our sense of vulnerability always increased at its margins. Thankfully, the late-night revelers were limited on this Thursday night. We slept unmolested, or at least Clyde did, snoring away. My feet and legs throbbed so badly I found it hard to conk out. Yet the inevitable always happened. Eventually, my weary body dragged me into some semblance of slumber.

Day

16

*M*y God, what a day, what a day. A day in which we walked *in the Kingdom of Weather and lived to tell the tale. So* began my journal entry for Day 16 of our Long Trail adventure.

Our morning unfolded calmly enough, revealing no hint of the drama ahead. In fact, the opening salvo was downright pedestrian, and highly unwelcome: Clyde's 5 A.M. wake-up call. I cracked open my sleepy-seeded eyes to a greyish day. No rain yet, but it was coming. I shut my eyes again.

"I am waking up in a parking lot," I thought, stretching my heels to loosen their night-shortened tendons. There at Lincoln Gap, I'd chalked up yet another experience that would have horrified my mother: sleeping by the side of a road. Still, *I* wasn't horrified—only slightly amused at the oddness of it. I sighed and opened my eyes again. It felt good to feel at home in a parking lot. Very liberating.

We assembled a few essentials to carry for the day (water, rain gear, lunch), stowed our heavy packs under the Subaru, and ate a light breakfast that included some wild raspberries. Then, packless and unweighted, we nonetheless huffed and grunted our way up the 1.8 miles to Battell Shelter. Even when we weren't carrying packs, hiking up mountains churned a sweat and sent our pulse rates soaring.

Branch and Stick had spent the night at Battell and were still abed. Clyde rousted them gleefully, calling, "Ho! Good morning! And how are we DOING this morning? Time to be WALKING! VER-mont waits for no man!" Branch and Stick were less than thrilled by our boisterous arrival; Clyde was lucky not to get impaled by a hiking stick that morning.

Battell Shelter offered a decent spring. According to our guidebooks, the ridge ahead was dry, so we cameled up and drew what would be our last water of the day. Water bottles full, we parked our shabby carcasses at the shelter's picnic table for a snack to fuel the next leg of our ascent.

A picnic table in the woods is a lovely thing for a weary hiker. My heart always gave a little thump of pleasure when I scanned a new shelter area and found one. A table, no matter how primitive, offers the opportunity to feel *somewhat* civilized when living in the woods.

We chatted that morning with an Audubon Society trip leader, who was in charge of six eleven-year-old boys in constant motion. Very laid back, the young leader remained untroubled by the chaos of the pre-teen energy roiling around him. The boys pulled horrid faces at their breakfast of reconstituted eggs and threatened to vomit—until their shepherd calmly suggested they try the hot-pepper sauce in his pack. "Oh! Yes!" they chorused, and ran off whooping happily to out–hot-sauce each other. Wise is the leader who remembers what it is like to be eleven years old.

We bade all good-bye and continued up Mount Abraham. Before long, the forest thinned out and the white blazes marking our path were taken over by cairns. Normally, the Long Trail is marked by white blazes painted on trees along the trail. In the high regions, where no trees are tall or broad enough for a paint blaze, the Green Mountain Club marks the way with cairns, or small stacks of rocks, which stand several hundred feet apart along the path. As we continued up Mount Abraham, I played the "little rock-cairn game," in which the intrepid and curious hiker sees if he or she can balance the next rock, or tiny pebble, on top of the existing pile. These cairns are everywhere. Everyone must play. It's an unspoken rule.

A cool wind cut past in little puffs, lifting goose pimples on my arms. What a contrast! These were my first chill-bumps of the day, and I was happy to have them. The day's hiking would be more comfortable with cool temps and sunless grey skies. Instinctively, since we were ascending our first treeless, or "bald," peak and would be fully exposed to the elements, I performed a mental check. Was I wearing enough clothes to stay warm on a "slack" without a pack? I smiled wryly—after the previous day's temperature meltdown, here I was worrying about hypothermia. Such were days at elevation. Rain gear? I had the rain jacket tied around my waist, along with my homemade "rain skirt," made from a fetching black trash sack. I had water, snacks, and I.D. in my waist pack. I'd be fine.

Amidst swirling clouds, Clyde and I finished the trudge up to Abraham Peak, noting the alpine vegetation left here 10,000 years ago when the glaciers retreated from New England. One of the protected plants I saw was a simple clumpy sedge with reddish foliage. The ruddy coloring was said to aid in capturing warmth in the harsh conditions. The short tufts looked like plain old fescue grass to me. Still, while these tenacious plants may have held their own for thousands of years, they were also fragile and easily crushed by boots, dropped packs, and hiking sticks. Their growth rate is so slow in the harsh summit environment that destruction could easily outpace re-growth. Only tiny mountaintop islands of alpine vegetation remained, found only on a few peaks in Vermont, among them Abraham, Camel's Hump, and Mansfield. We would eventually walk over all three peaks on this hike. Ascending Abraham, I kept to the stony paths to minimize impact on the little plants. Life grew so slowly up here; much of it survived simply because no human or animal had ever directly disturbed it. I respected its unyielding stand against the elements.

The fishbelly grey skies above us grew thicker. Cloud-smoke blew through the balsam and spruce below. The rock surrounding us was a plain, dull grey, shot through in places with seams of white quartz. One hulking quartz boulder, lodged in the slope just above us, stood apart from the rest; the swirling clouds gave it a mysterious air. A pure, white quartz chunk in a sea of grey rock, the stony orb resembled a singular, massive snowball. All it lacked was a protruding sword to complete the mythic setting.

"Makes you wonder, doesn't it," said Clyde. "Maybe took a hell of a volcano download to blow it there. Hope it doesn't roll down on me."

Clyde, as usual, had survival on the brain. It made sense, though. After surviving the military, a heart attack, and the last hot, hard half-month, he could claim kinship with the tough, knee-high spruce and

"We bade all good-bye and continued up Mount Abraham."

weather-worn sedges that eked out their living on these high, stony margins.

Feeling playful, I put my hands to the white stone and pushed. Of course, nothing shifted. I leaned into it, hard. I goofed around, pretending to hold the snowball rock off Clyde, then straining to roll it upward like Sisyphus while Clyde snapped a picture.

We reached the craggy, treeless summit of Mount Abraham (or "Abe," as the locals called it) and took in our first natural, unimpeded view from a bald Vermont peak. Cloud-cover blocked our scrutiny of the valley below. A few heavily pruned conifers—bonsai crafted by nature—clung to cracks off to the side of the peak, but the summit of Abraham consisted mostly of rock and more rock, dry as the moon.

With nothing to break its force, the wind pushed hard that morning, batting the grey clouds around and chilling us rapidly as our sweat dried and our funky scent blew away to some unfortunate valley below. We found a stone circle, a sort of low, roofless "hut"—clearly a gift from previous travelers to this open, wind-beaten peak.

Simple comforts like relief from the wind, cessation of a climb, or a chug of clear water, would have blended unnoticed into my daily, much softer home life. Here they stood in stark relief. On the trail, we appreciated every bit of ease we encountered, probably because there was so much discomfort in contrast. The stone circle was a welcome windbreak for us.

We rested there awhile with one other hiker. Our stone-circle companion was a friendly 56-year-old former dairyman who had sold his Vermont farm out to some "city slicker" and now delivered fuel oil for a living. He liked looking down on his former domain in the pastoral valley below. He told us he frequently walked up "Abe" for exercise in his slick-soled work-boots—no hiking sticks, no rain coat, no water bottles, his shirt open. With our high-tech, lightweight gear, we felt like coddled babies in comparison.

Clyde in particular took a shine to the Vermont native, who loved a good "outsmarting" story as much as Clyde did. The two men swapped lies and shared a few laughs at the expense of those silly "city folks." Now, Clyde was a man who gave both his daughters a college education, who could don a tux and hold his own with dignitaries and national figures in service of a variety of community and environmental causes. Clyde was someone who would one day, at his eldest daughter's request, take waltz lessons and learn a father-daughter routine that would wow the crowd on her wedding day.

Yet Clyde loved to play the country redneck. A child of a large, struggling family, he had worked himself up to an elite soldier, then to a college graduate on the G.I. Bill, and then to a prominent, highly successful landscaper with contracts to develop Jacksonville's waterfront. At one time, he even considered a run for Congress. Clyde understood the value of education, and he gave his family an easier life than he'd ever had. But he respected people who scrabbled for a living, who worked hard with their backs and their hands. He actually seemed to prefer their company.

We asked our new friend to snap our picture in the rock ring. Views were hard-won in the peak-fog, but every once in a while the thick clouds blew thin and offered a glimpse of the slopes below. With nature's elements supplying the mythic ambiance, the peak of "Abe" truly felt like the top of the world.

After soaking up the misty view and chill wind of Mount Abraham's 4,006 stony feet, we bade our local friend good-bye and started down to Little Abe Peak—at only 3,900 feet in elevation, the wee babe. Half an hour and less than a mile later, we were on nearby 3,975–foot Lincoln Peak, snacking on the windy observation platform in the cold Vermont air. Mind, now, we had to go *down* in order to go *up*. Such is the nature of the Long Trail. We looked back at Mount Abraham in wonder: "Did we walk that far in only thirty minutes? Really?"

As we hiked toward the Sugarbush Valley Resort ski area, the clouds shed a spit of cold rain—a portent of things to come. The rain was still spitting when we lunched on Sugarbush's observation platform. With clear skies, we told each other, what magnificent views we would have. Sometimes, when the winds tossed back the cloud curtain for a moment, we could glimpse the farmland far below. But then the curtain would close again, and the chilly, high-elevation winds would nudge at us once more.

All day we traveled a long ridge, a handsome, rocky ribbon, the frequent ups and downs of which included Nancy Hanks Peak and Cutts Peak. At 4,080 feet, Mount Ellen offered the highest climb of the day. The gondola platform there provided a clean, flat place to sit, so we stopped in for another little snackerooni. There was no view from the wooded mountaintop, but we seemed psychologically unable to stay off fire towers and gondola platforms. And really, why should we?

The Long Trail's stony spine presented rich and interesting hiking that afternoon. Despite the low clouds obscuring the horizon, the immediate foreground sights engrossed this pair of southeastern flatlanders. We marveled at the low stunted spruce, rocky outcrops, and mineral shelves galore. We passed "sweating rocks," wet from the cool and humid air condensing on their warmer surfaces. When the cloud ceiling lifted momentarily, we were treated to stunning vistas that would make a stone man weep. I never imagined that such grey, shivery weather could provide such fantastic hiking.

Clyde was a lot of fun that day, joking, goofing around, and offering hilarious commentary on the local climbs and the stoic nature of Vermonters. Never committed to hiking the entire Long Trail with me, he now allowed that walking to Canada "might be all right." I attributed his change of heart to the cool air that lifted our spirits and put a bounce back into our step—although hiking without a thirty-pound pack just might have helped the "bounce" part. Clyde pooh-poohed my climate theory, saying no, that he was from Florida and loved the heat.

"Okay, whatever," I replied. I was just pleased to see him enjoying the hike, regardless of the reason. Goofing around on one of the day's gondola platforms, he'd draped himself from a nearby chair so I could snap his picture. He repeated his desire to ride a ski gondola, a word he took pleasure in pronouncing "gon-DO-la."

From open vistas to the world at my feet, the Long Trail always offered something unusual or beautiful to examine. Among the fir and spruce, the mossy forest carpet was overgrown with a low, shamrock-like plant that sprang from the moss-covered ground. I knew it wasn't clover. What was this merry upland dweller? Other floral wonders entertained us that day. On the ski runs that sliced across the Long Trail—cleared slopes that would be crowded with skiers five months hence—wild summer phlox and fall goldenrod vied for our acclaim, their seasons overlapping in this special August cusp. Though the world around us bloomed greenly, fall hinted at an early arrival in these windswept elevations.

The clouds darkened as the afternoon progressed. "We are truly in the grip of the Kingdom of Weather up here," I thought, "and there is nowhere else to go." Wind was our constant companion. Distant thunder growled at us. We hustled off the tops as fast as we could. There were a lot of tops.

I set a new personal record that day: one whole week without a proper shower. Our original plans called for a town stop that night. I was more than ready. As we raced over the exposed peaks, under threat of the weather, I imagined the comforts that awaited us. I could hear the hot water calling my name.

But Mother Nature had other plans for us first. The skies boiled over our ridge, their leaden bottoms darkening ominously. Our maps showed no way off the knife's edge. What had started as a light, spitting rain strengthened to a drizzle, and soon became a full-scale downpour. (You want *water*, Sugar Plum? Well, you asked for it. Here it comes!)

KAAA-BOOM!

Water falling on stone does not sink in. Within minutes, a torrent of rushing brown liquid churned down the trail. Drenched, we waded through a cold, ankle-deep river, the water soaking our socks and filling our boots. The relentless rain made a dicey business of climbing the boulders and rock shelves in our path. The sideways-blowing wind compelled us to walk with our heads ducked against its force. Water poured into my eyes and dripped from my nose. Seeing and breathing became difficult.

The thunder crashed closer. We glanced up nervously. Our metal hiking poles could well act as little lightning rods, but we needed them because we could no longer see the uneven footing of the rock-strewn trail beneath the rushing brown water.

I anxiously counted the seconds between the thunder and the lightning.

"ONE one thousand, TWO one thousand, THREE one thousand, FOUR ...

"Damn, less than two miles away ...

"ONE one thousand, TWO one thousand, THREE ...

"Wow, less than a mile now ...

"ONE one thousand, TWO one thousand ... whoa!"

Then the strange and unexpected happened as we huffed across the ridge. The thunder was crashing close above us, the lightning following so soon afterward that I no longer bothered to count. The situation was intense. I was downright terrified—and something else, too. I could feel my heart beating in my ears—with fear, with terror, with ... exhilaration. Suddenly I started to whoop.

"YEEE-HA-A-A!"

I felt alive! Even if the next second vaporized both of us, the rush of "RIGHT NOW!" was sharp and wild. Clyde looked back to see what I was hollering about.

Right then, a blinding flash, a snap, and simultaneous BOOOOOM! exploded directly overhead. *Right overhead.* Instinctively, I dropped to my knees in the icy water. I didn't think I was praying; it just seemed the thing to do. Clyde, ahead of me, never even flinched. I could smell the acrid ozone.

Upon realizing life still continued for us both, I whooped again. We were alive! The weather was definitely in control up here—not us. We were mere playthings of the weather-gods. It was *great* to be alive and vulnerable up on that wild ridge, soaked to the bone, wind-lashed and hiking, living in the very thick of it.

We splashed on through the torrents and puddles, cautiously descending and ascending rocks lubricated to a dangerous slickness by the running water. The trail led over house-sized boulders, and climbing required much care and attention. Traction was a sometime thing. To avoid slipping on the rocks, we tested each footfall before tentatively releasing our full weight into each soaked step. Water ran into our shoes, and a fine, loamy grit worked its way into our wet socks, rubbing blisters afresh as our toes and heels pruned.

And the mountain rain was *cold.* "I swear, the sky water in Vermont is barely a degree-and-a-half shy of a Slushee," I later wrote in my journal. Rain struck my back and neck, and the cold seeped through my short-sleeved shirt, causing me to shiver despite the physical effort of hiking. Ordinarily, the bulk of my pack would have shielded my back from the chill; I realized then that my foot-crushing, thirty-pound burden could also be my friend, an insulating mass to protect me from hypothermia.

Just when I thought I could get no colder and no wetter, I slipped off a stepping-rock into black, ankle-deep ice water swirling with loam and needled duff. The shock of the cold blast left me squealing in outrage. Still, the experience of clambering up the slick rocks in such angry weather was spectacular; no terrain—no experience—like this existed back home in the mild, gentle sandhills region of central North Carolina.

Despite the odd, unexpected thrill rendered by our vulnerability in the storm, we were relieved when the thunder finally passed to the east. Fear and discomfort paired with exhilaration: another paradox of the trail. The Long Trail rarely offered straightforward either/or situations, I was discovering. Most days, it gave us both the terrifying and the exquisite faces of adventure.

At such times, it seemed I had no choice in life about hiking. Something—whether the taste for adventure, the desire to prove myself, the need for personal growth, or something else—had gotten under my skin, and it had to be worked out. Long-distance hiking was my way of working it out. There was no other obvious explanation for it. Learning to embrace such paradoxes was merely a part of it all.

By the time Clyde and I reached the warming hut at the Mad River Glen Ski Area, we no longer needed the shelter it provided. The rain had stopped, and with the absence of a constant cold wetting, I'd warmed up. We sat anyway, enjoying the clearing views from the deck while we wrung our socks out multiple times. The sun popped fully out as we rested. "We had it all today," Clyde said, "except for snow." I shot him a warning look—no sense in tempting fate there, buddy. Such epic conditions lent themselves easily to superstition.

Our break occurred on our last high ground of the day, General Stark Mountain. The Mad River Glen management had kindly opened their ski hut, "Stark's Nest," as emergency shelter, and we appreciated both the respite and their concern for mountaintop travelers. But then, Mad River Glen was no ordinary ski area. In1995, a large group of fans of the mountain had formed a co-op and sold shares in the enterprise, and it became the only cooperatively owned ski area in America. This non-corporate aspect lent the understated ski area a delightfully quirky and personable air. We admired Mad River's ancient, primitive ski lift, a unique one-seater. Later we learned this is the only one-seater lift remaining in America. Clyde and I both searched our adventurous souls and confessed that, were the tiny lift running, neither of us would have the grit to dangle precariously from one of those chairs as it descended the mountain, bouncing airily in space.

I found it hard to get moving again; sitting and drying in the sunny breeze was proving most pleasant. Would this gravitational tendency of mine to sit, contented, gazing out, be a hindrance to completing the

Appalachian Trail next year? Here was another paradox to sort out, I thought—but there would be time to ponder that later. Now it was time to climb off the mountain and find a shower. Little did we know what lay between us and respite.

The descent to Appalachian Gap was a pure jaw-sagger. On this stretch, we were again babes on the rocks. We were astounded to discover what constituted a "path" in these parts—steep, near-vertical rock in places. Clyde and I would still be talking about it on the bus ride home from Vermont. We couldn't stop asking each other, "What kind of people build *trail* like this?" It boggled our flatland minds. In a city park, such terrain would be roped off, topped with concertina wire, and guarded by Dobermans against liability. Here in northern Vermont it was the damn blazed trail! We lowlanders were dumbfounded.

There was virtually no "hiking" involved in the "hike down." We slithered, crawled, and butt-slid. We clung to ladders, root-holds, and small trees where we could. The greasy, organic slickness of the wet, duff-covered rocks threatened traction and complicated the precarious descent even further. "Hiking" absorbed my complete attention. I did notice that, were I to slip, the neighboring trees and bushes would prevent a complete free-fall. Thank God for organic matter! How hikers of the future would descend when some of these roots had disintegrated was beyond me.

For us, it was a measure of the trail's rough going to observe that, after walking eleven miles already that day, we actually felt sorry for the guy we saw climbing *one* mile *up* this section of trail. The descent wore us out, and we greeted the sight of the Highway 17 with whoops of relief. We had survived the drop into Appalachian Gap.

Thanks to Clyde's finely honed conversational skills, we caught a quick hitch with two young women to the Hyde Away Inn and Restaurant at the base of the mountain, one of our planned stops. I was grateful for the easy ride from this spot in the middle of nowhere. A ride to town always seems like a minor miracle. Hitching when tired is a desperate game. One is *there,* close to town, but not really *there yet.* One can almost smell the hot apple pie and brewed coffee. At the same time, one's appearance is intimidating, and one's odor is rather earthy. A quick ride is a blessing.

Or so it seemed at the moment. As it transpired, our two trail angels were drunk. To top it off, halfway down the curving, steep mountain road, the young woman driving turned to her companion and declared that the old car's brakes weren't performing to expectation. Actually, her exact words were: "I have no brakes, hee hee." The girls giggled as we rocketed around the curves. Life was just one adventure after another on the Long Trail. Somehow, after our day of thunderbolts and harrowing descents, this wild ride seemed par for the course.

Miraculously, we landed safely at the lovely Hyde Away and were taken with its charming gardens full of blooming daylilies and other colorful perennials. Clyde headed directly to the bar and knocked back several colas in a row; the bartender was amused by Clyde's great thirst and evident pleasure in drinking cold, caffeinated liquids. I believe the man gave Clyde his last refill on the house, in appreciation of such a demonstrable capacity to hold his cola. I myself wondered if Clyde would sleep, caffeinated as he now was.

My first priority, now that we were in civilization, was a hot shower. I found one immediately. Luxuriating in the cleansing—my first real shampoo in over a week—I heard a toilet flush somewhere below. The spray in my stall immediately turned to ice water. It was a mark of my growing toughness that I hardly flinched.

After I checked in with my elderly father by phone, Clyde and I went to dinner. The meal was good and plentiful, we agreed. Nothing beats tasty calories for hikers. Buoyed by this satisfactory dining experience, Clyde ordered a $3.50 slice of apple pie for dessert. He had dreamed of apple pie for a week; in his mind's eye, he said, was a vision of what this dream pie would be like. I'm sure he was expecting homemade pie, like his mom made. Imagine his disappointment, how it must have pained him after all that anticipation, at having to declare this particular piece of apple pie tasteless. In fact, my partner—who liked to squeeze a nickel, by his own admission—found this pricey-but-bland pie an affront. I heard about that $3.50 piece of pie for the rest of the trip. Clyde did admit, though, that our stay exceeded expectation in every other respect, as the hosts were most generous.

In the warren of rooms above the bar, we met Smoothie, a fellow guest and former A.T. thru-hiker. A gentle and friendly man whose legs were covered with colorful tattoos, Smoothie was an avid cyclist and very fit. He'd thrown on the backpack again to hike the Long Trail that summer and liked it so much that he'd turned around at the Canadian border and started back south. Such there-and-back hiking is called "yo-yo-ing" in trail culture.

Such is the lure of long-distance hiking. Journeys like these create repeat offenders. With all the hardship and discomfort promised by a long-distance trail, there seems to be no accounting for it. Yet another paradox to consider.

While the Long Trail was proving to be a beautiful and unexpectedly satisfying adventure of its own, in the back of my mind I couldn't stop assessing my abilities to walk that gold standard of American long-distance pilgrimages, the Appalachian Trail. Since Smoothie had hiked both trails, I pumped him for intelligence. How did the A.T. compare to the Long Trail? Was it harder? Steeper? Though I didn't say it aloud, what I was actually asking was, "Can I hike it? Me, Jan, the slow of limb and broken of foot, the lollygagging, backpack-avoiding, too-easily-spooked-by-the-steep-bits hiker?"

Smoothie reassured us we were doing just fine. He told us he'd also had trouble pulling big miles in the Long Trail's northern half. He also mentioned that the feats we'd just accomplished—dropping down the steep face of Appalachian Gap, in particular—were as hard as most of what the A.T. offered in the White Mountains, where the rolling trail consisted more of ridge-walking than of the steep ups and downs we were hiking.

I welcomed this as good news, very good news indeed. In times past, whenever I mentioned that a given stretch of the southern A.T. had been hard for me, certain veteran thru-hikers would warn, "Just wait till you get to the Whites." Fear of the unknown had allowed doubt to creep in. If nothing else, the challenges of this Vermont adventure were pointing to a better way of preparing mentally for the Appalachian Trail. Rather than let fear of the unknown undermine me, I would learn to reserve final judgment until I could discover the truth for myself.

Day

17

The Hyde Away Inn and Restaurant
to Cowles Cove Shelter

Today's Miles: 5.5
Trip Miles: 167.8

At the Hyde Away Inn's generous all-you-can-eat breakfast buffet, I consumed enough food for three: coffee; scrambled eggs; OJ; half a pig's worth of bacon; whole-wheat bagels; more coffee; sweet cantaloupe; blueberry pancakes with real Vermont maple syrup and real butter; a third cup of coffee; more OJ; some apple strudel; more bacon; a handful of grapes; and one last cup of coffee. I knew I would be hungry again in an hour, so I saved some yogurt and a plum for a snack.

Breakfast came with the room, and I had a hard time understanding how the management was going to earn a profit on us. Clyde and Smoothie packed it in for all they were worth, too. Long-distance hikers can eat like that. At home, I would bloat and fall into a food coma after ingesting such a breakfast. Here on the Long Trail, those calories wouldn't even hold me 'til lunch.

Our wood-paneled room, located over the bar, had turned out to be noisy and hot. Deep sleep seemed destined to escape me on this hike; part of my brain would never shut off, always alert to the strange, new surroundings each night brought. After tossing and turning until 2 A.M., I stumbled to the bathroom to splash cold water over my face and arms. Then I wandered downstairs and found a box fan blowing into the empty common living area. Relief! I brought the fan back to the room with me. Its breeze helped a little, but I still slept fitfully and awoke with a heat headache.

Smoothie, the yo-yo End-to-Ender, was a self-confessed "gear-head," someone who loves anything and everything about backpacking gear and, more specifically, lightweight hiking. After breakfast, he sat on our beds, watching as we sorted through our paraphernalia. Our tattooed, ponytailed friend was good company; he had a pleasant energy and was a veritable fountain of Long-Trail information. That morning, he told us that the previous day's astounding descent, that so-called "trail," actually had a name: Stark's Wall. And Stark's Wall wasn't the last of the Starks for us; Clyde and I still had to ascend Baby Stark and Molly Stark Mountains that afternoon.

"Everyone *hates* the Starks," he informed us genially, with the insouciance of one who knows how tough a section is and doesn't much care. "Beware the Starks!"

I pondered that statement. Impressed as I had been with the rocky drop into Appalachian Gap, I didn't "hate" it. Quite the contrary. Truth be told, I realized that the intensity of Stark's Wall had actually added further spice to an already exhilarating day.

My mental response was a revelation to me. Something was shifting. Where is that imaginary line in our heads that an aspirant crosses from a "wanna-be" to a "be"? Upon reflection, I believe this was the very moment I recognized myself—hopelessly, haplessly, happily—as a real long-distance hiker. I tried the new identity on for size: *long-distance hiker*. It felt good; it felt livable.

At some point that day, we would also cross the invisible line on the map that put us less than one hundred miles from Canada. The dramatic scenery and terrain of the north were just beginning, Smoothie told us, and he urged us not to hurry through this last, grand portion. Besides, this was genuine moose country and, as Clyde, Moose-Spotter Extraordinaire, so magnanimously put it, "It's time Jan saw her first moose." Taking Smoothie's advice, we agreed to throttle back to ten-mile days and savor the rest of the magnificent north country.

Smoothie informed us that the clear, abundant water of the southern Long Trail was far less frequent in the northern portion. (Thinking back to the past week, I wasn't too sure about either the "clear" or the "abundant" parts.) In any case, for the final stretch, Clyde and I decided to carry enough water to get us from shelter to shelter. Water weighs about eight pounds a gallon, so shedding every single ounce of unneeded gear would help.

Since we would hike right through the little hamlet of Jonesville in two days, Clyde and I decided to mail ahead, or "bounce," all but two days of food to Jonesville. We saw no sense in dragging the extra, unneeded weight up the infamous Camel's Hump, our second bald peak of the Long Trail. Let Uncle Sam carry the extra weight for a few days, we reasoned. Our daily choices were always a balance between freedom and security.

That wasn't all we "bounced." In the Camel's Hump portion of the Long Trail, camping is prohibited above 2,500 feet (except in shelters) in order to protect the fragile ecological area. Thus, along with those two days of food, I also "bounced" ahead my hammock, stakes, and bear-bag rope, eliminating nearly two pounds from my pack. That put my pack weight at twenty-nine pounds with food and sixty ounces of water.

Before I became a long-distance hiker, I would have thought "Two pounds? That's not much. I can carry two extra pounds"—and I could, if I *had* to. But my body respectfully requested that I please no longer heft even one unnecessary ounce. With the added weight of extra water, I, of course, had to comply.

Hopelessly plugged with the green scum of Skylight Pond, Clyde's water filter also hit the discard pile. Clyde decided to go with iodine as his water-treatment method. Yuck-o-la! I mock-gagged and asked, "Do you know what color mashed potatoes turn when re-hydrated with iodine water? Blue! They turn blue, for Pete's sake!" Clyde just shrugged, and I shook my head. Even hikers have their gustatory limits, and iodine was clearly mine, if not his. I continued with my chlorine-based water treatment, which not only preserved the God-given color of spuds but carried little aftertaste. Although Clyde wouldn't miss the extra weight, I suspected we would miss the filter, which could rest in a mud skim and suck up the low stuff, turning dregs into drinking water.

Margaret Hyde, our big-hearted hostess, shuttled us to town so we could do chores. Acting as tour guide as well as chauffeur and proprietor, she pointed out the ridge of General Stark Mountain, which we had traced during our wild-weather adventure. From the ground, we were startled by how massive the mountain appeared. An interesting thing, perspective. I struggled to adapt that vast scale of "mountain" to the small scale of roots and rocks we saw at our feet each day. There was no middle ground, visually speaking, unless one came to a bald or a peak. Only then did the mountain traveler, feeling the stone underfoot while gazing at the panoramic view, gain a certain focal perspective.

Back on the trail, our packs cruelly laden with both water and eminently edible fresh deli sandwiches from the local store, Clyde and I walked over Baby Stark Mountain. It was steep, but no problem for us. Our growing fitness was becoming evident, and we congratulated ourselves on our newfound, hard-earned strength and endurance. We started up Molly Stark Mountain with a well-carbed, town-fed ease in our step.

"C'mon, Molly!" hollered Clyde, feeling punky. "Your husband the General couldn't whup us, and your young 'un couldn't whup us. Show us what *you* got!"

Mindful of the previous day's ferocious descent down Stark's Wall into Appalachian Gap, I hollered back "He's just *kidding*, girlfriend!"

Clyde was in a great mood, even with the lingering disappointment of his $3.50 apple pie. I was glad of that. When Clyde was in a good mood, everything was easier. I, on the other hand, was in a funk about some developments back home. So far, hiking with a partner had proved to be a fortunate balance; when one was down, the other supplied the requisite daily dose of optimism.

Partway up Molly, Clyde stopped and pulled me aside.

"Here," he said with a grand flourish. "Step up onto this here rock." Dully, I stepped up and took in the sweeping view that spread from the rocky outcrop known as Molly Stark's Balcony.

"There," he said, pointing east with his hiking pole. "See that dip out there in the farthest mountains?" I nodded. The distant blue line of a far-away mountain range—almost smoky enough to be mistaken for clouds—had a dip.

"Smoothie told me to show you this," he said. "That's Pinkham Notch, in the White Mountains. You'll be walking there next year." I could hear the pride in his voice.

The presentation was perfect. I was moved. Nature, once again, had taken me out of my head and into the present. I suddenly knew that, barring an accident, I *would* be slip-sliding down that dip next year.

Clyde looked pleased with himself, gratified at the impact of his staging. He also pointed north to Camel's Hump, our next major summit. It looked too far away to walk to.

As we climbed out of Huntington Gap that afternoon, we couldn't resist stopping and feasting on the ripening mountain blueberries. The original organic food, wrested from the minerals of the mountain, these hard-won, dusty-blue bursts were tiny but abundant. We gorged. The little fruits yielded veritable blueberry explosions and tasted so much more potent than the large, watery southern berries back home. Everything just flat-out tasted better on the trail, I decided—though I conceded aloud that this might only be a perception on my part. But inside, secretly, I thought not.

"He also pointed north to Camel's Hump..."

By late afternoon, we reached the simple Cowles Cove Shelter, an elegant, spare log lean-to anchored on a natural rock slab. Exhausted from lack of sleep, I fluffed out my bag on the shelter platform, crawled in, and passed out. I vaguely heard two women arrive, then two more, but I was constitutionally unable to rouse myself to greet them. That shows the extent of my exhaustion: for days, I had been starving for some female energy. The Long Trail was dominated by male hikers, and while I enjoyed their company, my social life needed occasional *balance*. I missed the conversation of other women.

Later, Clyde would write, "The trail is a strange place. To spend the night with five women would not be socially acceptable anywhere else. Here, it isn't given a second thought." That, I thought, is probably because hikers are all worn flat-out, smell bad, and can barely remain civil in conditions of extreme heat, uphill trudging, or dehydration. It's a poor recipe for mischief of any kind.

Later that evening, I finally roused myself, emerging from the sleeping bag. Never the shrinking violet, sociable Clyde was holding forth, entertaining the entire group. People flocked to Clyde, who was a natural leader and storyteller. Our social shelter band had grown while I slept; it now included a Bernese Mountain Dog and a sweet, endearingly goofy young southbounder named August. I visited awhile with my new female neighbors, Liz and her sister, who had spread out their bags directly next to mine. All together, we were a full house, squeezed into the shelter cheek-to-jowl. How odd, I thought. In seeking solitude in the wilderness, here we all were, sardined into a shelter. Humans are funny creatures.

I walked down to the watering spot. I needed a refill, and not just of water. My internal batteries were running low. On all my hikes, I had been deeply drawn to springs and creeks, but on this journey was especially so. I take water for granted in "real" life, like most other Americans. At home, potable liquid flows out of a faucet when I turn the handle. Who gives it a second thought? On the Long Trail, water was a living, plastic, elusive substance that demanded attention, effort, and respect.

This particular icy little pool turned out to be a honey—a secluded grotto, ringed with mossy, cracked rock shelves that released a little musical trickle down the broken stone above. Despite the summer's drought, this abundant spring brimmed full and clear.

Though I felt the urge to join the social scene above—I could hear merry bursts of laughter washing down—I couldn't tear myself away from this secret place. The birds, settling in for the night, flitted through the trees, fluffed about, then stopped rustling. Dusk fell.

In this healing little spot, as I grew quiet, it was perhaps inevitable that some of the sadness that accompanies the sweetness of life should leak out. It leaked and leaked, and kept on leaking, too, until young August came down for water. That flushed me, and I returned to my bag and slept the sleep of the dead—black-hole sleep, at last.

Day

18

E verything was hemorrhaging. My favorite water bottle, now a veteran of several hundred trail miles, had begun to leak, soaking me from shoulder-strap to knee as I hiked. My food bag had developed a rip, and I'd been dribbling crumbs, Hansel-and-Gretel style, across Vermont for days. My self-inflating sleeping pad had recently sprung a leak from contact with a splintered floorboard. Even my body was leaking; I'd lost gallons of sweat, and I was forced to limp because the raw skin between my toes had begun to blister and weep. And that morning at Cowles Cove Shelter, when I realized I'd lost my very special red bandanna, I felt like shedding tears of my own.

Long-distance hiking is rough on the body, but it's rough on equipment, too. Gear is poked by trailside branches, dragged on rocks, slung to the ground at summits, and used for backrests at breaks. Sometimes it's just forgotten; water holes and shelters tend to be prime "forgetting" spots. Gear can be repaired, but I felt an unaccountable sadness at losing the bandanna. Mentally, I hunkered down with my disappointment and wrote it off, beloved though the bandanna was.

Clyde wasn't doing so well, either. For starters, we'd begun the day under a self-imposed deadline and felt rushed from the moment we awoke. Our plan *de jour* was to crest Camel's Hump early enough to enjoy its rocky summit and avoid possible afternoon thundershowers. Seven rugged miles and three peaks lay between us and our goal. We couldn't waste any time.

We packed and started hiking at 7 A.M., which seemed grindingly early to us. Clyde struck out fast and strong, a man on a mission. I struggled in his wake, stiff and weary. But one hard, rocky mile into our day's journey, Clyde stopped dead at a trail crossroads and cursed. He'd forgotten his red fanny pack, which contained his heart pills, among other essentials. He had to go back to the shelter, two stony miles round-trip. Red was proving the unlucky color of the day.

Rather than walk on, I chose to wait at the junction of the Hedgehog Brook Trail. I was craving a rest, actually; the hard miles were exhausting me. A car-sized rock, clasped by a spruce, offered a seat, so I leaned against the tree trunk, content, and caught up on my journal. My writing momentum had slowed over the past few days as the tough terrain took its toll. The best I could do each day was to jot down a few phrases I hoped would jog my memory later.

I'd planned to use this unexpected break to fill in some of the empty spaces, but instead I thought about my special bandanna—lost. It was just a simple, ordinary print bandanna, but it had belonged to my mother, and it had kept me company on every backpacking trip I'd taken since her death in December of 2000. The passing of a parent is one of life's checkpoints. Scarcely a month after her death, I read *There are Mountains to Climb* by Jean Deeds, the story of one woman's solo journey on the Appalachian Trail, and out of my quiet pondering, almost overnight, sprang a passion for backpacking. One moment I was at home, wondering about the life I'd created to date; the next, it seemed, I had thirty pounds on my back and was planning to hike the entire Appalachian Trail. In little more than a month, I had sloughed off many of the trappings of my previous life, but my mother's bandanna had stayed. It made the crossover with me.

And so the red scrap accompanied me on every hike. It came on every exploratory backpacking step of the A.T. in northern Georgia, North Carolina, Tennessee, Virginia and now, Vermont's Long Trail. The bandanna was a slender red thread of connection that extended into both my past and my future, and I hated to lose it. Had I dropped it? Gallant young August had taken my address and promised to search as he walked south over the same ground we'd hiked the day before, in case I'd dropped it before landing at Cowles Cove Shelter.

My sadness left me in a ruminative, thoughtful state. I still wasn't sure why backpacking had emerged after my mother's death and not a more sedate pursuit, say, knitting. Certainly, my overprotective mother would never have approved of her only girl-child going days without a shower, or scrambling up steep rocks with sudden drop-offs just inches away. This was a woman who had frantically initiated a search party when three-year-old Jan took her dolly for a mile-long wander down to the Milwaukee County stadium and was gone for hours. After a later outing left me with a cracked front tooth, her lifelong parting caution became, "Watch your teeth!"—even if I was only going to the corner store.

Throughout my adult life, I'd overstepped the boundaries of what my poor mom considered "safe"—riding horses, traveling abroad, living an unconventional life by her standards. After she died, I realized, in that period of clarity that comes when time stops, I could claim nothing in life as a given. More than ever I wanted to be in the thick of it. Backpacking offered such an opportunity. It immersed me in the living, breathing world of nature and provided a freedom, an adventure and a simplicity that appealed to me.

So here I sat, on a giant rock in the middle of nowhere, as Clyde— breathless, red-faced and fuming—returned with the essential medicine pouch in hand. Two of the women back at the shelter had noticed it and planned to bring it forward to us, he reported. They probably would never have caught us, however, since we had begun at a faster-than-usual pace. Clyde was understandably aggravated at the wasted time and energy; while going back for the medicines was the right choice, no hiker likes to backtrack miles, especially when on a deadline. We resumed our hustle, and once again, I struggled to keep up with Clyde's adrenaline-fueled steps.

Eventually I gave up and downshifted to a pace I could comfortably sustain. Not only did this cool my burning feet, but it allowed me to drop into my own rhythm. I would impose all sorts of goals and "shoulds" upon myself each day, but my mental map rarely took into account my physical abilities or the terrain ahead. Still, my body adapted quite well to the tasks at hand, when I listened to it. Once I found my own rhythm, I could sustain a pace for miles.

In addition, I had little desire to keep up with Clyde that day. He was mad at the trail, and my normally sociable soul was lately craving more and more time alone. I pondered this new wrinkle in my personality. Was this what happened to people when they took to the woods for a while? Would I become a veritable hermit after six months of hiking the A.T.? Well, I rationalized, as long as I returned a happy hermit, it probably wouldn't matter.

Perhaps the solitude of a long-distance hike would adjust my priorities, I thought. Maybe I would get so bored with my own company that I would come to welcome each person, each rock, each tree for the miracles they were. Long-distance hiking offered a balance of social and solitary living that suited me. Another discovery. Another paradox.

With Clyde about five minutes ahead, we climbed up on the beautiful and demanding Burnt Rock, a craggy outcrop we followed for at least thirty minutes. My heart quickened. This was precisely what I had come to Vermont for: bare rock, space, and wind. My excitement vibe shot up, and a holler exploded from my lungs. Very unladylike, but these things happen. My steps lightened as I breathed in my surroundings. Energy! Life!

A woman above me, unseen, laughed at my audible pleasure. I felt an instant connection to her, as sometimes happens unbidden. She knew! I rounded a clump of shrubs, and she soon came into view.

"If you like this," she said, smiling down at me, "you'll *love* Camel's Hump!"

I finally caught Clyde at the top of steep Burnt Rock Mountain. In the clear air, we could see distant mountains all around us—some climbed, some unclimbed, and some yet to be climbed, including the forbidding Camel's Hump. The hearty ascent had settled Clyde; he seemed happier. He'd been stripping small blueberries from the tiny bushes that wedged themselves into the cracks of the rocks and the thin soil alongside the trail. The bushes were laden with ripe, sweet-tart fruit. I sat on the cool stone to feast on several handfuls of the pure mountain blueberries.

We'd first caught sight of Camel's Hump days before; the third-highest mountain in Vermont had then been a rounded, faraway peak, hazy in the distance. The 4,083–foot mountain had slowly drawn closer as we approached it, looming larger with each vista. The trail had also grown rougher and was less of a footpath and more of an unstable staircase. Now we scrambled up boulders, lifting our knees to our belly buttons to heave our weary, weighted carcasses up the next step. In the same breath, we cursed the rocks and praised our hiking poles, which did much to ease the climbs. Although tired from the exhausting labor, we could tell our limbs and backs were growing stronger.

At one point, substituting momentum for strength while boulder-hopping, I felt an electrical snap and knew I'd pulled a muscle in my left calf. My inner hypochondriac immediately piped up: *Hope it doesn't become chronic. You're out in the middle of nowhere, did you know that? What are you going to do if you can't step-and-lift? Did you bring enough ibuprofen?* I hiked on and did my best to shut out the questions.

We climbed up ladders, over boulders, and across "steep-ass pitches," as Clyde put it. He described one ascent as "one hundred and eighty-nine McDonald's Fun Houses stacked right on top of another."

"Is this legal?" I asked rhetorically, on one climb that left me shaky with anxiety.

"These steps are not up to code," he replied dryly, heaving himself upward.

Before reaching Camel's Hump, we had to summit Mounts Ira Allen and Ethan Allen. Named after Vermont's famous Allen brothers of the Green Mountain Boys' fame, they were tough climbs in their own right. Ethan was a workout, and I found Ira Allen particularly rough. I could feel my low back and rump muscles burning from the bursts of effort needed to clamber up and over every boulder. Clyde read in the guide-book that a Professor Will Monroe had named these two mountains. "I don't know if Professor Monroe realized it or not but he sentenced these two pillars of Vermont history to constant condemnation," Clyde later wrote in his journal, adding, "Let's just say that every time someone hikes up Ira they will have unflattering things to say about its namesake."

The difficult terrain made it impossible for us to keep to our anticipated schedule, though we strained to reach our mileage goals. Still, we forgot about the effort of climbing each time we reached a peak; we would pause and look out, time standing still. The sights atop were wildly exciting to me. My cliff-side yowls had a way of startling poor Clyde. He thought I was toppling into space, I guess—as if he could save me once gravity took hold! I had no way to predict these wild upwellings, though, and I thought it best not to suppress them.

Doing so would surely cause cancer, or baldness, or something equally wicked.

On the backside of Ethan Allen, we arrived with great relief at Montclair Glen Lodge, a log shelter five miles from the day's starting point. We slung our packs to the ground and rested with another hiker, Old Man Sam, in the shelter's cool darkness. Clyde and I were so whipped by the heat and the rugged climbs that we discussed abandoning our original plan of summiting Camel's Hump and calling it a night. In the register, we read that Jester, a 2000 A.T. thru-hiker, was a day ahead, as were Branch and Stick. Could we possibly catch up with them? Putting off the question for a while, I chatted with Old Man Sam, who had thru-hiked the A.T. in 2001 and thought parts of the northern Long Trail were even rougher than the A.T.

Here was another veteran thru-hiker saying that if I could do this part of the Long Trail, I could hike the Whites and Maine. While I certainly appreciated the support, I was gratified to note that such confirmation now was almost moot; I myself was feeling the same thing. Although I had yet to see the roughest parts of the A.T., my confidence was brimming from the inside as I met and overcame each challenge of the Long Trail.

The physical effects of the climb overtook us that afternoon, and we passed out on the shelter bunks. After only a half-hour nap, I sat up while Clyde continued to snore. Thunder grumbled, and I wondered where my raincoat was. It never failed to amaze me how capacious a little backpack could be. Stuff could rattle around inside it for weeks, unfound, tucked into unseen nooks and crevices. I started to unpack my gear in order to repack for possible rain. Somewhere in there, I shook out my silk sleeping bag liner and out popped—oh, yes!—my special red bandanna. Together again! I felt both foolish and joyful.

After an all-too-brief rest, Clyde awoke and announced that he still wanted to climb Camel's Hump that day. Despite his earlier declaration of exhaustion, I'd thought that possible, which was why I'd repacked. But I still felt a deep, weary reluctance to set out again. The day's hiking had been very hard for me; it had included a stepping-up type of climbing that used new muscles of my lightly muscled frame. My back ached. Now it was late afternoon, 5 P.M. The last time we had tackled a big climb late in the day, we'd exhausted ourselves. We still hadn't learned the lesson of Stratton Mountain.

Inevitably, my internal litany began: I was genuinely bushed and didn't want to leave the shelter; my left calf still hurt; a thunderstorm was grumbling; and we would be ascending an exposed peak. It was late, I was inert, and I wanted to socialize now that the hiking had paused. Liz and her sister had come in, and I was enjoying their company. But Clyde was hiking, no matter what. I considered staying the night at Montclair Glen Lodge, but at the rate Clyde was charging up these hills now, I might never catch him. I wistfully bade the sisters good-bye and told them how much I'd appreciated their female energy.

"Yes," said Liz, with a knowing wink, "and Clyde's a real male-type male." I laughed.

Clyde and I had eyeballed the famous Camel's Hump for days, and now we were about to ascend this distinctive peak. Ira Allen had originally named it "Camel's Rump." In truth, the bony summit did seem an ugly, rafter-hipped thing from afar, a tall stony carbuncle atop an otherwise forested peak. The top of this mountain had loomed large in our consciousness, like the Devil's Tower from the movie *Close Encounters of the Third Kind*. Its very apex looked like a pimple, and I had wanted to pop it for days.

We approached the base of the mountain like scruffy supplicants and looked up in wonder. Camel's Hump just flat-out didn't look *climbable*. The first four-fifths seemed like a typical Long-Trail mountain ascent—difficult, with hardwoods giving way to spruce. The actual peak, however, shot straight up, a column of naked stone, big and bald, several hundred feet above treeline. I didn't see how we could climb the bare column of rock without ropes.

Yet climb it we did. Perhaps the nap and rest had helped; I was full of energy and climbed with anticipation percolating inside me. Always, just when we thought the trail would end at a cliff or a wall, another way up unfolded. We summited Camel's Hump about twenty minutes before sunset. My litany of protest long forgotten, I planted my feet on the stone, looked out, and felt that peculiar wild excitement welling up again. I suddenly remembered feeling that same sensation as a child anticipating vacations and other family-travel adventures. Perhaps this journey was a link to my natural temperamental heritage.

The woman from Burnt Rock Mountain had been right—I *did* love Camel's Hump! We surveyed the 360–degree view of the fine feral world, rolling at our feet like a cat. Gusty and cold, with no trees or other ground disturbance to break its force, the ripping wind of the bare peak forced me to don my rain jacket as a windbreaker within the first minute. Clyde grinned widely and commented that it was fine kite-flying weather. My beloved red bandanna whipped sideways in agreement.

"The top of this mountain had loomed large in our consciousness ..."

We lingered as long as possible, alone on top of the world. We'd found the stony summit bare as we crested and had it completely to ourselves—a rarity on a peak that some 15,000 people visit annually. Admittedly, few climb Camel's Hump for the sunset on a Sunday evening. In the clear, cold air of the peak, we took the customary pictures, raising our poles in triumph and celebration. We knew full well it wasn't just the mountain we had conquered that day.

Before descending, Clyde relented to my wild impulses, saying, "Okay woman, have at it. Let 'er rip." I did, unleashing a barbaric YAWP! that would have done Walt Whitman proud. I YAWPed for us both—for our tired legs, for our sunburnt faces, for our strained calves, for our weary backs, for our blistered feet, and for our shelter-bruised hips. For our summit. I YAWPed my vocal cords raw. It was only right. This was a hard-won ascent, and it deserved acknowledgment.

We descended, walking north down stony flanks for a good two hours, watching a perfect pink sunset smolder across the west. How many people get to take in such a sight from such a height? A fat, three-quarters moon rose in the east as the sun melted into the far horizon, and for a brief time, we held both in view. In a couple of days, we would be able to night-hike by the full moon, if we wanted to. A few sparse lights blinked on far, far below and away in the valley. Mars shone hotly on the horizon. But for the wind, silence overtook us, and we grew quiet as we walked. This site, away from it all, on the top of the world, would have been the perfect ending of our day.

Alas, we had miles to go. The adrenaline of our peak experience quickly wore off, and a bone-deep weariness set in on the tricky, quad-jellying descent. The downhill trail was steep and difficult, and we had to don headlamps for the last hour of this too-late hike. Clyde and I were very tired, muscle-sore, and cross with each other for reasons neither of us can now recall, although the origin was certainly exhaustion. The new Bamforth Ridge Shelter, a lovely construction smelling of fresh wood, rose up like a beacon in the dark forest. Finally, at 8:30, we stumbled in and roused some prone figures (always a hazard when arriving late to a shelter way past "hiker midnight" of 8:00).

Someone hailed us, and we discovered Branch and Stick lodged here. We dug in our packs and, with a flourish, presented the fresh apples they had craved; we'd been toting them for two days and offered them as our belated thank-you for saving my suppers that one day, and also for spotting and rescuing Clyde's heart pills another day. I also handed them a roll of salty Ritz crackers, which they wolfed down immediately. Those boys were nearly out of food. Luckily, the Long Trail led through the town of Jonesville the next day, and they were planning to re-supply there.

"YAWP!"

Seeing how absolutely staggered we were, Branch and Stick rose from their bags and proceeded to cook Clyde's supper for him. I wasn't hungry and immediately collapsed into my sleeping bag. Nonetheless, unasked, Stick brought me a hot mug of chamomile tea—a nurturing token of care, from one hiker to another. This simple act of kindness from a virtual stranger brought tears to my eyes. I enjoyed the soothing tea, and in no time at all, was sleeping the slumber of the well-used.

Monday, August 19, 2002

Bamforth Ridge Shelter
to Duck Brook Shelter

Today's Miles: 7.8
Trip Miles: 186.3

W e slept hard and woke early. In the light of day, I could
see the lovely Bamforth Ridge Shelter, a structure so
recently built, the guidebook didn't even mention it. The
shelter looked like a three-sided log-cabin kit, with a large overhang and
a bench at the back. The new walls shone with a graffiti-free gleam, and
the damp morning air carried the pleasant odor of fresh wood.

Branch and Stick began to stir as Clyde and I ate breakfast. Our plan
for the day was to deal with a temporary detour in the Long Trail. We
would first walk the trail down off the mountain, take a side trip into
nearby Richmond for some town grub and a telephone, then hit the
trail again. Branch and Stick were planning to get a room in Richmond,
while we would walk on. I wondered if, after today, I would see these
kind young men again.

After morning chores, all four of us walked together toward River
Road and town, just a few trail miles away. As we descended from the
mountains, the rocky footing of the past several days began to smooth
out, becoming a footpath once again. Cracked stone no longer dictated
foot placement, and we were each allowed to enjoy our natural strides.
On either side of our descent, the upland balsams gave way to birch,
leafy hardwoods, and ferns.

We hiked comfortably in single file down the wooded path: Stick in
the lead, then Clyde, then me, with Branch taking up the rear. Branch
and Clyde began to argue politics. Because I was between them, I

listened for a while. I sighed as the argument morphed into of those no-win debates gentlemen seem to enjoy. Branch didn't know it yet, but he would never win; Clyde could be a pit bull when he sank his teeth into a juicy argument. My opinion was neither sought nor offered, which suited me just fine. When I grew tired of listening, I flashed Branch a grin and drifted to the rear of the line, leaving the guys to it.

Almost immediately, details of the Vermont woods swam into focus. I noticed the bright lime-green of a surrounding fern garden and wondered at the out-of-scale massiveness of the large slab of stone we'd all just descended unaware. I had been looking but not seeing. *Jeez!* I thought. *I love being out here!* How could they talk politics when surrounded by … this?

I could discuss political affairs in less compelling times. For me, for this special month, a period I'd carved out of my working life, I wanted to be in the woods, and I didn't want to waste a single minute. The trick, I was finding, was to make the choice, over and over, to remain in the woods—physically and mentally, every day, every hour, every moment.

Choosing, of course, involved remembering—never my strong suit. Old habits and thought patterns proved stubborn. Too often, I focused on my own inner dialogue, and not on the beauty and freedom that comprised my days. Time out here was growing shorter, too, with less than eighty miles now to Canada. The miles would be hard and slow, to be sure, but I wanted to enjoy every lichen, every ache, every Ramen noodle.

We soon reached River Road, but no traffic passed. We peered hopefully up and down the empty street. On a "town day" like this one, the absence of traffic can be anticlimactic, as well as disappointing; an eager hiker bursts forth from the woods, pregnant with expectation, stomach growling in anticipation of hearty—preferably fried and fatty—edibles, ready to have the senses filled. That didn't happen that morning.

The men sat down in the shade near the woods to continue their conversation. I stood near the road, listening for the sound of an engine. Within a few minutes, I heard one. Deliverance! When the SUV drove toward us, I stuck my thumb out with authority. I was learning fast; almost immediately the vehicle slowed, doing my old ego a world of good. The driver looked surprised when Clyde, Branch, and Stick jumped up to join me for the ride, but he good-naturedly allowed us all in.

A young electrician on his way to work, our driver Mike was wiring the basement for a fellow who worked as the light-board man for the Vermont rock band, Phish. Mike expressed his utter delight at landing the job, since he was a light-board man himself. He worked with a Massachusetts group with the unusual name of New Pond Fondle—named for a painting, he explained at our wondering looks. He played some New Pond Fondle cuts on his car stereo as we rode toward town, and the bluesy-funk tunes sounded good to my music-starved ears.

Mike dropped us at a clean, breezy, bakery-eatery combo in the town of Richmond. Clyde took one look at the bistro-style menu and dismissively declared it "yuppie food shit."

"I want groceries," he said indignantly, "not damned goat cheese." He left us, crossing the street to eat at a diner that served every manner of fried food.

Inside the café, I found plenty of good "groceries": French toast with real butter and genuine Vermont maple syrup; a side of thick-sliced bacon; scrambled eggs; home fries; substantial slabs of homemade bread with homemade peach preserves; plus a bottomless cup of organic roast. After breakfasting on little more than granola bars and stale bagels for the last several days, today's abundance refreshed and filled not only the senses but the belly. Branch and Stick ate the "yuppie food shit" with me before departing to find a room and shower.

After a pleasant morning catching up on my journal, I prepared to leave this pretty little town with its Victorian homes and flower-filled yards. We saw Branch and Stick again, and said goodbye to them; unknown to us, this would be the last time we would see our companions of the last three weeks.

Clyde set about solving our next little challenge. From trail guides and shelter notes, we'd learned about the washed-out Winooski Bridge ahead, damaged by the area's violent storms. The bridge was part of the Long Trail near Jonesville. Acting quickly, the Green Mountain Club had arranged for volunteers to shuttle hikers from River Road around the miles-long detour, making the car ride part of the official trail. Coming out of the woods, we'd been an hour and a half early for the shuttle.

Our stomachs had taken first priority. We'd caught the first hitch into Richmond.

Now, we had to get from Richmond to the Jonesville post office to pick up the food and gear we had mailed from the Hyde Away Inn. An easy problem to solve—if you have a car. On foot, it required creativity. In such situations, Clyde is nothing if not creative.

I don't know why I was surprised. Clyde secured us a ride in no time; Mindy, a coordinator in the Vermont Youth Conservation Corps, was the latest victim of his yogiing skills. People loved conversing with Clyde (who loved conversing back), and before they knew it, they were falling over themselves to be of service. He had the gift. Mindy drove us to Jonesville.

While waiting for our shuttle, we milled around the old-fashioned Jonesville General Store. Being hikers, we simply couldn't resist buying more food, though we were about to pick up our mailed supplies. My needs were simple: sugar and calories. I bought a chocolate bar, a pack of peanuts, and a chocolate milk.

Clyde, however, required more, and my eyes widened when I saw his purchases: a loaf of raisin bread; a jar of mustard; and a half-pound of braunschweiger—a rich, highly fattening smoked liver paste that was certainly off-limits for former cardiac patients. Because I was keeping an online journal, and because his nurse-wife Sandy was one of my readers, I was forced to dissemble, mentioning the braunschweiger in my journal only as "lunchmeat." From the start, Heart-Attack Clyde had warned me against accurate dietary reporting; if his wife learned he ate cholesterol-laden food on the trail, he said, he'd "catch hell for it." Several minutes later, as we sat at a picnic table outside the general store, I watched in awe as Clyde proceeded to consume every crumb of his massive purchase—bread, mustard, and "lunchmeat."

Soon we met Bob, a local retiree and our volunteer shuttler. He kindly took us to the Jonesville post office first, where once again I discovered I had packed too much food. When I offered Bob an unopened jar of peanut butter, he accepted with surprise and delight. Depending as we did upon the kindness of strangers, I passed the jar over with pleasure. It was nice to be able to give something back, even if it was just peanut butter. On the trail things so often worked out nicely, fitting neatly, like pieces of a jigsaw puzzle. We re-packed our packs and piled back into Bob's truck for the ride to the trailhead.

Minutes later, Clyde and I were walking toward Canada once more. The trail turned upward—it always went up, unless, of course, it went down—and our packs were again heavy with fresh supplies. I downshifted into trudge mode and prepared for a long, arduous climb out of the Winooski Valley toward Duck Brook Shelter, our destination for the night.

But our day of socializing wasn't over yet. When we met two Long Trail Patrol Crew members during the first mile, we took advantage of the opportunity to pause for breath and visit. Two pleasant kids, barely twenty, carried shovels and told us they were looking for a dead dog on the trail. After earlier hikers had reported it, the two had set off to find and bury it.

When the pair learned I was from North Carolina, they asked about my return plans. They needed a ride south, they said. Unfortunately, while I would have enjoyed their company, my travel dates didn't line up with theirs.

"Why are you going to North Carolina?"

Annually, they explained, they rode in a special summer bicycle rally called "The Superhero Ride." Every year, they—along with twenty-five or thirty of their closest friends and family, including parents—picked a state, dressed themselves up as superheroes, climbed on their bikes, and set off to travel the back roads of their chosen state. Last year's state was Maine, and this year's was North Carolina.

This was more than just a wacky bicycle adventure, they said. The real purpose of the ride was community service. The madcap crew would descend upon a small town en masse and go straight to the local Chamber of Commerce. Then, the flourish they enjoyed the most: twenty or more "superheroes" would burst into the Chamber offices, declaring, "We are *here* to *help!*"

After the initial astonishment—I could just imagine the scene—the towns usually put this enthusiastic volunteer labor force to work on such jobs as cutting brush, helping on park projects, and picking up trash. Sometimes officials steered the homegrown superheroes to individual citizens, such as the single mother who needed a babysitter for the day, or the man with polio who needed a winter's worth of wood cut. These two were genuine ordinary adventurers, and just the sort I would have loved to run with in my youth. They were an irresistible combination of high spirits, innovation, loopy humor, journey, heart, and service, their bike-ride project an in-house, free-form Peace Corps with a twist.

We wished them luck—both on their ride and in finding the dog— and continued our hike, unaware of the adventure that lay ahead for us. It began when Clyde and I actually found the missing dog, which lay dead at a very inconvenient skid of slick, steep rock. I felt a tug of sadness; the creature looked domestic, a pet Newfoundland rather than the feral mix I'd imagined.

Distracted, we lost the trail as the slick rock diverted us to a false path that would eventually peter out. Before we realized our error, we traveled some truly scary trail, cutting across a slope that grew steeper and steeper. Would the Green Mountain Club put trail on such a precipitous slope? It was possible. We'd seen our share of flabbergasting trail over the last few days. The faint track finally disappeared on a precarious slant of wet forest soil. We stopped, uncertain. Backtrack or go forward? Either way, we were in danger of falling down the steep slope. Our backpacks skewed our balance, making the effort even more dangerous.

Hoping the trail lay just ahead, Clyde pushed on, bushwhacking up the hill. I wasn't so sure. Clinging to thin bushes, I backtracked. I eventually found where we'd gone wrong, but the effort had frightened me.

I stopped to center myself, and then whooped for Clyde. No answer. Twenty more minutes of whooping brought no response. I dropped my pack and traversed the dangerous non-trail for the third time. No Clyde. Had he crashed and hurt himself? I saw no skid or claw marks in the muddy slope. Strained his heart? I saw no body. Did he find the trail higher up and continue alone? Was he being cranky and bloody-minded? I didn't know what to do. The weight of responsibility pressed down upon me; I didn't want to risk leaving him in potential trouble in the deep woods, but I couldn't find him. I decided to go to the shelter, about a mile distant, to see if he'd found it after all. If not, I'd drop my pack and return unencumbered, with a headlamp and another person if possible. Torn, I returned to my pack and started for the shelter. The implications of our isolation left me uneasy.

The Long Trail wound along the side of a hill. About a quarter of a mile down the trail, I heard a call above me. Clyde appeared at the edge of a shrubby cliff, bee-stung and mad as hell. He'd found a way to the top, stumbled over some ground wasps, and now, thwarted by cliffs and brush, he couldn't find a way down. Gratitude and relief washed over me. He was pissed, but he was safe. I guided my irritable friend over to a wooded slope I could see past the cliff. Before long, he was back on the Long Trail with me. We arrived at Duck Brook Shelter well before sunset.

The shelter was nestled in a fairy-tale setting above playful Duck Brook. I perched atop its lively falls, my rump anchored on a stone bump not five feet from where the water dropped some fifteen feet onto a refrigerator-sized rock, then flowed to a stone-choked channel below. The churning tumble of water on rock filled my ears. A bear could walk up behind me and I wouldn't hear it, I thought. Even as I smiled at my paranoia, I checked over my shoulder. It was early evening, about the time the local nocturnal stock began to stir. Nonetheless, I cooled my feet in the icy flow and journaled until the real predators—the mosquitoes—chased me back to the shelter.

Despite our very social day, we'd noticed the trail becoming more isolated as we hiked farther north. It looked like Clyde and I would have Duck Brook Shelter to ourselves. I built a small fire with a few fragrant pine sticks that burned cheerfully and drove back the skeeters. I felt happy and peaceful in the solitude; it had been a busy day on the trail, and it was nice to relax and enjoy the fire.

I crawled into my sleeping bag shortly before dark and was drifting off to sleep when two young men, burdened by heavy packs, hiked in. They gave their names as Jonah and Jeremiah. I wanted to ask them if those were their trail names or their real names but fell asleep before I managed to speak a single word.

Day

20

Tuesday, August 20, 2002

Duck Brook Shelter
to Taylor Lodge

Today's Miles: 13.2
Trip Miles: 199.5

A much-needed rain fell that night and continued to patter on the shelter's old tin roof as we awoke. An intimate, relaxing sound, the gentle drumming reminded me of an old cabin I'd stayed in one summer at a mountain camp where I'd been a counselor. Though I'd always loved the outdoors, I had no idea then that one day I would strap on a backpack and live out here for an extended time. I lay in my bag and enjoyed the sound of the rain until everyone else began to stir.

Clyde sat up, a stunned expression on his face. After a motionless minute, he began grumble-singing, "It's a beautiful day in the neighborhood ..." "Mister Rogers" moved slowly that morning—unusual for him. But it was wet outside. No one rushed to step out of the dry shelter and into the soaked woods. Also, we had a daunting hike today: nine rugged uphill miles to the summit of Bolton Mountain, then a couple more hours to camp.

Fortunately, the rain stopped and the sun broke out while we were packing up, quickening our desire to walk. The cool morning had dawned fresh and full of that rich damp-earth smell. We were now in the very north of the United States, and we could feel it. My energy returned with the drop in temperature. I was ready to hike.

Clyde and I chatted with Jonah and Jeremiah as we packed. The "J-Boys," as I called them, appeared to be good kids and trail companions, and seemed competent for youngsters of sixteen alone on a long trek in the backcountry. For their main grub, they had packed an enormous bag of couscous. I expressed some surprise at that. Couscous was not part of my diet at age sixteen; I may have been twenty-nine before I even knew what the stuff was.

Kids today are exposed to all sorts of different things, I thought, then caught myself: *Kids today.* I shook my head. I sounded like my grandfather. That stood in contrast to a unique aspect of the trail I enjoyed: the breaking down of age-related barriers. Young or old, most hikers out here were simply peers and fellow travelers.

Clyde and I left the shelter at 8 A.M. The rain had drenched the foliage, and soon I was as soggy as my surroundings. Chest-high nettles and grasping raspberry bushes saturated what the dripping spruce and beech branches hadn't soaked. My thin wool hiking socks, sopping wet now, bunched under my toes, rubbing new blisters afresh. This was nothing new; three weeks before, however, such conditions might have kick-started an internal drama, evoking worry and attention. Now they were unremarkable facts of life simply to be dealt with.

My focus had certainly shifted. Physical awareness had heightened, for one thing, but in an offhand way. Subconsciously I tracked my breathing patterns and heart rate; almost by reflex, I would adjust my pace to stay within a useful zone. I approached aches and pains the same way: absently noting the pulled muscle in my calf that morning, I managed my stride accordingly. I'd rested the muscle after the previous day's five-mile hike, but on today's upgrades it reaffirmed its zinky presence. A pulling pain in my heel, which I felt only on the steepest grades, had also pushed into my awareness. Something new was being stretched back there—or torn. The beginnings of plantar fasciitis? Whatever it was, it had me hobbling in the mornings. Only an hour or so of hiking would relieve the painful tightness. I patiently walked out the pain each day, only to meet it again the next morning.

All this I accepted as the price of walking to Canada. Not that "acceptance" precluded a generous amount of companionable bitching; to be sure, griping aloud about aches and pains—along with food, and the weather—were simply what constituted vigorous conversation for Clyde and me most days. What else would we talk about? Politics?

Jungle steam rose as we walked though the white paper birches of this northern rainforest. Margins sharpened in the clean, moist air;

every stone seemed in high relief, every leaf distinct, etched against the sky. Plant life was exceptionally verdant in the post-rain stillness. The mosses in particular grew ecstatic in this wet, nutritious world—so green and so, well, *mossy*, that they fairly vibrated and wriggled. The fuzzy mounds of moss on the rocks invited patting. Time and again, I cupped my palm around a springy tuft, just to feel the life in it bounce back.

The first hour of a morning's hike often yields wildlife sightings, and today proved no exception. Early on, we came across two moosey-looking ponds, and I perked up, alert and stealthy—alas, no moose. Still, we were not alone; in the upper pond swam the resident beaver. The creature eyeballed us but did not slap its tail in alarm as we eyeballed it back.

The lower pond looked more like a mud-hole than a pond, and sure enough, the trail blazed right through it. I groaned. Slogging through squelchy, knee-high muck was *not* my idea of a fun morning activity. As we paused before the path, we noticed that recent hikers had taken a detour—right across the top of the dam between the two ponds. Good engineers, those beavers. Their work held as we tested it. We crossed the woven "bridge," muck-free.

A few yards after we rejoined the trail on the other side, we met beaver-humor head-on. Our path was blocked: A small beech tree with a white trail-blaze painted on it had fallen where a beaver had chewed it. Its trunk was at an angle directly across the trail, and the effect was much like the classic circle-and-slash symbol.

"Humans, do not tread here," Clyde interpreted solemnly.

We hiked on. The trailside plants changed back to upland flora, first appearing here and there in a few shady spots, then abundantly in the high mossy woods. I was gaining a new awareness for the entire micro-world—the plants, mosses, and fungi—that thrived at my feet and along the edges of the trail. The northern plants fascinated me. By querying people and reading plant guides in town, I'd learned the poetic-sounding names of some of these new plants. There was clintonia, the low-growing shade plant with the non-edible, blueberry-like fruit on a stalk. Bunchberry was the cheerful upland dweller that sported edible red berries above its low, dogwood-like foliage. But my favorite new plant was wood-sorrel.

Clover-like wood sorrel grew in abundance along the Long Trail. I'd nibbled some upon learning its lemony leaves were edible. I'd read that wood sorrel is a "refrigerant," meaning it cools a fever and refreshes hot, thirsty travelers—of which I certainly was one. Lacking as I did the "gouty and rheumatic tendency" said to be aggravated by the plant's acids, I chewed on the leaves like gum as I hiked. A little green salad, I figured, could only assist my vegetable-starved diet. Once sampled, a sorrel patch never got past me without a taste.

When I first considered this adventure, my mind's eye never imagined this intimacy with trailside plants; instead, it conjured constant sweeping vistas from majestic mountaintops. Views did abound on the Long Trail, certainly, but I had yet to master the art of walking while taking in a vista. I'd try but was likely to slip on a root or tangle my hiking poles in my feet and go down with a withering thud. A falling backpacker is not a pretty sight. The awkward weight of the pack pushes down like a hand; once in motion, a hiker can do little to stop a fall.

So I spent most of my hike looking down, maneuvering the tricky footing, noticing the plant life at my feet, and taking occasional glances for moose, Clyde, or mountains. Opportunities for big, scenic views abounded and were usually, and conveniently, coupled with my desperate need for oxygen. When the legs began to burn and the breathing grew ragged, I'd scan for the nearest rock outcrop or sitting-log and head for that. At various times during the climb toward Bolton Mountain, I stopped to rest while admiring the views east to the White Mountains and west to Lake Champlain and the Adirondacks.

After about six miles, Clyde and I arrived at a side trail to Buchanan Shelter. No one loved a load-shedding shelter break more than Clyde, except possibly me. But we decided against a visit, as it was an unnecessary third of a mile off the trail. Long days under pack had taught us to save steps, and a trip to this shelter would add over a half-mile, round trip, to the day's hike. Since the guidebook warned us that the approach to upcoming Bolton Mountain was peppered with numerous energy-sapping ups and downs, we needed to conserve strength anyway. We continued, remaining at an easy pace and stopping whenever we felt like it.

I hiked ahead, but Clyde soon called me back to admire a champion moose track in the middle of the trail. We could tell the beast had passed recently, as the print margins remained distinct and uncrumbled by the morning's rain. The cleft hoof's deep imprint was now filling with water, which seeped into the depression from the ground below. A moose! So close! I stuck my lip out. Clyde had seen a moose in Vermont weeks before, and I had yet to see my first.

We broke for lunch at sunny Harrington's View, which my modest partner rechristened "Clyde's View." He promptly arranged a front-row seat, pulling out his sleeping pad and sitting back in comfort against his pack, looking out. From here we glimpsed Mount Mansfield, our future destination and Vermont's highest point, wreathed in dramatic clouds that hinted of the epic. We shot some photos, commenting that Mansfield's bare rock, which reflected brightly in the sunlight, made its monumental peak appear capped with snow.

We rested a while after eating. All morning we'd climbed the wearying up-and-down approach to Bolton Mountain, and we needed the long break. Optimistically, Clyde checked the maps to see how close we were to the day's goal, but we were disheartened to learn the summit was still hours away. At 3,725 feet, Bolton stuck into space only 23 feet lower than gut-busting Glastenbury Mountain, Clyde's early nemesis—and it was only 150 feet lower than Stratton, where I'd feared Clyde was giving himself a heart attack. I'd explored the Rockies out west on horseback, and while Vermont's 3,700-foot elevations seemed tame next to Colorado's 14,000-foot mountains, the jagged and peak-ridden Long-Trail terrain walked large to a novice long-distance hiker.

I left Harrington's View while Clyde stayed behind to chat with some incoming hikers. Again, the plant life in this northern stretch enchanted me. On the way up Bolton's slopes, I spied a veritable Indian-pipe garden popping out among little tuffets of lush green moss, the ghostly white stems forming the perfect elvish landscape. Like a spotlight in a jeweler's case, another tilt of sunlight illuminated a white quartz globe that was lodged in blander rock and framed by the day's ultra-green moss. Perfect! Magical mini-landscapes for future classics of children's literature. All that was missing was a Kenneth Grahame, a Lewis Carroll, or a Tolkien to populate them with quirky characters.

Clyde caught up and we walked together awhile, searching for Bolton's top. We crested knobs time and again, only to discover the mountain had thrown us another false summit. Formed by a hiker's shortened perspective, a false summit is both an optical illusion and a searching test of mental flexibility. Hiking strongly today, Clyde marked each one with genial curses and marched steadily ahead toward the actual apex. Not me; I stopped for a few restful, heartbeat-slowing "views." Finally, at 4 P.M., I topped Bolton. There were no views from the tree-covered summit, but a sign reassured me that, yes, this was indeed the true summit—no more climbing required today! The remaining trail—at least the next four miles of it—led mostly downhill.

Even with the day's long climbs, I had enjoyed the hike. Finally, I realized, I didn't mind walking *up* mountains. After twenty days on the Long Trail, my climbing muscles had kicked in, working strongly with an increasingly efficient cardiovascular system. Even when I felt the burn while ascending one of Bolton's false summits, a short pause always brought the body-machine back to normal—whatever *normal* now was for my ever-changing physique. Though the mountains continued to work us hard, their sharp slopes no longer evoked that wash of novice dread.

While we didn't linger on the top of Bolton—the breeze chilled every damp part of us, and there were many damp parts—we both took a few minutes to let our progress sink in. In spare phrases, we reflected on our trip so far, and on what we'd accomplished. Cardiac Clyde announced, with some pride, that he'd fulfilled one of his major goals for the trip: walking all the way up a real mountain without stopping. I smiled, remembering. Early on, his goal hadn't seemed possible. Now it was; he had proved it to himself. I could see it in his face. His vision of himself had expanded. He had marched up the mountain like a soldier under orders, and now he leaned comfortably against a rock, a seasoned long-distance backpacker with a leisurely air of confidence.

I believe we both had something to prove. Clyde pushed his physical limits, exploring those reset cardiac margins. ("The Way of The Guy," I called it.) Certainly, I pushed my body—sometimes to stumble-footed exhaustion—usually trying to keep up with Clyde. But my process worked more on the inside. I'm sure Clyde felt this internal downshifting as well, though he didn't speak of it much.

Days of quiet, deliberate walking naturally encourage a meditative calm. Aggravations grow less aggravating, even when they *are* aggravating. Insights, inner promptings, and memories often bubble up, unbidden. Like water on stone, gently persistent, the act of walking dissolves the surface material, revealing the core; one settles down, tends to become more one's own person. One meets *oneself*—newborn today and different from yesterday.

Reflecting on that mountaintop, I was reminded of something a North Carolina farmer had once said. It went something like this:

"Having a simple rhythm of life that ties us down to this pretty farm isn't so hard. I often think about the monks and the nuns who live in work communities. They always talk about their work as a sacred thing … that really is true when you live close to the land."

I think I understood what he was getting at. Life on the trail was so simple. Though my "work" on the Long Trail did not—yet—produce an external harvest, inside new ground was being plowed. I had the daily rhythms of nature and of walking a long-distance trail to thank for that. The simple cycles—eat, walk, sleep—while repetitive, never presented themselves in the same way on any given day. The very act of walking became a living routine that opened me up.

My world seemed new again, full of possibility. This is how I felt when I was young, I reflected. Time moved more slowly, and a lot of life packed itself into a 24-hour period. I wasn't, say, counting the minutes to the weekend. Today was just another day to see what came my way. Out here, I came closest to the cliché "live every minute." At night I would look back and think, astounded, "Did that happen *just* this morning?" Recent incidents would seem like long-ago occurrences.

By feeling my way into what I was capable of, my vision of myself had expanded without my realizing it. I told myself bigger stories; I considered previously overwhelming dreams. I thought, I *can* thru-hike the Appalachian Trail—if I want to.

The life-force seemed to flow through me on that mountaintop, and it would flow for days to come. Walking offered a freedom from the maddening, at times overwhelming, details and routines of "real" life. The simplicity out here acted as a mirror, reflecting my life back to me from a fresh perspective. Excitement and wonder brought new richness to my days. Appreciation grew for comforts previously overlooked: flush toilets, sinks with soap, towels, and hot water—such luxuries! What abundance I lived. I saw that life as I'd known it would not remain the same. I'd be making some changes.

I'd find better-fitting shoes, for one.

The chill finally drove us off our reflective rock and down Bolton's rugged backside. Within half-mile we stopped for a late-afternoon snack at Puffer Shelter. I checked the register, the only reading material around. Scanning recent entries, I saw that a woman I knew, Mama Lipton, had camped at Puffer three days earlier. A hiker named Flatlander had signed the register with her.

I perked up at the memory of Mama Lipton, a nutritionist who had given a lecture on backpacking food at the most recent fall gathering of the Appalachian Long Distance Hikers Association. I'd listened intently while she argued that hikers sometimes skipped on protein in their diets. She suggested hard-boiled eggs as one convenient source, since they could be packed out for several days and were a compact, nutrient-dense food. I'd filed the tip away as useful information. Now here she was, in the same woods as I. The long-distance trail community, I was discovering, was a small world.

I mentioned Mama Lipton's suggestion of hard-boiled eggs to Clyde as we ate our snacks. In clearing him for this hike, Clyde's strict cardiologist had ordered him to eat a protein bar every day to support his heart muscle. Dutifully Clyde ate them, complaining with every bite and making screwy faces. He claimed they tasted like "sawdust and wax." But he did eat them. Maybe hard-boiled eggs would be more to his liking.

Two friendly young men joined us in the shelter, graduate students who were surveying the Bicknell's thrush for the Vermont Institute of Natural Science. The men explained that these rare, little-seen birds live only in the low vegetation at treeline on isolated mountaintops in the northeast. The Bicknell's habitat is not increasing either, they said, given the fixed number of mountaintops and the continued development on so many of them.

We talked for a while, but I knew I had miles yet to go on this long day. On the north side of the mountain, the sun had already set and the cool of dusk was descending. I hoisted my pack, reluctantly said goodbye to the two men, and began the last stretch of the day. Clyde stayed to chat awhile longer.

Hiking alone, I crossed a bog bridge over the second beaver pond of the day and saw its resident, too. The beaver tried to sneak casually away underwater, but the channels in the reed-choked pond were shallow. Little waves preceded the creature's passage, and I was on it, visually, when it emerged. The beaver looked at me, dripping. "Busted," I said, marking the glossy animal.

A little after seven o'clock, near Taylor Lodge, I crossed the 200–mile mark of the Long Trail. Two hundred miles didn't seem very far for all the sweat and energy packed into the last three weeks. What a puzzling activity this was—to put *so much work* into walking a distance a car could travel in a few hours!

The long day might have colored my perceptions. After almost fourteen miles of foot-grinding up and down, I finally reached home for the night, Taylor Lodge. I found that young Jonah and Jeremiah had beaten us there by an hour and a half. Clyde scuffed in a few minutes later and dumped his pack, and we set off on the nightly ritual of finding water. The "J-Boys" told us the spring was piped, which was good news; it was always a pleasure to find water delivered directly from the source to my water bottle with no intervening bird-droppings or dog-lappings.

A small waterfall also flowed near the pipe, they told us. Excellent! For the second night in a row, I would soak my hot, beat-up feet and refresh my tired soul at a waterfall. A weary hiker had to work, however, for this waterfall; the water source flowed a quarter-mile downhill from the shelter, and our tired legs would have to climb back up with full, heavy bottles that held enough water for cooking, breakfast, and the next morning's walking. Still, the lengthy visit to the small cascade proved a delightful end to the day.

Back at the shelter, I capped off my evening with a veritable feast of chili Ramen, thickened with refried beans and dried sweet corn re-hydrated by the icy spring water. From a little bottle I carried, I added extra olive oil to the Ramen pot. I needed the calories to power up these hills, and the olive-oil booster was another tip I'd picked up from Mama Lipton's lecture

After supper, I considered stringing up my hammock for a comfortable sleep, but the night air had already chilled me, and an un-insulated hammock sleeps cold. I opted for the ease and warmth of the shelter, though I knew my hipbones would pay the price; my inflatable air mattress had leaked for days and offered little protection from the hard shelter platform.

A yellow moon, near-to-full, rose on the horizon. What could be a better capstone to a fine day? Already asleep, the guys snored in their bunks, missing the lunar spectacle. I sat on the rock outside and said hello to the night. I took a few minutes to write in my journal before turning in myself.

The next day we would tackle Mount Mansfield, the biggest mountain in Vermont, and the one we had seen from afar earlier that day. I looked forward to climbing it and smiled again at my shift in attitude. Mount Mansfield was the omega of this trip; it promised to be a difficult climb, but it was a climb I was eager to begin.

The next morning's chill confirmed my judgment to sleep in the shelter rather than in my exposed, uninsulated nylon sling of a hammock. However, as expected, my flat air mattress offered little cushion against the shelter floor. Once again, I tossed and turned all night. I awoke cranky, wondering if I would ever get a decent night's sleep. Then I forgot my miseries in a flash of realization: "It's Mount Mansfield Day!"

Clyde and I packed quickly, chattering with animation. We had long anticipated climbing this iconic peak. We'd heard all the stories about mighty, exposed Mansfield, how we should tuck our tails and run across the summit—or else avoid it altogether, opting for an alternative side trail if the slightest dark cloud passed on the far horizon.

We hiked out earlier than usual, with crisp purpose. The trail unrolled swiftly in the cool morning air, which breathed so easily into the bottom of the lungs. We made short work of the first four miles. We caught occasional, ever-growing glimpses of what is known as Mansfield's rocky "Forehead," the first stony promontory we could see of the peak-drama awaiting us. Viewed from a distance, from certain eastern angles, Mount Mansfield resembles a sleeping human face; the imaginative viewer can pick out a forehead, nose, upper lip, lower lip and chin. The mountain even sports an Adam's apple, making Mansfield a man, I suppose. At 4,393 feet, the "Chin" stakes its claim not only as the highest point of the mountain, but of the entire state of Vermont.

Not long past an intersection with the Butler Lodge Trail, we squeezed through the Needle's Eye (an "eye" of a natural stone "needle") then reached the bad-weather detour of the Forehead Bypass. Our blue-sky day showed no hint of a storm, and we marched on, eager to climb this mountain. The mountain, however, was about to open our eyes.

Treeline—the altitude at which trees can no longer grow—occurs shortly below 4,000 feet in northern Vermont. We scrambled up Mansfield's steep Forehead, the full trees giving way to the tough, stunted spruce of the krummholz. We clambered over sun-washed stone, snaky naked roots, exposed rock slabs, and even man-made ladders that were bolted to the mountain with cables. We were thankful for our dry, gloriously sunny day; the mountain air was intoxicating, and we climbed with sure, competent moves that would have been difficult on rain-slicked rocks.

Halfway up the Forehead, we stopped near a flat boulder that offered some purchase and a place to sit. Our legs and backs were aching, and we needed to rest and refuel. After a snack, Clyde stretched out on a sunny rock for a power nap. Black dragonflies rattled their wings as they buzzed and settled about us. I savored my favorite lunch of tuna, crackers, and a Snickers bar, hoping it would give me strength to ascend the rest of the mountain with grace and vigor. We'd needed both already. Mansfield's high, rocky trails required finesse and balance to negotiate its stomach-turning drop-offs and ledges.

"Empty the side pockets of your pack," advised the guidebooks. "Tight squeezes ahead."

We hiked on. After a few tight, tight squeezes in high, high places, we climbed a ladder to confront a truly jaw-sagging bit of trail, which I christened the Mother of All High, Tight Squeezes. The Long Trail simply stopped at an open gap. Simply stopped. To our left was open space; to our right, a cliff wall. Below was a long, rocky drop. The Long Trail seemed to dead-end right there, but it resumed on the other side of that drop. Without a pack, we could simply hop over the drop-off. With a pack, I doubted my balance. To the right we saw a narrow horizontal crevice or cleft cracked into the cliff wall. A very skinny person could possibly squeeze through and use that as a bridge. Now, Clyde had lost a good chunk of weight, but it would be a stretch to classify him as "skinny." We had a decision to make: squeeze into a narrow cliffside cleft, or leap over a drop-off into space. What to do, what to do?

Confounded, we employed that most useful of strategies: we dithered and kvetched. *This* was a trail? Weren't there *laws* about these things? For veteran rock-climbers, such an obstacle would be a non-issue; for ordinary flatland adventurers, the gap was epic.

"I didn't know I had a fear of heights until I got up here," Clyde said sincerely. "I didn't know it would be dangerous."

After pondering our situation from all angles, we formulated a workable plan. We would remove our packs and go singly through the crevice. After one of us had crossed, we would pass the packs across the void. Anything dropped here—cameras, water bottles, us—would be gone forever. We stuffed any loose gear deep into our bags.

Clyde went first, wedging himself into the cleft of rock. With his back to the cliff wall, he flattened himself and "became one with the mountain," as we joked later. Using the cleft as a bridge, he shimmied past the drop-off and stepped onto the trail on the other side. He crouched at the gap, and I passed his pack, and then mine, awkwardly across the void. Now unburdened, I felt more secure. I hopped nimbly across the empty space.

We laughed with relief on the other side. *Ha! Piece of cake! HA! HA!*

"I was squeezed in tighter than a June bride in a feather bed," said Clyde, grinning with the giddiness of a survivor.

Ha! "Yeah, and you weren't thinking about the IRS or your cash flow, were you?" I teased. "That's being in the moment, eh?"

"If I fall off here," said my Type A, hard-driving partner, "the IRS can have anything that's left of me." *Ha-ha! Ha!*

Still hooting from our adrenaline high, we continued our upward climb. Near the summit of the Forehead, Mansfield's scalded grey rock rolled in waves and creases. Blueberries grew in small patches, scattered among bonsai spruce and other low vegetation. I saw a wooden sign ahead and knew we were cresting the peak. "The top!" I cried in triumph, ever-ready to celebrate.

"No," said Clyde, "we still gotta walk to the Chin. This is just the first peak. This ain't even 4,000 feet." He was correct; the sign announced that we were at 3,940 feet and offered us yet another bail-out trail off the exposed rock of the summit. (No *way!*) We could see Canada ahead, and Camel's Hump behind. (We *walked* that?)

We dropped off the Forehead and into a shallow saddle—Mansfield's Eye Sockets? Our next challenge was the Nose. Here we passed the far end of the foul-weather route that had bypassed the Forehead. (What, and miss all that *fun?*) Again I was grateful that our day brimmed over with such fine conditions. Climbing again, we emerged onto a gravel service road that led to the Nose. Its peak looked like a small city of TV and radio towers; they bristled up from the Nose like sprouting hairs.

"This was a trail?"

Here we overtook Jeremiah and Jonah. We were happy to see these adventurous teens again, but were sorry to learn that Jonah had fallen ill. In low spirits, they'd called home on their cell phone that morning. Once they reached the parking lot on top, they would meet their mother, who would take them home.

"What? People can *drive* up there?" After a morning of hard walking, I was baffled to learn this.

"Yep," Clyde said, "You can pay a toll for the privilege of driving almost to the summit."

"Someday," I said, "I would like to come back in a car. I may not be able to walk after this hike."

Since the boys wouldn't need their trail food anymore, they gave us anything we wanted. Included was the gift I will always remember: big, chunky pretzels encrusted with large salt crystals. On the hot, dragging days ahead, once the pretzels were gone, I would eat the salt chunks from the bottom of the bag.

We soon arrived at the Mount Mansfield Summit Station, which houses a visitor center with displays of natural history. We filled our water bottles at a nearby spring, used the portable johns and, after looking around the visitor center, chatted with Jonah's mom for a few minutes. But we needed to keep moving. Soon we stepped back onto the spare upper ridge of Mount Mansfield.

Tundra plants led us upward, and signs directed us to leash our dogs and stay on the marked path. Though the day's breezes ruffled my hair affectionately, I knew the ridge-scouring winds could play rough on short notice. As we passed a cairn that marked the spot where a visitor was killed by lightning many years before, I was reminded again of the potential danger of hiking these high trails.

Early that afternoon, we clambered over Mansfield's Upper Lip. The Long Trail bypassed the Lower Lip, so our next facial feature was the Chin, a rugged ascent to the highest point. By 2:30 P.M., we reached the circular metal survey marker that marked the summit. Along with a handful of other visitors and hikers, we stood as high as anyone could in Vermont.

After admiring the 360–degree view, Clyde set down his pack "I think we got something *real* to celebrate this here summit with," he said slyly, his eyes twinkling. I looked at him curiously; so did a few of the day hikers and car visitors. He was up to something.

He grinned. "I got a loaf of bread."

"Bread?" I perked up. Carbohydrates fueled walking, and I craved them constantly on the Long Trail.

"Not just any bread," he said. With a flourish, he reached into his food bag and pulled out a veritable treasure: a beautiful, rustic brown loaf, freshly baked, crusty, and dusted with flour: Elmore Mountain Sourdough Rye, given to him by Jonah's mom several hours before, probably while I was getting water or using the bathroom. I was wowed, and exclaimed as much.

"Yeah. Yuppie shit," he pronounced, clearly pleased with himself and the impact of his presentation. The visitors chuckled, enjoying the show.

"There's also a tomato," he added offhandedly.

"A tomato!" My eyes widened. A fresh summer vegetable of the tastiest sort!

Someone nearby offered a knife and we commenced slicing the fresh loaf and the red, ripe tomato. Juice squirted everywhere, running down our arms while we drooled and exclaimed. People laughed at our heartfelt appreciation of "this here tomato," of "yuppie bread," of our soulful lust for *food*. Our delight was all we had to offer, but up there, at the tip of Vermont's highest peak, it was big entertainment.

"If only we had a Vidalia onion, this would be the max," I said, biting into my tomato sandwich. A shy little girl, who introduced herself as Briella, offered us a big bag of salt-encrusted potato chips. We thanked her heartily and saw her parents beaming in the background. (*Feed the pretty hikers, baby. Mind they don't nip. Careful of your fingers, darling!*)

Moments later, a burly man brought us a brick of extra-sharp white Vermont cheddar, crumbly and rich. "Don't hold back," he told us. "We got more in the car."

Overjoyed, we were up to our eyeballs in delicious non-hiker food, real food—food not long from the oven, cow, or vine. Abundance on a spare mountaintop. A loaves-and-fishes moment. Our teamwork was increasing; Clyde and I had just pulled off our best joint-yogi to date, and all we'd done was be ourselves: hungry, appreciative, and dramatically aware of our audience. We both had a little P.T. Barnum in our souls. Of course, we hadn't *expected* to be fed; at the same time, we were always open to the possibility.

As we feasted, we watched as Briella and her daddy searched for the very tip-top of the summit, all 4,393 feet of the Chin. Dad found the marker and said to her, "How about a hug on the very top?" She lifted her arms up to him. He gave a mighty hoist, lifting her far up above his head. "Now you're the highest thing in Vermont right now," he said. Before he lowered her to the ground, he gave her a kiss.

The easy company and the bare, windy 360–degree sweep of Vermont's largest mountain compelled us to linger there for over two hours, and we feasted and chatted with the dozen or so of our newest best friends. Mountains, mountains, mountains stretched in every direction. To the west, we could clearly see Lake Champlain and the Adirondacks. To the east were the Whites. Mythic Mount Washington was the large, peaky smudge far to the east. We learned from Chris, the summit caretaker, that such a clear day was rare on Mansfield.

"A loaves-and-fishes moment."

I had never been so deep in mountains. Clyde and I were both reluctant to descend, but we still had miles to go. As we packed up, an ebullient young woman bounded up, breathing hard. Her damp red curls sproinged everywhere. She threw herself down and kissed the survey marker at the summit.

"I made it! I *made* it!" she exclaimed. "I need to sing the music from Rocky *right now!*" Her operatic, loopy pleasure in her feat—she was overweight, out of shape, and breathless—infected everyone, and we all smiled. I noted the intimacy of the mountaintop. Up there, we were all community.

"Some people yell when they get to the top of mountains," she declared to the assembled masses. "Me, I sing." Clearly, Clyde and I were not the only ones channeling old P.T. Barnum. Like a diva, she announced that she was taking requests. When someone called out "Amazing Grace," I saw Clyde grimace and shoulder his pack to leave. As we descended from our big day on Mount Mansfield, after nearly five hours of rocky exploration, the moving *a cappella* strains of the young woman's excellent voice wafted down Vermont's tallest mountain. While I felt not a whit the "wretch" the lyrics spoke of, I was caught off-guard by the unexpected beauty of the moment.

Clyde, the self-described Florida redneck, felt the twinge too. He was silent until the song ended, then silent for a few beats more. "That was kind of goofy," he finally said, "but kind of nice, too." High praise from a man who does not care for goofy.

The trail dropped off steeply. Our easy spirits were soon interrupted by two butt-sliding little washes: stone alpine slides. The slicks looked almost like creek sluiceway stood on angle, shiny and scoured smooth. The polished native stone would be no problem normally, except that these washes ended in blue sky—wide open spaces. No nanny to catch me at the bottom of the slide, either.

The trail turned immediately to the right after these washes. Not even a tree offered hope of a desperation-grab. (*This* is the trail?) I doubted my trail shoes' ability to grab enough ground to prevent my hurtling off the thin lip at the bottom, and off the edge of the world. Mere rubber on stone. Was it enough? Would it hold?

As it happened, it was, and it did. I shut my eyes, sat down, and slid, grabbing just enough trail at the bottom to stop me. Rump-friction helped too. In rain, that little stretch on the backside of Mansfield would have been non-negotiable. How would one ascend? The mind boggled. It was as vulnerable a moment as I'd felt in my long-distance hiking career. Nothing but traction between me and a ski-jump hurtle. *Thank you, dear Traction. I am grateful for your patronage.*

Another survivor-relief moment. I did a giddy little riff: "We continue this ongoing broadcast of 'The Jan and Clyde Show,' *live* from Mount Mansfield, but first a word from our sponsor, Traction."

Clyde raised an eyebrow and watched me. I continued. "Ladies and gentlemen, without Traction, 'The Jan and Clyde Show' would be flying through empty space before dispersing into the molecular components from whence it came. Yes, Traction is your friend. Traction: it's what's for dinner. Traction. Thank you for your support."

But one cannot live on the adrenaline-fueled edge of life all day. We resumed our downhill walk. Once again, gravity pulled Clyde far into the lead. The hike toward green-roofed Taft Lodge was so pleasant that I missed the side-trail turnoff. By the time I heard Clyde shouting my name above me, I had already dropped well below the shelter. I groaned. Uphill to go back! Long-distance backpackers don't backtrack, I thought, and certainly not uphill. How badly did I want to see the renovated shelter? Not badly enough. I called back to Clyde and told him I was trudging on, since we were planning bigger miles anyway, and settled back into the long walk down Vermont's highest mountain. About an hour into the descent, though, my body told me, in no uncertain terms, that it was done for the day.

Experts always tell you to listen to your body. But what if your body hasn't read the map? I still had two hours to go on this footpath we sometimes called "The TOO-DAMNED-Long Trail," and the remaining miles were mostly uphill. Camping beside the trail wasn't an option; a road marking the Smuggler's Notch area cut through the forest below, and the roadside climb, with its rock staircase, offered no camping spots. Hiking on such rugged terrain—from 7:30 A.M. to 7:30 P.M., no less—leaned hard on my small frame.

Water, which had been scarce on the peaks, flowed parallel to the descent. I stopped to fill my bottles at a lovely cascade. The leafy spot gave me privacy, so I also stripped off my salty shirt and bra to rinse and wring them out. I put them back on, knowing the wetness would evaporate quickly enough. Ahh … I was newly cool and clean, relatively speaking. Refreshed, I walked another twenty minutes downhill toward the road.

Not far from the road at Smuggler's Notch, I realized I'd left my special bandanna behind. "My God!" I thought. "I'm attached to that red scrap. I *have* to go back up."

Back uphill—what a disheartening thought. The long, steep downhill had left me with jelly for legs. The spirit was willing, but the flesh just laughed at the thought of ascending those steep steps for a two-dollar bandanna. I dithered, unwilling to just walk away from the little keepsake that had belonged to my mother. Maybe Clyde would see it tucked away in the creekside woods. I hoped.

I looked up to see two southbound hikers coming toward me. One of them was … *fate!* Smoothie! What was he doing here?

When he reached me, Smoothie explained he'd taken a day off from his Long-Trail thru-hike to take his mother day-hiking up Mansfield, good son that he was. I was so glad to see him again and said so. He introduced me to his mom, a down-to-earth, sensible sort. I told them about the bandanna and asked if they would keep an eye out for it. If they found it, I would gladly pay them to mail it on. Smoothie said he would be happy to take charge of the bandanna search. His own mother beamed. There are many everyday heroes out there. Once again, the trail met my needs.

The two hiked on, and Clyde soon joined me at the road. Together, we started the final leg of the day's hike: a hot, wearisome slog uphill. Clyde confessed to deep fatigue; he'd considered stopping at Taft Lodge. I wish I'd known! I was also exhausted and could barely climb the steep slope up from Smuggler's Notch. My feet seemed stuck in slow-motion. To make matters worse, a lithe, gazelle-like woman passed us with two dogs. Effortlessly, she stepped lightly past us and up the rock steps, making us feel like salty, sluggish snails in comparison. I'd say it was a viewless climb, but Clyde felt the "view" had proven worth it. But for me, coming as it did at the end of the day, that climb may have been the most exhausting of the entire Long Trail.

By the time we reached Sterling Pond, 1.2 miles up the mountain, I was out of gas. I stopped, dropped my pack with a thud, and ascended a lakeside rock to pick up a little breeze. The early evening sunlight slid across the water, highlighting a lodge far across the pond. Nearby a woman tossed a stick into the water for her enthusiastic Labrador retriever, and a mellow couple looked to be smoking a joint on the shoreline to my right. Where did all these people come from? Smugglers Notch? Up that hot and unhealthy climb?

Sunset's chill finally drove me off the rock. I stumbled the last ten minutes to Sterling Pond Shelter, too tired to cook once I got there. I finished off Briella's potato chips, dressed my blistered toes, and watched as a merry group of college freshmen cooked dinner nearby. They were part of an orientation group and had been hiking together for an entire week. This was their last night in the woods, and they were giggling and scaring each other with references to the movie *The Blair Witch Project*. Several New-England colleges use wilderness hikes as a bonding experience for new students. I can assure school administrators that a person certainly comes to know his or her hiking companions on a long hike. Even if they're as different as chalk and cheese, a respect among hikers grows because they understand the physical costs of doing what they've done. Character proves out among the rocks, long ascents and high peaks.

The freshmen made me smile with their good-natured, hormone-fueled energy, but at the same time, I wondered how I would sleep amid the animated chatter. I was so worn-out that my head buzzed. *Ah, Sleep, be kind to me,* I pleaded silently as I lay down on the hard shelter floor. I'd earned a good night's sleep this time. Tired as I was—exhausted, really—I felt peaceful and grateful, even if the gratitude stemmed from now-motionless body parts. My mood and the nighttime quiet lent themselves to reflection, and I looked at the rough-hewn shelter ceiling, thinking.

I would make changes after this hike, I decided. I would re-create my life. Not that I'd had a bad life before, but I wanted to adjust some things. One harmony-stealing culprit was the accelerated pace of my "normal" existence. Nothing like traveling at 0.9 miles an hour over uphill, unstable rock to slow a person down long enough to realize such a thing. As my world had sped up in the last two decades, my time seemed to shrink. So many distractions in daily life clamored for my immediate attention, and I spent my days rushing from one distraction to another.

I had no one but myself to blame. It was so easy to over-commit and lose focus. I piled my plate high, then wondered why life seemed less fulfilling despite all of the interesting things I had selected to do. I supposed even the day's long hike could be seen as an example of over-committing. Were I to hike Mansfield again, I thought, I'd end my day in triumph at Taft Lodge on the downside of the mountain, basking in that rare balance of harmony in body and spirit. Nonetheless, our focus on the day's rugged hike had been laser-sharp: Climb that mountain! So yes, my over-committed body rebelled in the end, but my spirit could claim vigor and a keen pride in the day's accomplishments.

As for my life, in that clear-seeing that sometimes comes with utter physical exhaustion, I saw that I needed to step back from some of my commitments back home. I didn't know what specific changes I would make, but I'd pay attention to my insides and find out. I was confident the answers would allow for more stillness, more relaxation, less stress. Blessedly, for several decades, I'd had interesting work that let me be myself, and not someone else. I just did too much of that work lately, letting it creep into all waking hours. Surely there were ways I could cut back without dropping out, ways to live a richer life in the slow lane. Quiet time paid big dividends, and I wanted more of that juice for the spirit. At the moment, time—just to hang out and look around—seemed the ultimate sort of life-leverage.

A bigger picture emerged that night, a recognition of a larger web. Crafting an existence worth living wasn't self-indulgent navel-gazing, I saw—quite the contrary, although the scared, the powerful, or the mean-spirited might paint it so. I felt this acutely, down to my pounding toe-bones. Taking time to imagine and create a rich life of experience, creativity, friendship, community, and peace would be a whole-hearted grab for sanity. To be effective, to contribute my best to any common cause, I first had to be centered myself.

I write as if I had these epiphanies all in a single moment, on a single night after climbing Mansfield. To tell the truth, the tectonic plates of my interior had been rumbling and grinding away for several years. Three weeks of hard walking had finally shifted them. It would be interesting, I thought, to see in what areas of my life the eruptions would occur. The last thing I recalled before sliding into oblivion were distant squeals from the lively freshmen. Somehow, all was well in the world.

Day 22

Sterling Pond Shelter
to Awesome View Hostel

Today's Miles: 11.0
Trip Miles: 221.9

The wind blew in overnight, and I slept anxiously. Like a nervous horse, I'd always felt uneasy in a gale; my sense of hearing sharpened yet was confined to the rushing sounds in the treetops. The wind was still roaring when we awoke, the weather cloudy and threatening to rain.

Looking for something good to eat, I fished around in my food bag. Raw pecans and Oreo cookies were all that remained to fuel the eleven miles into the town of Johnson where our maildrops waited. The college kids camping near us faced a similar predicament; all they had left were packets of instant oatmeal. I watched, amused, as they pooled their various packets and cooked one big pot of multi-flavored oatmeal. The community gruel provided both variety and solidarity, an edible metaphor for their new melding. Their youthful banter once again put Clyde and me into a pleasant, indulgent mood. We laughed at their clever give-and-take; fun seemed to be their *raison d'être*. Their prankish, fresh enthusiasm made me smile wistfully for those younger, more innocent days—though I wouldn't want to be nineteen again. On the other hand, were a wish-granting genie to offer me some youthful cartilage today, I mused, I wouldn't turn it down.

Back on the trail, under the moody skies, I searched backward to glimpse the demanding mountain we'd climbed less than 24 hours before, but sailing clouds obscured the view.

"I'll bet there's a whole lot less traction up on Mansfield this morning," I said to Clyde.

"Yep, and I'll bet a kite would really sail up there now," he responded.

Our first trudge *de jour* snaked up Mount Madonna. Neither of us could find our zip today. Our muscles, still aching from yesterday's climbs, protested in fatigue. We looked at that first big upslope and sighed in unison.

"We can do it," said Clyde.

"Step by step," I agreed, psyching myself up. "Trudge mode."

"Like we whupped every other mountain so far," he said.

"Like water on stone," I concurred. "Relentless."

"Shoot, it ain't nothin' but a *thang*," Clyde concluded.

This exchange, and variations of it, comprised our hill-climbing mantra for the rest of the Long Trail. Such pep talks seemed to help power our tired selves up the remaining mountains.

The trail up Madonna's upper flanks cut across several open ski runs where we found splendid natural stands of goldenrod and fall asters. Autumn was announcing its intention to crowd out the Vermont summer, and sooner rather than later.

"Upper Chilcoot" declared a nearby sign, designating a ski run we'd just walked up as "More Difficult," marked by a blue square. Well, *that* surely was a relief to know—at least we weren't climbing black-double-diamond runs; I didn't have the legs for those most difficult of ski hills. I bet the winter skiers seldom think of people walking *up* their favorite slopes.

Mid-morning, finally atop Madonna Peak, a ski resort, we rested and chewed the fat with some workmen running big machines. They'd been blasting portions of Madonna's hard rock for some ski project; only as we walked away and began our descent did we come upon the warning signs the project had placed along the trail. Pausing at the hut for water, we looked back—and up—at the high point of the Mansfield Chin, now scoured clear of clouds by the wind. We could peer down on the east flank of Mansfield, where we saw Stowe's steep ski runs. Even farther down, we spotted Sterling Pond, where we had started hiking that morning. Did we walk all that way already? I was constantly surprised by our distance accomplishments on foot.

The wind whipped on Madonna too, swooshing noisily through

the compact, upland balsam, pushing the clouds away. The weather certainly changed quickly in Vermont. We trudged on over Morse Mountain and the other, smaller rises of the trail. On the ascent up Whiteface Mountain, a deep fatigue plagued my suffering quadriceps. I would step up onto the next rock but had little energy for the push-and-lift power moves the northern Long Trail was demanding of me; the spirit was willing, but the transmission was weak. My lower back ached. I longed to lie down. I craved my power lunch of tuna and crackers.

Before reaching the summit, we stopped for a nap, water, and snack at Whiteface Shelter. Across the valley some entrepreneurs had poured concrete chutes down the side of a mountain. As we munched, we speculated that people would pay to slide down. The air was chilly so I took time to brew some coffee—both for the warmth and for the caffeine, which would help reignite my enthusiasm for further hiking. When we stood up to hike, though, our legs buckled for the first few steps, and we laughed ruefully; the slightest rest now caused our muscles to shorten up. The final push to the summit of Whiteface looked very steep, but then, the guidebook had told us it would be.

"It ain't nothin' but a *thang*," Clyde pep-talked.

"Step by step," I returned. "Like water on stone."

Part way up, on a near-vertical portion of the slope, our tired legs and lower backs began to rebel, heavy with lactic acid. Too winded to speak, my mental dialogue grew desperate, arguing for a stop.

"Just a few dozen yards further," I pleaded silently with my arguing mind and muscles. "Then we can rest. There's no place to stop now."

It was then that we met the paper birch. The medium-sized tree skewed across the narrow, rocky jumble at an impossible angle, blocking our way. Going under it would demand a snaky stretch, but going over it on this steep slope would be worse. Our legs shook from fatigue as we paused, pondering. I thought about my next call to my father and friends back home and began to laugh.

"Clyde, there is just no way to convey this to people," I said. "Even to those who have done the Long Trail. It's like they say about childbirth. One simply forgets how painful it is."

"Just say it's a sixty degree rock pitch with a damn birch tree a'crost it," he declared. By clinging to the trunk and carefully removing my pack, tugging, and wriggling, I managed to navigate the birch and continue upward to meet other confounding obstacles.

Many times, when confronted with a sheer upward slab of rock to climb, I couldn't immediately see any toeholds or handholds. But if I sat still a moment and studied the obstacle (and rested the quads), tiny nicks and crevices—little spots of possibility—leapt into focus. Impossibly small, yes, but somehow they got the job done. Up we went, overcoming hurdle after hurdle, and finally topping Whiteface as we had so many other peaks.

On the descent, I reflected that three weeks of walking had given me a new lightness of foot. I hadn't set out to develop this novel grace; the phenomenon had just happened with miles and miles of hiking. I'd noticed it several days before, particularly on downgrades of loose, cobbled stone—leg-busters, certainly, for a novice hiker. But I was no longer a novice. Planting my hiking pole like a slalom skier, I would carve a graceful arc around the upcoming rock moguls. With such practice day after day, I grew more confident in my footsteps. My pace also grew more efficient, with little wasted motion.

On the other side of Whiteface, the low-hanging clouds let loose and began to drizzle. Once again, we spoke of our good fortune at climbing Mansfield in the previous day's sunny breezes. New grace notwithstanding, I knew better than to tempt the traction gods. Whiteface was the highest peak of the day, so our final seven miles were mostly downhill, although the terrain rolled enough for variety.

As Clyde and I crossed a boggy area in a mountain saddle, we came upon the Long Trail Patrol and recognized Melanie, one of the women we'd met several days earlier. She was one of the young people who participated in "The Superhero Ride" and had been looking for the dead dog on the trail. Today, she and her crew were working in the rain to replace rotting bog bridges in the area. Heavy spruce 8x8s had been airlifted to a clearing near the trail, but the crew had hand-carried the raw lumber a fair distance to the bog. Impressed with their industry and sturdy willingness, I thanked the patrol for their efforts. Without bog bridges in this area, visitors could do untold damage to the fragile terrain. Bog bridges also relieved hikers of the unpleasant task of slogging through boot-sucking mud.

Once we left the crew, the drizzle spattered harder then turned into a real rain. I just *knew* I could smell Canada—or maybe wet spruce was the evoking scent. Clyde and I paused to stow our cameras in our packs and break out the rain gear. My trail shoes were already soaked through and, once again, my wool socks bunched up under my toes, blistering them in short order. I could see that, as a long-distance hiker committed to the lighter type of footwear (trail runners rather than heavy, waterproof hiking boots), I would have to resign myself to wet feet on many occasions. The upside was that, unlike boots, my cooler, lighter shoes dried quickly once the sun came out. As I walked, my feet buried in unwieldy folds of wool, I wondered if I would need to replace my beloved wool socks with a synthetic blend that could hold its shape better and dry more quickly.

We called a rain break at the lovely Bear Hollow Shelter, three miles downhill of Whiteface's summit. I checked the register and saw we were only a day or less behind Mama Lipton, the nutritionist hiker. I hoped we would catch her; I wanted to pick her nutritionist-brain for information and compare notes. I could tell from the register that she was hiking with someone named Flatlander. I was thinking about hurrying forward to catch up with these hikers when Clyde suggested we stay at the shelter and wait out the hard rain. I laughed and reminded him we had no food left. That got Clyde back on his feet in a hurry.

Continuing toward town, we hit a side road and walked along it for a while before making our entrance on the lightly traveled main drag of VT 15. We needed a ride into town, but circumstances looked dire in the lonely rain on this quiet road. Lady Luck walked with these two soaked, bedraggled hikers, however; we found a ride into Johnson on the first thumb lift when a Ford Explorer pulled onto our road from a side street and stopped for us. Our benefactor dropped us at the Laundromat, where we washed every item of clothing we could while remaining dressed.

As our clothes sloshed and cooked, we walked to The Plum and Main, a nearby café, where I ordered a massive Angus burger. It arrived with a fat slice of onion and tomato atop it. Delicious! Though normally I ate little meat, my system demanded the protein on the "Long and Hard Trail." Fat, sweet, and salt were three other cravings. I added a huge chocolate milkshake to my caloric intake, relishing its cool, creamy sweetness. In just a few days, when I would put my backpack down and stop hiking—and burning so many calories daily—I knew such indulgence would have to end. I savored the treat and the moment.

As we finished our lunch, a man approached us and asked if we were hikers—we hadn't showered yet, so our woodsy status must have been apparent. Yes, we told him, and he smiled and introduced himself as Flatlander, Mama Lipton's hiking partner. We'd caught up! He led us across the café to meet Mama Lipton. As we chatted, we learned that they were spending the night at the Awesome View Hostel, same as we were. After paying our bill and collecting our laundry and maildrops, Clyde found a phone and called the hostel. Our host, Al, arrived, and we all piled into the shuttle together.

Alice, Al's wife and our generous hostess, opened her walk-out basement to us. A striking woman in manner and appearance, she reminded us of Katharine Hepburn Vermont-style, with great cheekbones, a dry manner, and an austere, no-nonsense, natural elegance. As long-time supporters of the Long Trail and its hikers, this couple offered a dry roof, a shower, a bed, and a towel to weary backpackers, all for a modest thirteen dollars. Alice then donated the small sum back to the Green Mountain Club in support of the trail.

Our hosts were both retired teachers in their 70s, and I had no doubt Alice could command a recalcitrant class to attention, as she seemed to be one of those rare sorts who knew exactly who she was. I would no sooner argue with her than with the Queen. I could tell that, while gracious, she would brook no nonsense. Of course we provided her with none. On this chilly, wet night, we all were grateful to be in such a cozy spot.

After showers and supper, we sorted out our maildrops and sifted through the hostel's well-supplied hiker box where previous hikers had left supplies they no longer needed. There I was able to refill my fuel bottle with cooking-alcohol from a larger tin someone had left. I donated several energy bars to the box for the next needful wanderer. I liked this simple, organic method of sharing with kindred spirits.

Hearing Clyde comment on how much he'd taken his pack belt in since the start of our hike, Alice brought down her bathroom scale. We joked about Clyde's trail name, which didn't seem so applicable anymore. "MAF Man," of course, stood for "Middle-Aged Fat Man." Early in the hike, he would slap his belly so it would ripple. "Two hundred and thirty-five pounds of chiseled fat," he would declare, much to the amusement of onlookers. Clyde, the Middle-Aged Fat Man, stepped on the scale with a flourish. We crowded close to read the flickering red numbers, which indicated he'd lost nineteen pounds in the past twenty-two strenuous, overheated days. I was astounded; that was almost a pound a day!

The scales disappointed Clyde, though; he'd thought he lost closer to thirty pounds. We kidded him, saying that, despite his hearty, high-calorie town meals, we would have to shorten his trail name to "MA Man." With his belly burned off, he looked more youthful, and his cardiac and hiking fitness had increased to the point where I was trailing him up mountains. I think it was about this time Clyde began to believe he would actually survive the trip in style. In addition to losing weight, he had grown significantly more laid-back in the past week, no longer so impatient with the incremental pace of life or the trail's emptier moments.

I stepped onto the scale after Clyde stepped down. Although my pack belt, too, snugged in tighter, I saw I'd lost only a little weight. I'd heard women packed on muscle during longer hikes, while men lost fat more rapidly. This seemed to be the case with us.

Clyde and I spent the rest of the evening talking with Mama Lipton and Flatlander, who, like me, were planning to thru-hike the Appalachian Trail the following year, when they would both turn 65. No strangers to the A.T., Flatlander had section-hiked it over a four-year period ending in 1999, and Mama Lipton was getting ready to retire from her job as town clerk of Salisbury, Connecticut, itself an A.T. trail town.

The two had only a couple of weeks for their "shakedown hike" this year and had chosen this tough section of the Long Trail for it. So we had much to talk about before I would sink into a real bed that night. I questioned Mama Lipton closely about trail nutrition and learned that they carried hard-boiled eggs and jerky for much of their dietary protein. Alice would willingly boil up a dozen more eggs for them to carry out the next morning.

A clean body, good food, pleasant company, warmth and a comfortable bed with ample cushioning for my hip bones—all in a single evening after slogging up and down cold, rainy mountains all day. Luxury! I snuggled deep into the warm covers, relishing the golden, sleepy feeling of cozy abundance and needs fully met.

Day

23

Friday, August 23, 2002

Awesome View Hostel
to Corliss Camp

Today's Miles: 11.7
Trip Miles: 233.6

After a comfortable night in the Awesome View Hostel's snug basement, Clyde and I awoke early and walked around the back garden, freshly scrubbed after the previous night's storms. Thousands of water droplets hung suspended like diamond stickpins from twigs and tall grasses, throwing fire in the rising sun. The hostel lived up to its name, for "awesome views" stretched out all around us. We could see Mount Mansfield to the south and Roundtop and Laraway—mountains we would climb later that day—to the north. Upon taking a quick internal assessment, I decided I felt up to the task. In fact, despite a persistent creakiness of limb, I'd decided to spare my stomach lining and abstain from the usual morning ibuprofen. I felt certain I could walk through the discomfort.

That morning at the Plum and Main Café, Clyde and I took our place among the flinty Vermonters who nodded at us and commented on the weather as we consumed enough sausage, muffins, eggs, orange juice, and coffee to choke a moose, or rather, *the* moose I felt sure I would see soon. Mama Lipton and Flatlander had opted to skip the rich café breakfast—imagine that!—in order to get an early start to their walk. By this point, I couldn't fathom skipping an opportunity to eat heartily. Well, the two of them had plenty of eggs, I mused, but a cold hardboiled egg sure didn't beat out a greasy sausage-scramble breakfast in my book. Not lately, at least.

As we ate, Clyde and I reflected on how our journey's end was in sight. Only fifty miles left! Onward to Canada! After breakfast, Al, finished with his town chores, swung by and shuttled us to the trail. We thanked him again for the welcome respite of last night and resumed our walk north. The day's climbs remained challenging, but we were stronger now. So were our appetites. The Long Trail was turning our bodies into metabolic furnaces. By 10:30 A.M., scarcely more than three miles from our monstrous breakfasts, our stomachs growled and we stopped for a snack at Roundtop Shelter, where we looked at the map and predicted how long it would take us to travel the 8.2 miles to the evening's destination, Corliss Camp.

Because of the large physical effort expended, backpackers learn to make constant mental calculations throughout the day: miles walked; miles to the next water or shelter; total miles to go. These numbers run almost automatically while the mind weighs and balances the information. If the guidebook says a shelter is 8.2 uphill miles away, a backpacker immediately takes all the circumstances into account— elevation, weather, current energy level, etc.—and predicts how much time it will take to get there. These field assessments proved fairly accurate after I got a feel for them. Early in our hike, thanks to the more moderate terrain, we could count on averaging two miles an hour, even in our out-of-shape condition. But the trail lately had changed the rules. On the rugged northern portion, predicting pace became a best-guess scenario that required us to consider the topographic maps, guidebook, and shelter registers before hazarding a wild guess and releasing any firm expectations. On the northern Long Trail, an 8.2-mile day could take four hours, or more than twice that. Our hiking pace depended on the number of "step-and-lift" sections we had in front of us on any given day.

With more than eight uphill miles between us and Corliss Camp, the guidebook advised planning for another five and a half hours of hiking—a pace well under two miles an hour. So much for the idyllic vision of short, easy ten-mile days we'd promised Smoothie, I thought. True, we were only going 11.7 miles, and 1.7 more miles doesn't sound bad from an armchair. However, coming as it would at day's end on the northern Long Trail, an extra 1.7 miles could mean either an invigorating end-of-day workout or an adventure in mind-numbing exhaustion. It was hard to predict. All we could do was trust our growing fitness and our ability to tackle what lay ahead.

Since Mama Lipton and Flatlander had skipped the town breakfast this morning, they were ahead of us on the trail. I could track where they'd snacked by the little flakes of eggshell left behind. A few hard-boiled eggs, if stashed deep in the pack and eaten within a couple of days, made a lot of sense to me as a hiking food. Carbohydrate-rich meals such as noodles and instant oatmeal were easy to come by, protein less so.

"Onward to Canada!"

I quickened my pace, hoping to reconnect with the couple once more. Rare were days like these: cool, sunny, and dry, with the trees a luminous post-rain Vermont green—the sort of day that makes a body feel as if it could fly into the blue skies above. But no flying was in store for me today. I found myself in trudge-mode, plodding sluggishly up the steep trail. The weight of full provisions seemed to crush my arches flat to the ground. Sometimes on the Long Trail I would actually forget I was wearing a backpack, but never on the day after a fresh re-supply. At one point, scouting a road-crossing for where the Long Trail picked back up, I dropped my food-heavy load with a thud by the side of a ditch. I immediately felt buoyant and practically skipped down the sun-dappled gravel, weightless and giddy.

"I feel like helium," I told Clyde.

About lunchtime we caught up with Mama Lipton and Flatlander and learned their plans to stay at the same camp as we were. On a long trail, such simple encounters are generally social occasions. They were getting water at a small creek and we joined them, visiting as we filled our water bottles. We'd seen many lovely streams that morning, swollen by the recent rains. The northern creeks reminded me of North Carolina's mountain streams, falling over rocky ledges and dropping into multiple clear pools. We lingered that morning at one lovely six-pooler, where Clyde, the professional landscaper, said, "People pay me good money to reproduce that in their backyards." Jokingly, I suggested he label his month on the Long Trail "developmental research" and deduct it as a business expense. Clyde liked the idea.

Despite its difficulty, the afternoon's hike offered numerous lovely flat stretches through the fragrant coniferous forest—a "walk in the woods," as it were. Whenever the usually rocky trail evened out to soil-covered softness, we would say to each other, "*Anyone* can walk to Canada on *this* trail." What pleasure it was to hike on forest soil, where I could choose the length of my own stride—rather than repeatedly heaving my weight up rocks higher than my hipbones. The trail over Laraway Mountain wasn't flat by any means, but the actual path invited the rock-weary hiker to stride out.

Partway up the mountain, a rock wall rose to our right. The edifice grew higher, eventually looming over us as we walked. Clyde compared the tremendous rock to the mass of a battleship in dry dock, explaining that he'd once been beneath one in San Francisco during an earthquake. "Hope the earth don't burp now," he said, survival instincts ever-honed.

While we hiked with purpose, we paused often to admire and photograph the curiosities of the northern Vermont woods: wall oddities like clefts, cracks, and holes; shining crystals; the sheer life-force of a cliff-dangling paper birch, pulled down by gravity and storms and then making a U-turn to grow upward again. A little higher, and we entered a cool, deep wash with thick moss fairly dripping off the rock wall to our left. Moody and elvish, this scene looked like a real *Lord of the Rings* movie set.

By 3:45 P.M. we stopped for another snack at Laraway Lookout, a sunny outcrop near the summit. Clyde stretched out on the smooth rock for a snooze while I rested, rubbed the knot in my bad calf, and treated a few new blisters—undoubtedly the result of the day's heavier load. As I sat there, I was buzzed by, of all things, a hummingbird. I informed Clyde's snoozing figure of this event, jokingly speculating that the hopeful visitation was most likely due to our flowery scent.

Mama Lipton and Flatlander, whom we'd passed earlier, caught up to us here and talked about spending the night right on the lookout. The idea was tempting; the sunset views, which stretched across the Lamoille river valley from the northwest to the southeast, would certainly be fine. Clyde and I, however, had other plans; we wanted to push on a few more hours to Corliss Camp. Only 39 miles left in our journey! We packed up quickly and hit the trail again.

We straggled into the shelter a few hours later to find two hikers we'd met briefly at Laraway Lookout: a New-Jersey father and his college-aged son, cooking their suppers at the picnic table. Shortly after unpacking, we joined them. Shelter camping is communal living, after all, and it always amused me to see the social structures start to build. Tonight I was particularly amused; the father had irritated Clyde earlier with his loud calling and full-of-himself opinions. Now they both inhabited the same small space. Of course Clyde could have camped farther away, but with only his tent fly and a cold night, he decided to weather any possible irritation.

Satchmo, a '96 A.T. thru-hiker, walked wearily into camp about an hour later.

Hiking south from Canada, Satchmo was trying to do big miles.

"Why the big miles?" I asked him, curious.

"Because I'm an idiot," he replied ruefully.

Wow. An honest man! I asked for his autograph just to make him laugh.

Mama Lipton and Flatlander hiked in at dusk; apparently they had decided against camping at Laraway Lookout. In obvious good humor, they set up their tent together away from the shelter, giggling quietly at their efforts, making the rest of us smile. In close company on a hard hike, with its myriad challenges and decisions, it can be hard to remain civil, especially for couples. Repeatedly the Long Trail had tested both Clyde's temper and mine, and we were merely hiking partners; I couldn't imagine how much harder it would be to hike as an actual couple. Yet these two seemed to genuinely enjoy each other's company, and they handled challenges with grace and tolerance.

The dusk air had grown surprisingly frosty by the time I finished my supper. As I scraped my pot clean and put away my dinner utensils, the cold seeped into my tired bones and brought on a shiver. Though it was still August, Vermont nights came down hard at summer's end. Clyde later wrote: "You could almost see the cold hiding in the cracks and shadows, waiting for October." I thought about putting up my hammock to spare my hard-used bones from the shelter boards, but it was again too cold to sleep out. My hipbones and I would, once again, seek the warmth of the shelter—this time, the four-sided, enclosed cabin that was Corliss Camp.

The father and son were staying in the shelter with us, but Satchmo elected to tent out that night. Concerned about porcupines chewing on his gear, however, he set his backpack inside the shelter's covered porch before retiring. Little did I know how his decision would affect my sleep during the night.

Snug in my bag, I thought less about my aching muscles than about the moose I hadn't seen yet. Our journey was nearly over. I couldn't leave Vermont without my moose-sighting. Could I?

Day
24

Saturday, August 24, 2002

Corliss Camp
to Belvidere Saddle

Today's Miles: 12.2
Trip Miles: 245.8

W e awoke cold the next morning. The fishbelly grey skies
threatened rain. A warning bell buzzed in my brain:
this was hypothermia weather. Everyone was sluggish, I
particularly so. I had again slept terribly, disturbed by my lack of hipbone
padding, three guys snoring, and Satchmo's watch alarm singing out at
10:30 P.M., well into the dreaming period for all good hikers. The watch
had been in his shelter-stashed pack, and it took time to find Satchmo,
who was tenting, so he could disable the alarm. Just another night on
The Long, Sleepless Trail. Clyde chuckled all morning about that alarm,
figuring it was poetic justice for my nocturnal Pocketmail faux pas of a
dozen nights ago.

I ate sluggishly too, searching for the heaviest items in my backpack
to cook, hoping to lessen the weight of the day. I felt worn out before I'd
even left the starting gate.

Our trail today took us up Butternut Mountain. After breakfast,
Clyde and I started the ascent, which led steeply up. And up. And up.
Straight-out-of-the-box up; no-warm-up up. A hearty climb first thing
in the morning, I ruefully thought, is just not the same as a mellow dark
roast, fresh-brewed and close to scalding, liberally spiked with half-and-
half, served up in one's favorite mug—along with time and leisure to
contemplate The Meaning Of It All. I decided that retirement one day
from the working world, so rough on many hard-driving types, would
not be the least bit traumatic for me. Until then, I would just have to put

my head down, pull into my shoulder straps, and face the trail ahead. Today, that trail was "little" Butternut, whose summit seemed a mere bump on the profile map.

"Worn out" was not the picture I'd had in mind when I first envisioned the freedom of a long-distance sojourn. I didn't enjoy the all-too-frequent weariness, but I had now come to accept it as the price of admission. Of the many rewards of a long-distance hike, one was the discovery that I could make significant up-trail progress even when feeling like a threadbare sock. On the final grade, long-legged Clyde pulled ahead while I labored in his wake. In a few minutes I heard a welcome call float down from the summit. It was Floridian Clyde, in his best Hernando De Soto imitation: "Tell the Queen: Butternut is ours!" Tough little Butternut stood only 2,715 feet high, but it wore me out.

"I go no further," I announced when I finally reached the summit, dropping my backpack with a thud.

Clyde just laughed. "You can talk shit if you want, but in two minutes up here, your butt is gonna be *cold!*"

The deep aching was probably a sign I need a serious zero-mileage day. The day's scenic hike just wasn't that tough; it didn't make sense for me to be struggling like I was. I longed for a substantial break, but Clyde was right of course. The chill-bumps popped out in no time as the cold breezes chilled my damp back. I shrugged my pack back on and we began the descent.

"Some days you're the windshield, some days you're the bug," said Clyde cheerfully. Today, I was clearly the bug. My feet throbbed with a hot, bone-deep pain, my pulled calf threatened mutiny, and both hips ached—not only from exertion, but from grinding into the wooden bunks at night. That last bit was my fault, as I was generally too tired to string up my hammock, especially when facing a cold night. But my overall low energy puzzled me. The trail wasn't that tough through this section, and was very pretty to boot. *Did* I need a day off?

Once we descended out of the wind, the temperature and humidity rose and I was soon sweating again. *So much for hypothermia.* Streams and waterfalls were abundant at the lower elevations. We found an old settlement now covered in trees; as we stopped to look at the moss-covered walls of loose rock, we wondered at the physical effort it must have taken to build their extensive length. Around noon, Clyde found his groove and strode ahead of me, faster than my aching muscles felt inclined to go. I let him walk his pace, knowing I'd catch up with him at Spruce Ledge Camp, our planned lunch spot.

When I finally staggered upon the sign for Spruce Ledge Camp, I read that it was only 830 feet away. Hallelujah!

But my moment of rejoicing was short-lived. I looked at the spur trail—*up*. Aaaargh! Of course it had to go *up*. So I trudged *up*.

Walking to an unfamiliar shelter can be a guessing game. Since you've never been there before, you're never sure where it is exactly, or what it looks like. When searching for an upcoming shelter, Clyde and I had formed the habit of scanning for a diagonal slash of roofline among all the vertical tree trunks. Sometimes we were fooled by the line of a fallen tree, but not often. Ours proved a useful technique, especially since many shelters, with their wood frames, blended into the forest.

My eyes searched in vain for the shelter at Spruce Ledge as I hiked up the steep ascent. One of these days, I thought ruefully, I'll drag up a spur trail's cruel final distance only to find not a shelter, but a sign tacked to a post: "HA HA!"

Not this time, though. The charming shelter at Spruce Ledge, with its cheery skylights and decked porch, swung into view about the time I decided the sign had been wildly optimistic. Stained a light grey and green, this clean, new structure had sliding doors. Its privy amused me; a whimsical little squirrel was cut high into the door, in place of the classic half-moon. Such sights served as a temporary distraction from my nagging disappointment with my body. Why did it ache so badly?

Lunch did little to restore my hiking spirits. I shifted and turned, trying to grab a nap of my own while Clyde snored away. I glared at Clyde's sleeping figure; that man could fall asleep so quickly. I hated him for that. I lay on my back in the shelter and raised my feet against the wall to see if elevating them would ease the aches.

Then I remembered I'd been off ibuprofen for two days. Two whole days! The trail had kicked my butt the whole time, too. I sat up and rummaged around in my pack, finally pulling out the big guns—Vitamin I. My stomach lining had rested, and the joints now demanded equal time. Stomach rest over! Time to kick back at pain and inflammation. I'll take two, please.

When Clyde woke up, I confessed my weariness and desire to stay at this lovely lodge. We'd already lingered two hours. Clyde admitted he felt the same way, but his work ethic was also pushing hard on him. This cozy camp sat only 6.7 miles out from our day's starting point. If we trudged three more miles, he reasoned, we would be at VT 118 and could camp there for the night. Roads were usually downhill of the trail; after consideration, I decided I had three more easy miles in me to complete a respectable nine-mile day on the Long Trail. We rallied, shouldering our packs again.

The trail offered us gifts for our fortitude. On the trudge down, we hiked through the delightful Devil's Gulch, a child's-block jumble of large, mossy rocks in a "fern-filled defile," according to the guidebook. Clyde liked the term "fern-filled defile" and repeated it several times on our traverse through the boulders and moist greenery. Water dripped everywhere, and temperatures fell a few refreshing degrees. The boulders invited a cheerful mood, and we obliged, snapping pictures of each other as we rock-hopped among the half-mile of giant, cubical boulders.

The shelters didn't seem to line up right mileage-wise on this section, so we would be making our own camp that night. When we'd hiked the three miles to the road, I felt remarkably peppy, despite the bad knot in my calf. I suspected the ibuprofen was working its magic. I certainly ached less.

"You know," ventured Clyde, "Anything more we get done today cuts miles off our fifteen-mile day tomorrow." He also mentioned that a fire tower crowned the next mountain, Belvidere, and proposed the summit as our new destination for the night's camp.

Fire tower? Say no more!

"Well, why not?" I returned optimistically. "It's only two and a half miles to the top, and it's only four o'clock now."

At the time it seemed feasible, even easy. But Clyde and I were nothing if not the slowest of slow learners.

Up Belvidere we chugged. Mama Lipton and Flatlander had opted to skip this section, so we were the first humans out on this sparsely populated trail that day. The cobwebs strung across our path told us this lonely truth.

As our stamina flagged on the flanks of the mountain, Clyde rang out with our Long-Trail mantra.

"Step by step," he encouraged.

"Ain't nothin' but a *thang*," I added, hoping the magic would not fail us.

But Mistress Belvidere was more than just a "thang"; she was a proud mountain who offered many false summits to waylay the tiny, overconfident creatures that crept up her sides. Time after time, we declared the summit close and claimed it for the Queen. But Belvidere persisted. At one point, after I proclaimed the ascent "Finished, Done, Ours," we were disheartened to turn a corner and meet yet another rocky, steeply ascending wash.

"*Take* that, *cocky human insects …*"

"*This* mountain doesn't *like* to be talked back to," I observed.

Clyde agreed. "It seems the Queen has just been handed her tongue in a bag."

Once we were forced to duck under a blow-down. The only way Clyde could proceed was to crawl under the fallen tree.

"Clyde," I teased, "Belvidere has finally made you kneel before her."

Finally, we shut our smart mouths and focused on climbing; subsequently, the mountain graciously handed us a saddle—a low spot on the mountaintop that was suitable for camping. Clyde kicked aside the abundant moose poop, dropped his pack, and headed down another trail to a spring listed in the guidebook—which turned out to be foul and filled with brush, forcing us to make supper with the meager bit of water we'd carried up.

After catching my breath, I decided to take the short summit trail to the fire tower to watch the sun dropping on the high peak. We'd discussed the possibility of camping up there, so I also wanted to assess the fire tower's sheltering potential. Thanks to the miracle of ibuprofen, I was able to scramble up a sharp, 0.2-mile slope—and forget to take my pack off first. Once on the summit, I began the tower ascent, anticipating the fine view. As soon as I climbed above treeline, however, the wind slammed me like a blast fan, and I grew so cold so quickly that I paused to don a raincoat, hat, and gloves. The sharp wind whipped my raincoat around as I sought the arms to pull it on to break the fierce chill.

It was here, too, mid-platform, that I remembered my fear of climbing ramshackle old fire towers. Halfway up the tower, doubt flooded in; some of these aged, flimsy structures never quite seemed safe to me. *Where is its most recent engineering certificate?* I wondered—but I kept climbing. The reward at the top was a fabulous view of Jay Peak, our last challenge. I could see all the way into Canada.

I called down to Clyde, who had just hiked up to the base of the tower: "Tell the Queen, Belvidere is ours!"

While I shot a few photos, Clyde climbed up to catch the sun's last rays. The tower platform was open and the wind far too frigid for sleeping. Mindful of the backwoods wisdom to "hike high, camp low," we agreed to tent in the saddle. I left Clyde, who stayed to watch the last gasp of sunset.

Back down in the saddle, I found no good ground to pitch a tent, so I left the only semi-flat spot for Clyde, who was using his tent fly as an emergency shelter. I strung my hammock up, even though I knew it meant I was in for a long, cold night. The dark shadows lengthened. I had yet to cook supper, so I immediately began searching for a pair of trees suitable for hammock-hanging.

On the thinly forested saddle, though, few trees were close enough. Of the ones there, many were stunted; of those that were mature, most were dead or dying. I found two good trees a little ways back down the Long Trail; unfortunately, they grew on opposite sides of the path and would have forced me to suspend my hammock directly across the trail. Those two trees stood solidly, beckoning, but I was reluctant—not because I thought a hiker would come along before I awoke but because the darn moose used the trails for nighttime travel. The organic evidence of *that* lay everywhere. I wasn't keen to add "moose-entanglement" to my list of life experiences.

My other alternative was a standing dead tree—which sounded wickedly hollow when I thumped it—and a deadfall, which was leaning against a second tree that, itself, barely clung to life. Great. Did I want to be moose-trod or tree-crushed? It was nice to have a choice.

After finding I could budge neither dead trunk, I strung up the hammock, hoping for the best. I cooked a hot supper of instant mashed potatoes and packaged chicken, gulped down a few more ibuprofen, emptied my water bottle then my bladder, and pulled on all my extra clothing, including hat and gloves, before turning in. I wasn't planning on coming out of my suspended cocoon until morning. Once inside, I took forever to arrange myself satisfactorily among the insulation— my layers of clothes and my down bag, which, compressed beneath me, offered no warmth. Wriggling, thrashing, turning, cursing, I hoped my jolts wouldn't pull down the deadfall.

Finally settled, I felt the wind pick up and heard my tarp snapping sharply with each gust. With this as my lullaby, I shivered into an uneasy, restless sleep.

Day

25

By 9:30 the next morning, I was huddled inside the small framed cabin at Tillotson Camp, the strains of an old childhood song playing in my head:
Hello Mudda … Hello Fadda … Here I am at … Camp Granada …
My hands numbly clutched a scalding titanium pot of peppermint tea and were starting to feel warm for the first time all morning. I was amazed at how a little heat so quickly lifted my spirits.

Six hours before, deep within the dreaming part of the night, the winds had ushered rain into the saddle. Mistress Belvidere continued to convey her displeasure with us; the rain was cold, and the increasing winds buffeted our modest campsite. Despite Belvidere's determined efforts, my hammock's tarp had kept me dry. I decided this was partly due to a lucky alignment with the storm; with so few tree-options that evening, I could hardly chalk my survival to woods-savvy. Also, because I'd donned every stitch of clothing I had, including my raincoat, I stayed warm enough. Not *warm*, note—just warm *enough*.

Clammy and in low spirits, I awoke early to the rainy fog and called out to Clyde, who was already awake. Yes, he said grumpily, he'd survived the rain from beneath his tent fly, but his sleeping bag was wet. Our food bags, hung away from our camp to discourage nighttime bear-visits, were soaked.

We decided to skip breakfast and hike the dreary 2.6 miles to Tillotson Camp and cook there. I tried to pack quickly, but doing so without saturating my down bag was an exercise in dexterity and ingenuity. I shivered as I packed. This was hypothermia weather, for sure. An easy one to chill, I knew I needed to be extra careful in this weather.

As we began to descend the misty saddle, the dripping bushes alongside the path instantly soaked our legs and feet. New blisters sprouted between my toes like mushrooms on a damp log. I could barely see ten feet in front of me, and a chill breeze blew strands of fog-smoke across our path.

Despite all the wetness, we were out of drinking water. I suppose we could have licked bushes, but we weren't candidates for "Survivor." Pausing wasn't desirable anyway; the shivers would set in immediately if we stopped. We trudged grimly off the flank of Belvidere Saddle, our inner fires as grey and damp as the skies. The Mistress of this Mountain had had the last word.

Take me home, oh Mudda, Fadda, take me ho-o-ome …

Finally the old shelter at Tillotson Camp hove into view. We slipped out of the drizzle and into the rickety 1938 shack, which to us looked like a four-star hotel. After spreading out my soggy gear to air in the humidity, I cooked the last of my oatmeal. I no longer liked oatmeal after three weeks of it, but the gluey stuff was *warm*. The real spirit-lifter, though, was the steaming peppermint tea. I was heating up my second helping when the sky suddenly brightened. Our cautious spirits did the same. A few minutes later, we watched hopefully as a bit of the valley below blew into focus.

Clyde snatched up his damp sleeping bag and ran outside. Stepping onto a nearby rock slab overlooking the valley, he began to dance, turning around and flapping his sleeping bag over his head. It looked like a knee-sore interpretation of the Twist, or maybe a survivor's attempt to attract a rescue plane.

"Clyde, what the hell are you doing, if I may be so bold as to ask?"

"That's my salute to the sun-god Anon," said Clyde. "You know, the Egyptian guy."

Anon? I'd never heard of that fellow. All the same, Clyde's dance seemed to work; the sun was burning a slow hole through the clouds, though we still weren't sure which element would win. Optimists always, we dragged our wet tarps and damp bags to the rocks where they quickly began to dry in the sunlight. With a full belly and drying gear, I felt my misery begin to lift. The Vermont-Canadian border was only 23.3 miles away—or a mere twenty-minute car ride to the end of the Long Trail!

Mudda, Fadda, kindly disregard this letta …

The trail was pleasant for the rest of the day, and it grew sunnier by the mile as the fog melted away, taking the frigid air with it. Clyde hiked ahead shortly before the trail led steeply up. Soon I was sweating alone up Tillotson Peak. I reached the wooded summit, then skittered back down the mountain on ball bearings of moose scat. So many moose droppings, so few moose! It wasn't right, I reflected, that Clyde had seen a moose and I hadn't. It seemed he was always running his mouth on political topics while I was the one quietly observing the plant life, the mushrooms, and the birds. Surely if a moose had been nearby, I would have seen it.

I eventually caught up with Clyde. He had stopped to talk to a group of southbound backpackers near the top of Haystack Mountain and had just scored some candy bars from the hikers, who were out for ten days. When they handed me a candy bar too, I knew they must already be weary of their heavy food bags. Appreciative, I ate as we chatted. Free calories, particularly when carried in by someone else, were always welcome in the woods.

The two-mile walk to Hazen's Notch was easy enough, but thereafter the trail grew steep. That last upward trudge of the day was the worst— as always. We finally off-loaded our packs at Hazen's Notch Camp. The four-bunk shelter felt cozy despite the great beams of sunlight that shone though walls with cracks big enough to pass a Number-Two pencil through. This old camp would be an interesting place in a sideways-driving, windblown rain, I thought. But in the afternoon's calm, the layout suited me fine.

Clyde soon found a good water source, better than the one indicated in the guidebook, at a small creek behind the shelter. After filling my bottles and taking a short, restorative nap, I cooked supper and laid out my night supplies: flattened air pad; sleeping bag; silk bag liner; water bottle; headlamp; toothbrush and toothpaste in a Ziploc bag; and a second Ziploc for toilet paper and hand sanitizer. I'd developed a nighttime shelter routine after three weeks; without thinking, I could grab my shoes, light, and toilet paper for an efficient nocturnal trip to the privy.

Before long we were joined by Scott, a pleasant, wiry man from Georgia who owned a company that repaired peanut pickers, and Clyde prompted him to speak more of it. We also learned that Scott was a trail maintainer and looked after Muskrat Creek Shelter, located just north of the Georgia–North Carolina state line on the Appalachian Trail. He had thru-hiked the A.T. a few years back under the trail name "Pilgrim." Here was yet another thru-hiker who assured me that the northern Long Trail is as rough as, or rougher than, the A.T. Once again, this raised great hopes in me for the next year when I would attempt that most famous of hiking trails.

Like Native Americans, we performed the ritual hiker-exchange of food gifts. Scott gave me a packet of hot chocolate while I portioned out some of my home-dehydrated pineapple for him. Because he was hiking with an older friend and was concerned for him in the heat and humidity, Scott walked outside several times to see if his buddy had arrived. The friend, Wayne from Virginia, finally entered the shelter, red-faced, mute, and sweating profusely. After resting, he admitted the day's hike had been a struggle, and that he was too tired to eat.

Experience had shown me that the "too-tired-to-eat" route is a dangerous one; fatigued muscles and other important organs need fuel to recover. Scott gave Wayne some water, which he had already fetched and filtered for his friend. This warmed my heart. Hikers just plain look out for each other.

Wayne soon perked up and joined the conversation. They were interested to learn of my A.T. plans and told us they would both be at the Appalachian Long Distance Hikers Association's "Gathering" in October. They urged me to attend yet again the informative and inexpensive workshops. Scott even offered to shuttle me to the trail the next spring, if I flew into Atlanta. Again, the generosity of hikers warmed me.

The next day we would tackle Jay Peak, the "twin peaks" we'd been seeing for days. I felt a buzz of excitement when I thought of it: our last big climb of the trip. While there was no gondola on Jay Peak, a tram did run from the summit to lodges at the base. Even better, I had heard rumors of pizza at the restaurants below, as well as a phone and a bathroom with running water. Clyde and I both looked forward to a trip to town, and then to the ride back up the sweeping flanks of northern Vermont's finest mountains.

Only seventeen-point-something miles left to Canada, I thought as I snuggled into my sleeping bag that night. I was ready to bring 'er home.

Day

26

Hazen's Notch Camp
to Laura Woodward Shelter

Today's Miles: 8.5
Trip Miles: 263.2

T he shelter's slatted sides gradually swam into focus as I awoke
the next morning. My first coherent thought: "It's Jay Peak
Day!"

After we packed up, Clyde and I went over the day's plan, as usual.
Seventeen miles lay between us and the Canadian border. The original
plan was to hike 8.5 miles to Laura Woodward Shelter, but Clyde wanted
to hike more miles. He pointed out that the extra hiking would allow us
to walk out of the woods earlier on our final day.

I considered this, rationalizing, *An extra mile and a half doesn't
sound like it'll require too much horsepower.* It might, however, given the
terrain and the day's planned side-trips. High on my list was the airy
tram-ride down the mountain; even higher ranked a pizza pie from the
restaurant below. The map showed seven hard miles up Jay Peak to the
tram, then a steep, rocky mile and a half to Laura Woodward Shelter.
Clyde's plan: to walk the additional miles to Shooting Star Shelter. I
proposed we just slog on, see how the day unfolded, and let our energy
levels make the decision later.

Buoyed by the mighty fine hiking weather, my spirits were high
as we began hiking. Sun glinted off every leaf and rock, and the dry
autumn air took my breath away with its apple-crisp tang. Fall came
early to these northern mountains. A light breeze sustained me, cooling
as needed.

Even on a cool, low-humidity day, I was astounded at how much heat I produced, simply by carrying a backpack up a mountain. In my other life I am a lizard, draping myself around sun-warmed objects and following the rays throughout the house as the light shifts. But on the Long Trail I produced enough thermal output to warm a few dozen lizards. Of course, this efficient calorie-burning mechanism, this metabolic beast of burden that was now my body, was precisely what allowed me to devour whole pizzas with impunity. It also allowed me to handle the day's hills with ease—another reward for feeding, watering, and resting the pack stock wisely.

After almost a month in the mountains of Vermont, the hiker's eye grows used to the color green. Any bright color stands out like a beacon. A spot of red caught my eye as I paused for breath halfway up Buchanan Mountain. Red survey paint? No. The redness radiated from two paper birches growing close together, long strips of their peeling bark nearly touching. The sun, shining just so on the birches' pink papery peels, glowed though the exfoliating bark as vibrantly as red stained glass. No cathedral rose window looked as uplifting right then as did that glowing red spot in a sea of Vermont green.

Clyde and I leap-frogged for several hours, so I spent most of the morning's hike alone. Whenever I came to a crest, I could see the looming Jay Peak ahead, a little closer each time. Descending from the last bump before the imposing sawtooth of Jay, I grew amused by an unusual rounded boulder by the side of the trail. In that whimsical way that long-distance hiking connects neurons, the fissured stone reminded me of an old anti-drug commercial involving an egg and a frying pan.

Kids, this is your brain …

Yes, the strange rock looked like a giant brain, down to the indents, curls, folds, and fissures.

This *is your brain on the* Long *Trail.*

(sizzling sounds …)

Any questions?

Here in late August, in Vermont's northernmost mountains, the earliest touch of autumn was apparent. The fern fronds and blueberry leaves, so green just a week before, had begun to redden from the chilly nights. In the mornings I noticed a fresh, untrod scattering of bright yellow birch leaves strewn across the path on the north slopes.

Partway down a rocky slope, it happened: I stepped between a rock and a hard place, fell down, and twisted my ankle. *No!* Seeing stars, I opened and closed my fists spasmodically to offset the sharp pain. Then I wept a little, out of a sense of both assault and astonishment. (Guys, you should try this sometime; it really works.) After that useful discharge, I rubbed my ankle for a while, wondering if I could make it to Canada on my knees if necessary. We were so close! I opened my pack, extracted an ankle wrap and a massive dose of ibuprofen, and administered both. With a few hearty curses, I heaved myself up with my sticks and hobbled to the gravel road below, where Clyde was waiting.

When I got there, I found he'd entertained a similar adventure, slipping on a slimy log and trashing his knee. Our injuries throbbed with every step. Loudly we catalogued the outrages. I think the bitching helped us steel ourselves for the remaining miles. Ruefully we observed that, as close as we were to the finish, the Long Trail was still toying with us like a cat with two mice. We treasured our hiking poles and ibuprofen, which at least improved the odds of us mice. I bummed some more Vitamin I from Clyde before we resumed hiking, so I'd have a few in reserve.

At Jay Pass, the southern base of Jay Peak, we took a long break at VT 242 to let things sink in. Ahead was our last 1,700–foot climb to a summit, our last big challenge of the Long Trail. Hiking 1,700 vertical feet is like climbing 170 flights of stairs with a pack. No *building* was 170 floors tall, I thought to myself. Shoot, the Empire State Building is only 102. No doubt about it, Clyde and I had a big final climb ahead of us.

Earlier we had discussed sending our packs up the tram and climbing Jay Peak unweighted. Ultimately we each decided—independently—to carry our packs. At 12:30 P.M., we rose and shouldered our burdens to ascend the last real mountain of the Long Trail. We both felt an underlying buzz of excitement.

"You lead, M'Lady," Clyde said, waving magnanimously. "This one's yours. Pull me up the hill."

Our sorry physical condition stood at odds with our high spirits, and we laughed at our pitiful selves as we hobbled across the highway. As we climbed our last big 'un, Clyde recited the litany of "All The Mean Ol' Mountains That Haven't Licked Us Yet," starting with the hellishly hot and steep Pine Cobble Trail back in Massachusetts. Was that less than a month ago?

It had been one grueling, transformative month. Everything hurt. Our bodies had grown thinner while our legs grew more muscular; we probably could have cracked walnuts with our knees. We both limped, but our hearts beat strongly and steadily, our muscles recovering quickly. We breathed from the very bottoms of our lungs. We were seeing more of the world—more of the "here and now"—and less of the interior of our heads. I had long stopped fretting about home; Clyde had quit drumming his fingers at every break. He now catnapped whenever we paused to rest. We fit in this world now, and we saw that. A long-distance hike was not about comfort, and we recognized that too, at a very visceral level. It was about Something Else, and while that exact motivation would be different for every long-distance backpacker, the very pull of it made us kindred with all other travelers.

The Long Trail up Jay Peak fell beneath our practiced boot steps. *It really weren't nothin' but a thang, now.* Around two o'clock, the trail emerged at a boulder field and we could see the very peak. With a wild excitement welling up in us both at the sight of the top, we hobble-ran the last one hundred yards to the rocky summit, yelling and hobble-hopping our way up the bare, beautiful terrain.

Tram-hauled tourists smiled at the grungy backpackers whooping up the rocks like idiots. *Energy!* The climb felt celebratory, significant.

Our last big peak. We did it!

"Tell the Queen, Jay Peak is ours," Clyde intoned.

I sat on a marble bench near the top to gather my wits and breath. I was surprised at how choked up I felt. We actually had ten more miles to walk before hitting the border and the end of the Too-Damned-Long-and-Hard Trail. But the conclusion of this giddy ascent felt like the psychological end. The Long Trail had been hard, and it was all downhill from here. We were going to finish. We were going to Canada.

Clyde joined me at the bench and an elderly gentleman snapped our picture for us. He added to the celebratory mood, congratulating us in that generous way some folks have of extending the gift of their acclaim. In the clear air, we picked out many familiar peaks in the distance, south all the way to the rocky pimple of Camel's Hump, east to the White Mountains, and southwest to the Adirondacks. Turning north, we could see the clear-cut in the thick coniferous forest that marked the 45th parallel. The Canadian border! The end of our journey.

But, of course, adventures never quite seem to end where they're supposed to.

At the summit, Jay Peak's ski complex opened its doors to any who ascended the mountain, whether by tram or foot. We found a drink machine nestled in a corner and Clyde sprang for a soda for himself. It cost two dollars, which irked him mightily—but he dug deep and paid the price. Not surprisingly, everyone in listening range heard about the overpriced soda—as well as the tasteless $3.50 apple pie, from way back in Appalachian Gap. That pie still bothered Clyde. After the mellowing effects of the Long Trail, though, the irritation was more a matter of style—a charming quirk, a part to play, a noise to make—than a cause for bad temper.

Next, we hit the indoor bathrooms for a wash-up. No hot water came out of my spigot, but I made do with the cold tap water; after all, I had the rare luxury of soap and paper towels to make up for the inconvenience. When I came out, I found Clyde looking chagrined. He'd surprised a young French female hiker who was taking a sponge bath in the men's room.

"She was buck nekkid, and not a bit embarrassed by me walking in on her," he exclaimed. "And she was a natural blonde, too," he added earnestly.

The young woman, who must have noticed Clyde's American embarrassment, came out later to apologize; there was no warm water in the women's bathroom, she explained.

No warm water? Tell me about it! I rinsed!

The next big adventure of the day was taking the tram down the mountain. Clyde decided to wait up top while I rode the car down the long, airy run of bouncy cables. He said he'd decided gondolas, trams, and other airborne, dangly things were not for him after all. He worried that if he rode the tram to the bottom, he wouldn't have the guts to come back up. And then where would he be? Ten miles from the Canadian border with another long walk up Jay Peak, which he didn't think he had in him in his weary, gimp-kneed state. Clyde was very practical, when you could follow his logic.

I went down alone. The views from the tram made it worth the ride, and the exits funneled me into the near-empty ski lodge below. I found the restaurant and bought a large, greasy pepperoni pizza and two sodas. Interesting, after I'd paid for my drink, I discovered I'd lost my taste for sugar water; I tasted it in the self-serve line, then dumped it out, refilling with ice and water. While I didn't care for the over-sweet soda, on this hot and droughty hike, ice was a Long-Trail novelty.

I was reminded of the scene from the movie *Castaway,* where the Tom Hanks character returns to a celebratory party in "civilization" after a long, lonely stint on a deserted island. He is astounded at all of the excess around him, such as the banquet remains that would have fed him royally for a week. The character reflects aloud on his return to abundance after living in deprivation: "And now ... I have ice in my glass."

Now, I had ice in my glass.

It took but eight minutes for the tram to ascend what had taken ninety minutes for boot and muscle to scale earlier that day. I'd meant to hold back, but somehow half the pizza disappeared down my gullet on the ride back up. Back on the peak, I surprised Clyde with a soda and the other half of the pizza; he ate some and packed the rest for supper. He told me he'd worked the phones while I was tram-riding, calling his family and making reservations at the "1893 House," a bed and breakfast near the end of the Long Trail.

Shopping and phone duties achieved, we left as the station closed down for the night. The trail dropped steeply off Jay Peak. As we descended, the sun drooped to the horizon, casting long shadows. My ankle pained me on the downhill terrain and I leaned harder on my hiking poles. The Long Trail followed a cross-country ski trail out of the area, and as we were about to leave the ski area's boundaries, we encountered a sign warning us that once we left this point, there would be no way back to the ski area. We laughed at that; we had no intention of returning. Canada was calling our names.

The air had cooled and the shadows grown long by the time we found Laura Woodward Shelter and set up our sleeping spots. Neither of us wanted to walk the additional miles to Shooting Star Shelter. While we cooked our dinners, Clyde admitted he'd felt mighty homesick. He wouldn't have long to wait. The next day we would complete the Long Trail.

Right at dusk, two hikers straggled in, exhausted. One of them was an unhappy woman who introduced herself as Merry Go Round, a former A.T. thru-hiker. It was the first day of their southbound Long-Trail end-to-end hike, and they were straining under heavy packs. They hated life at the moment. Clyde and I felt—I confess it—smug.

We had already turned in when Merry came over to visit. I was nearly asleep in my bag. Clyde, ever-gregarious though drowsy, rallied from his sleeping bag and gave her the lowdown on the trail ahead, just as every southbounder for the past month had done for us. I could tell he was enjoying that part. Clyde could pass out casual advice with the best of them.

They talked a bit more, and I was nearly out, cosseted by the murmur of nearby voices. Suddenly I heard Merry say to Clyde, "Wow, you're so laid-back." I twitched violently and nearly choked on my own spittle. They both looked over at my snort, Merry uncomprehending, and Clyde grinning like a hound.

Was it just back at the Inn at Long Trail that Cous-Cous was advising Clyde to "like, CHILL, man … Ommmmmm …" Was that so long ago?

Well, Clyde *did* admit he had quit drumming his fingers.

Tuesday, August 27, 2002

Laura Woodward Shelter
to Canada

Today's Miles: 8.7
Trip Miles: 271.9

"*B*ONJOUR, *tout le monde!*" I wrote in the Laura
Woodward Shelter register on the morning of August
27, 2002, a few minutes before we started hiking. "Today,
monde, we are going to walk to QUEBEC!"

Via Pocketmail, our friend Smoothie had asked, "Can you smell
Canada yet?"

"Is *that* what that smell was?" I'd responded. "And here I was thinking
I'd have to burn this shirt!"

But we were slow getting up on that final, frosty morning on the
Long Trail. All of us in the shelter cooked breakfast without emerging
from our sleeping bags. The Canadian cold pinched my fingers every
time I reached for my pot. Canada certainly wanted us to know she was
in the neighborhood and could, on a whim, breathe a little August frost
upon us.

I groaned as I rolled over to pack up. Clyde, already up and ready to
go, offered me some ibuprofen, as I'd exhausted my own supply. We left
camp at 8 A.M., a late start by our newly acquired long-distance hiking
standards. I hobbled stiffly away from the shelter on my twisted joint
while work-ethic Clyde, despite his injury, hiked ahead.

I walked with care, eyeballing every footfall and envying Clyde his
morning looseness. Little did I know that a few hours later I would find
him sprawled flat on his back, silent, unmoving. Naturally, he knew I
would think the worst ("*You* bastard, *your heart gave out on the last day,*

and your family is going to kill *me!"*). However, hearing me approach, he waved his poles gamely, signaling that he wasn't in full cardiac arrest, but had only slipped on a rock and knocked the breath out of himself.

On this last day on the Long Trail, I turned my thoughts from the hiker ahead to the natural world around me. I walked with eyes wide open, trying to pull it all in to some inner reservoir of nourishment and inspiration I could draw upon in less pine-scented times. I heard the wind hissing through the tops of spruce. I saw the tracery of lines on the naked bedrock, the orange and yellow mushroom in the moist duff, the seams of milky quartz lacing trailside boulders, the dappled play of sun on moss. I peered past every bend, anticipating that elusive Vermont moose, so promised by the abundance of scat.

The sun poured down on the Long Trail, warming me. The dry air smelled like wine, heady and full of fragrance, and I drank it down in large, greedy gulps. My sore ankle loosened up and began to function more like a joint as the swelling reduced. I hiked without incident past the summit of Doll Mountain, our last significant uphill of the Long Trail. I was still on the sun-striped ridge when I saw the pair of slim hawks high above me.

The birds *cheer*ed to each other, pirouetting through the air in unison. I stopped, mouth open, to watch their aerial exuberance. These weren't the red-tailed hawks of the Carolinas; their tails struck me as square, and their bodies slightly smaller, built for speed. They dove though the ridge-top branches, firing through high, hidden passages of fir like feathered bullets, never flapping. Then they burst through into the ridge sky again, arcing away, high into the scalding blue.

All of a sudden—magic!

I stood motionless beneath a spruce, looking up, mouth open in wonder and focus. I was craning for another view when one hawk zoomed in, right at me, to a pin-point halt on a spruce limb slightly above face height. *My* spruce. *My* face. I froze.

We stared. A glassy black and gold hawk's eye met mine square on, life meeting life.

A pause. An eternity, a heartbeat.

I could have reached out and touched the raptor. I was certain that, in the giddy rush of its dance, it hadn't noticed me. It saw me now! Had I ever been this close to such a purely wild thing?

Then, with a defiant *cheer* and a bluster of wings, the hawk exploded off its branch and re-joined its partner in the sky. Though I recognized my sheer, dumb luck—nothing more, nothing less—the moment still felt like a benediction.

As I walked the ridge, the raptors continued to wheel above me, calling to each other, doing their exuberant hawk thing. I hiked on, surrounded by paper birches. I decided I would miss these northern birches the most. The Carolinas have river birches, but they're not the same. The paper-like bark of the white birches, so plentiful in the northern forest, peels constantly, like a snake shedding a skin. Such peeling is necessary for growth. Often, as I passed a birch on the trail, I would slip my hand beneath a white flake and touch the smooth, newborn places—soft, like an infant's bottom. Baby-flesh pink with a subtle sheen, the new bark is a tender thing of beauty. It is a promise—and, at the same time, it is next year's flake. Everything changes. Nothing stays the same.

I had mixed feelings about completing the Long Trail. I was going to miss this ever-changing landscape, these quiet chronicles of peeling bark.

Yet I also missed friends and family at home. I missed my work, my dog, the horses, kayaking, soft beds, hot showers. It would be lovely to ramble *without* a backpack and the necessary chore of "miles per day." I just plain missed the Carolinas, and I was utterly, completely worn out.

Clyde felt much the same way. He wrote in his last register entry, "Had a heart attack in '97, and I guess you could say I am cured. All the mountains of Vermont couldn't kill me, so the flatlands of Florida don't have a chance." He had walked through the heels of his socks. He was ready to go home.

I had a bone to pick with the Green Mountain State, though. Vermont is stunning with vistas to spare, yes. Its leaders had the foresight not only to preserve these wild places but to thread a footpath through the beauty. A dedicated crew maintains the Long Trail and digs its privies. Vermont even produced a bobcat and a hawk for us, up close and personal.

But—and this is a big *but*—Clyde Dodge had seen a moose and I hadn't. You don't hike a month with someone without knowing

"... like a snake shedding a skin."

whether or not he's the sort who wouldn't ever let you forget a thing like that. Clyde even claimed he had the pictures to prove it. Can I ever forgive Vermont for that? Writing in the register while taking a break at lovely Shooting Star Shelter, the last on the Long Trail proper, I let Vermont know in clear terms that it only had four more miles in which to produce this wondrous, improbable creature.

About two o'clock, step by step, we ascended Carleton Mountain together, our very last bit of uphill ground, and stopped to look back at Jay Peak, so impossibly far away now. How did we ever walk that far—and in one day? The trail still boggled our perceptions of reality.

"If there's one thing I've learned on this trip," mused Clyde aloud, "it's the value of 'step-by-step.' Little by little, it gets the big jobs done." He pulled his gaze from Jay Peak and looked toward Canada, then back at me. "Well, Foots, you ready to go?"

The rest of the Long Trail rolled downhill from there. Six-foot-two Clyde pulled ahead with long strides while I hobbled behind on my twisted ankle. No worries. We were going to Canada! There was no doubt now. "You're close enough for me to tote you from here," Clyde called before he disappeared around a bend in the trail.

I hobbled steadily. Two miles. One mile. Half mile. Moose?

No moose. An ordinary adventurer cannot always craft that fairy-tale ending.

"Ah well," I thought, "I'll have another crack next year on the Appalachian Trail—if I go."

If I go. I considered those words. Right then, the thought of backpacking one more day was more than my spirit could bear. In fact, this end-to-end backpack in the August heat and drought had drained my batteries so deeply, it seemed entirely possible I'd never backpack again.

Suddenly, I broke out of the woods and into the open. As I emerged into the clearing, limping, Clyde sat at the base of a massive boulder. I figured he'd touched the Canadian finish line, completing his journey, but no—he'd waited for me. I found this gesture unexpectedly sweet for such a tough-acting hombre.

"You drug me into this thing," he said. "I figured you could drag me out." While this was not entirely true, the sentiment pleased me. Despite the strains of adjusting to our different personalities and paces, we would finish this testy trail together, as friends.

We consulted the guidebook. The trail continued on, right over the colossal rock. On the other side was Canada—and the silver cement obelisk that marked the end of Vermont's Long Trail. We crawled over the stone and there it was, the obelisk that signified the completion of our journey.

"It looked like Canada was giving us the finger," Clyde said later. We high-fived. *We did it! Done!*

We touched the end point, and a month of sweat and hardship fell behind us like a curtain. Clyde snapped a picture of me kissing the obelisk. I took one of him pretending to break his hiking poles over the thing. We took one of us together, using the auto-delay function on his camera.

"We crawled over the stone and there it was ..."

And then we walked on. No cheering throngs. No soul-stirring vistas. We felt gladness, but no big emotion, except maybe relief and the intense desire for a shower. The half-mile slog down the Journey's End Trail to the creepy Journey's End Camp seemed anti-climactic. Though we checked out the dark little shelter where southbounders typically start their journey, the inexplicable, unpleasant vibe of the place discouraged lingering.

We emerged into a clearing, a small trailhead. Here I learned that three more miles lay between us and the main road. Three more miles! The torture of food fantasies began. Though I ate little meat at home, my internal fires demanded more substantial fare out here. I told Clyde I was salivating for a Carolina pork barbecue sandwich, loaded with fresh coleslaw, and served with a side of hush puppies, sizzling hot from the fryer grease.

"Oh yeah," said Clyde, warming to the idea. "And the bun so loaded with meat it squirts out the side and you're embarrassed to eat it in the restaurant. When you're done, you have barbecue sauce from ear to ear."

While I could stand to eat such carotid-clogging sandwiches twice a year at best, my mouth watered hard at the thought of one of those greasy delights. Clyde then talked about one of his favorite places back home, Jacksonville's Beach Street Chicken. He and his father-in-law Redman enjoyed sneaking down there for a heart-attack special. "One of those barbecued boneless rib sandwiches would be real nice right about now," he said philosophically.

The "food talk" helped the boring miles roll by, but my body ventured close to mutiny. My stomach growled and my twisted ankle throbbed. The trail had turned to an asphalt road, and my feet burned on the unforgiving pavement. Traffic was sparse to non-existent, with a pronounced lean toward the non-existent. Except for some pastured horses, a nearby dairy farm looked uninhabited. It was late afternoon, and we had multiple road miles to town. Something needed doing.

We collapsed, discouraged, when we reached the main road. After several minutes, an old Cadillac turned into the dairy farm near us. We watched as a woman got out and began watering her horses.

"There was our ride to the bed and breakfast," Clyde said later. "She just didn't know it yet." We limped pitifully to the woman, and Clyde asked for directions to the "1893 House," our night's destination. The woman, a little older than us, was polite but reserved. She gave us directions but offered no ride.

While she and Clyde talked, I approached the horses, transfixed. I hadn't touched a horse in a month. I tried to entice the bay to approach, and the gelding considered it, taking a few steps toward me. The lady looked up from her conversation with Clyde and smiled. She explained that the bay was a natural-born mustang from out west, and that she'd acquired him through a Bureau of Land Management program for relocating wild horses.

Fascinated, I queried her about the gentling process. She went about her chores as we talked, and I offered to help water as I saw the opportunity. So I talked Horse awhile, and Clyde talked Directions, and even though she'd said she couldn't take us to the "1893 House," it wasn't long before the nice horse-lady was driving us to the very door of the B&B in the tiny town of North Troy, Vermont. We fell over ourselves in expressing our gratitude, and she knew our sentiments came from the heart.

"She didn't have a *chance*," Clyde said later. "We *gang-yogied* her!"

We found a note pinned to the unlocked door of the B&B: "Welcome Clyde Dodge and hiking partner." Clyde loved that, my being the sidekick. Our hosts, Rick and Pat Shover, had written that we should make ourselves at home. We entered the lovely inn, mindful of our scruffy state now that we were back in the land of civilized aromas. We admired the elegant old Victorian home, lovingly restored, with inlaid walnut-and-maple flooring in the foyer. I chose a room for myself, then drew a genuine hot bath and soaked off the last of my trail dirt.

Dressed and relatively clean, we walked into town to rustle up some civilized supper—no more dehydrated noodles for *these* campers. Both of the small town's restaurants were closed on Tuesdays; after the afternoon's food fantasies, this was a deep disappointment. Luckily a modicum of our trail-flexibility remained. We found an old country store and purchased thick sandwiches, chips, sweet cakes, ice cream, and drinks from the deli section. We lugged our grub over to the front porch of one of the closed restaurants, sat in their outdoor café, and ate until our bellies distended. We were as comfortable as ticks on a puppy. A quiet pride descended upon us as the fact of our completion sank in. That satisfaction would only grow deeper in subsequent years.

Deep in my aching bones, I now knew I could climb any mountain on the east coast if I didn't think about it too much; it ain't nothin' but a *thang*, never was. I was glad I'd attempted the entire Long Trail of Vermont. And I was glad I'd finished it.

So, I mused, adventures are not merely for those extraordinary "others" unencumbered by the baggage of life. Did such people even exist outside my envious imagination? Everyone yearns for unaccustomed freedom, freshness, simplicity, transformation. Plain old ordinary people could cast off the weight of complicated lives for a time and undertake significant journeys of both the external and the internal terrain, then return home, renewed. Perhaps even altered.

However, I also saw that life would not reach out and place adventure gently into anyone's lap. Such journeys are labeled "risky" by the hall monitors of our minds. Opportunity must be wrested from the static bedrock of life's routines. Inertia remains a powerful force, and few command the will to circumvent it. Those who do, however ordinary, possess an aspect of the extraordinary.

The next day, we would head back south to our everyday lives. We would no longer force aching, cold bodies out of warm sleeping bags. We would no longer will our hot, grimy, overloaded selves up steep and stony grades when a perfectly good road went around the mountain. We would have hot showers on demand. We would have ice in our glasses.

Hiking the Long Trail was by far the most difficult sustained physical work I had ever done. I even wondered if I would have undertaken the task if I had known what the road ahead contained. Never had I worked so hard, so hot, so full out, for so long. I hoped the Appalachian Trail would be more forgiving, should I be so foolhardy as to set out from Springer Mountain, Georgia, the next year, to carry heavy weights up mountains yet again.

But for now, our extraordinary adventure—undertaken by two ordinary, out-of-shape citizens with day jobs—was over.

And I thought, as I rooted through the wrappers for the last of the Twinkie crumbs, "I have *got* to stop eating like this."

Epilogue

Clyde wrote his version of this story, which you can find online at www.trailjournals.com. Use the "search" function for "MAFMan," and only believe half of what you read.

Photos from our adventure, as well as basic information on hiking the Long Trail, can be found at my web site at www.FunFreedom.com. Visit the official Long Trail web site, www.greenmountainclub.org, for maps, guidebooks, trail conditions, volunteer opportunities, and more.

Our chatty friend Art was not able to thru-hike in 2003, but a year later completed the entire Appalachian Trail under the trail name "Gabby."

In 2003, Suz the priest transcribed my A.T. thru-hike journal. She later married, and she and her husband live in a house in the trees in New Hampshire.

We never saw Branch and Stick again. Perhaps this book will be an agent for reconnection.

R-Kid, Mo, Valley Girl, and Cous-Cous completed the Appalachian Trail.

The Stratton Mountain warming hut is no longer generally open to hikers.

Mrs. Gorp finished two more hikes of the A.T. and in 2007 undertook a cross-country bicycle trip.

Bramble did take up backpacking, and hit the Appalachian Trail to hike in 2004.

Ted Anderson, the prankster who sent me the care package, planned to thru-hike with me and two others in March 2003. Ted died unexpectedly four days before leaving.

Flatlander and Mama Lipton went on to thru-hike the A.T. in 2003. Pilgrim delivered them to Springer Mountain, Georgia.

On June 15, 2006, Clyde started the A.T. southbound from Maine wearing the special bandanna his mother-in-law sewed (and that I never lost). He climbed Katahdin and kissed the sign, then slipped and broke his leg on the way down. He came home to heal and was able to witness the birth of his second grandson.

After the Long Trail, I thought I'd never backpack again. But long-distance hiking is like childbirth: you forget the hard times and remember only the coos and smiles. In March of 2003 Pilgrim made good on his promise and delivered me to the Appalachian Trail in Georgia. When I limped into Hot Springs, North Carolina, at 275 miles, Clyde e-mailed me: "You've now walked farther than the Long Trail. Is the A.T. as hard?" I could honestly answer: "No." Not yet, anyway.

In Maine on September 18, 2003, I summited Katahdin and kissed the sign myself.

Acknowledgements

You don't have to be a fantastic hero to do certain things ... You can be just an ordinary chap, sufficiently motivated to reach challenging goals.

—Sir Edmund Hillary,
Mountaineer and Explorer

I am indebted to my fantastic heroes, in no special order:

My Long Trail journal transcriber Kahley Hubitsky, now scattered to the four winds. Perhaps she will see this book and feel a small glow of pride.

My fierce proofers, Linda "eArThworm" Patton, Smith "Old Ridge Runner" Edwards, Cindy "Mrs. (Yolanda) Gorp" Miller, and Maureen Sutton.

Editor and irrepressible wordsmith Nina Baxley Rogers, thru-hiker and author in her own right. I was lucky to have her guiding hand. Nina possesses that rare gift of not only honing a work but of making the editing process more fun than "one hundred and eighty-nine McDonald's Fun Houses stacked right on top of another."

Jonathan Scott of Lotus Advertising and Graphic Design, and Middleton Press, whose beautiful cover design and early encouragement were critical in the shaping of this book.

Ken Westcott, whose creative help with all things photographic sustained me on the Appalachian Trail. In preparing my cover photo, Ken also kept me laughing, saving me from too much seriousness.

David "Awol" Miller, 2003 A.T. thru-hiker and author, whose vigorous eleventh-hour assistance and can-do attitude saw this book to print.

Leif and ZipDrive of Trail Journals for their most excellent web site for long-distance hiking journals. (www.trailjournals.com)

My beloved AT-L hiking list, for growing me from a seed. Your support over the years has been immeasurable.

Jean Deeds, whose book, *There are Mountains to Climb*, put a match to my tinder.

Wendy "Philosophy" Cronkite, who got me out there before I could change my mind.

My brother Tuck for all those late-night emergency computer fixes, and for just being an all-around terrific bro. The folks would be proud.

Michael, for his warmth and patience.

Of course, my improbable hiking buddy, Clyde Dodge. Different as we are, I am not exactly sure why Clyde and I remain fast friends, but we do, and I'm awfully glad to have him at my back. I'm also indebted to his family for parceling him out that grueling August of 2002.

We live in a wheeled society—a relatively recent phenomenon. Nowhere is that scale and those implications more evident than while walking. To hike around America is to experience a peculiar vulnerability. So finally, I'd like to thank anyone, anywhere, who has ever helped a human afoot. You know who you are.